Critical Perspectives
on Social Media and Protest

Critical Perspectives on Social Media and Protest

Between Control and Emancipation

Edited by Lina Dencik
and Oliver Leistert

ROWMAN &
LITTLEFIELD
INTERNATIONAL

London • New York

Published by Rowman & Littlefield International, Ltd.
Unit A, Whitacre Mews, 26-34 Stannary Street, London SE11 4AB
www.rowmaninternational.com

Rowman & Littlefield International, Ltd. is an affiliate of Rowman & Littlefield
4501 Forbes Boulevard, Suite 200, Lanham, Maryland 20706, USA
With additional offices in Boulder, New York, Toronto (Canada), and London (UK)
www.rowman.com

British Library Cataloguing in Publication Information Available
A catalogue record for this book is available from the British Library

ISBN: HB 978-1-78348-335-8
ISBN: PB 978-1-78348-336-5

Library of Congress Cataloging-in-Publication Data

Critical perspectives on social media and protest : between control and emancipation / edited by Lina
Dencik and Oliver Leistert.
pages cm
Includes bibliographical references and index.
ISBN 978-1-78348-335-8 (cloth : alk. paper)— ISBN 978-1-78348-336-5 (pbk. : alk. paper)— ISBN
978-1-78348-337-2 (ebook)
1. Social media—Political aspects. 2. Protest movements. 3. Social influence. 4. Social control. I.
Dencik, Lina, editor. II. Leistert, Oliver, editor.
HM742.C75 2015
302.23'1—dc23
2015017431

∞™ The paper used in this publication meets the minimum requirements of American
National Standard for Information Sciences Permanence of Paper for Printed Library
Materials, ANSI/NISO Z39.48-1992.

Printed in the United States of America

Contents

Acknowledgements

We would like to thank all the authors in this book for their great contributions and for engaging so positively with our edits and comments. We are also grateful to Anna Reeve and Sinéad Murphy at Rowman & Littlefield International for their encouragement and support in the publication of this book. We hope it will make for a useful and insightful contribution to the debate on contemporary protest.

—Lina and Oliver

Introduction

Lina Dencik and Oliver Leistert

The relationship between social media and protest illuminates some of the most pertinent questions regarding the place and role of digital media technologies in contemporary societies. Often marred in narratives of modernization and progress, the interplay between technologies and social and political change is rarely properly scrutinized in public debate. Instead, we often find ourselves with rather simplistic and one-sided explanations for how new developments in technologies have transformed society, caused major events and pushed new actors to the fore. Frequently we are left with a decidedly apolitical understanding of not only the uses of media technologies in different social and historical contexts, but also of the design and infrastructure of the very technologies themselves. Particularly when it comes to political uprisings and protests in recent years, a dominant narrative has emerged that celebrates the advent of social media platforms as simple tools to be used for liberating purposes by a host of progressive social and political actors. Although such a narrative appeals to inherent modernist sensibilities and Enlightenment ideals of technology as the midwife to social and political advances (Curran 2010), it does little to illuminate the complexity and contradictions of contemporary forms of protest in an age of social media.

This book seeks to address some of these inadequacies that have marked much of the discussion on social media and protest. In particular, we want to politicize and contextualize the architectures of what are predominantly commercial social media platforms in terms of their use for the purposes of antisystemic and progressive protest movements. Although there are aspects of social media technologies that have greatly benefitted activists and social movements in terms of their ability to organize and mobilize protests, closer inspection also reveals the myriad of controlling forces that permeate these technologies in many different respects, creating an evermore contradictory and paradoxical protest terrain, leading at its most extreme to severe repression and ultimately incarceration of activists. In highlighting these contradictory issues with the collection of contributions in this book, we seek not to add further ammunition to the tiresome binary debate between cyber-optimists and cyber-skeptics, but seek rather to provide a more considered and nuanced understanding of how social media and protest can be understood in relation to each other in current *context*. Abstracting social media technologies from the social, political, economic and cultural processes that embed their development and uses leads, otherwise, too frequently to a strategically driven interpretation of events. This starts with the term 'social media' itself, as it requires caution if not even rejection since it euphemistically refers to the services of large companies that shape and ultimately redefine—in the interest of their shareholders—the very nature of sociality.

What is more, critically interrogating the relationship between social media and protest is an interdisciplinary task. We cannot reduce this debate to merely questions of either media or politics. The study of the interplay between technologies and social and political change spans across different approaches and scholarly trajectories and it demands cross-disciplinary dialogue and understanding. With this book we want to encourage and advance such dialogue by collecting contributions from leading scholars across a diverse range of disciplines and theoretical frameworks—from media theory to critical technology studies to anthropology to social movement studies to political economy—that each highlight different, but central, aspects of social media protest. Each of these contributions illuminate and explore key, but often neglected, questions of emancipation and control in contemporary forms of protest and situate the nature and role of social media in cultural, social, economic and political context. In bringing these together, we want to show how these different traditions can speak to each other and, in conjunction, help us advance a more comprehensive understanding of developments in media technologies and the conditions of contemporary societies.

SOCIAL MEDIA AND PROTEST DYNAMICS

Protests of various kinds have in recent years taken centre stage as an expression of resistance and dissent towards prevailing systems of order. This was epitomized by the iconic cover of *TIME* magazine proclaiming the 'protestor' person of the year in 2011 following uprisings in the Arab world, occupations across Europe and North America, and riots in the UK. This story has continued with further revolts and mobilizations playing out across a diverse range of countries and contexts, such as the Yo Soy 132 movement in Mexico, the Gezi Park protests in Turkey, the Free Fare movement in Brazil, the Umbrella movement in Hong Kong and The New University movement in the Netherlands, to mention a few. These movements and uprisings speak not only to a period of crises and instability in the contemporary neoliberal world order, but indicate also new infrastructures of possibility for protests to emerge.

In his overview of the literature on social media and movements, Haunss's chapter in this volume illustrates the velocity of this growing field and the range of arguments emerging, both proven and disproven, in their assessment of the role of social media in protest mobilizations. As Haunss makes clear, the question of how movements engage with new technologies is not a new one—it is one we are familiar with within groups such as the Association of Progressive Communication, bottom-up, collectively run independent news sites such as Indymedia and the advancement of tactics such as online petitions and mailing lists. However, the development of so-called 'social media' has renewed the discussion, introducing numerous different aspects and approaches to the debate on how dissent and resistance are said to be changing in such a digital environment. Haunss provides us here with a dissection of this 'new' protest culture and the ways in which social movements are said to engage with it. Much promise has been attributed to social media with regard to new organizational capacities for movements to emerge and mobilize. Said to overcome long-standing restrictions and limitations for protest by lowering transaction costs and minimizing the kinds of resources traditionally needed for building and sustaining social movements, such as time, space and personal risks, protest in an age of social media is said to have become easier, faster, more spontaneous and ultimately more decentralized, horizontal and participatory.

However, as Haunss points out, empirical evidence based on studies of social movements and protest does little to support these claims in practice. And when it does, it also highlights numerous other forces at play that simultaneously can be seen to undermine some of these very possibilities that the technologies of social media are said to provide for protest and dissent. Movements need more than just faster and more widespread forms of communication in order to emerge and be sustained, and collective action commonly requires individual costs and personal risks to be taken in order for significant social change to come about. What is more, leadership and hierarchy is not necessarily done away with in this 'new' protest culture, but instead, new forms of leadership and hierarchies emerge within these movements, often contested and opaque at the same time, and activists are forced to negotiate new types of challenges and dangers both online and offline. As such, the story of social media protest is not one of simply enabling potential; these technologies have not birthed our emancipation. Rather, we find ourselves continuously confronted with the restricting structures and limitations that are inherent in these technologies, and the ways in which they enforce social control.

As Leistert's chapter makes clear, most of these social media platforms are commercial entities, first and foremost, a point woefully neglected in many discussions on social media and protest. They may be perceived to widen reach, potentially constituting a new form of mass media in the eyes of protesters, but they do so on terms primarily concerned with capital accumulation and profit, and predominantly, if not entirely, engineered to maximize advertising revenue and consumer consumption. As Leistert points out, this has significant implications for their use in protest activity. The algorithms that shape this kind of social media interaction are steeped within a business model that is designed to target individual affect and cognition in order to sell advertisements, commodities and data, which increasingly shows to be today's most growing resort for capital expansion. As such, the politics that is nurtured and promoted on such platforms is not a politics that is conducive to collective action and emancipatory ideals as pursued by progressive social movements, but rather a politics that becomes void of any genuine meaning, formed as it is around the corporate ownership of data points, based on a 'like economy' of individual expressions of (happy, consensual) emotions, contained within continuously changing and obscure terms of services agreements and permanently monitored and managed for the purposes of state-corporate surveillance. In such a context, social media platforms are not merely 'tools' that activists can utilize to advance their causes and ideals as they wish, but, instead, the algorithmic design of these platforms is shown to be deeply political and intrinsically constraining of emancipatory practices and ideals.

As such, Leistert illustrates how the shift from activist developed and owned technologies to commercially developed and owned technologies for the purposes of protest introduces a fundamentally contradictory juxtaposition for the pursuit of genuinely meaningful social change. Obscured behind benign-looking personalized interfaces, we are confronted, here, with the ideological dimension of datafied publics and activity. The politics of algorithms, in this regard, manifests itself not only at the point of ideals, but also has significant implications for the very organizational patterns and dynamics of how groupings come together and movements are formed. In particular, the logic of social media has been said to encourage 'ephemeral' forms of protest. Milan elaborates on this issue in her chapter by focusing particularly on the implications of the technical properties of commercial social media for the question of collective identity in social movements. The entrenchment of social media into everyday life has changed and subverted familiar dichotomies between the individual and the collective, the intimate and the public, and copresence and distance. With Milan's contribution, we see how the fundamental notion of identity within any group or collective has been replaced by a politics of visibility in which online presence trumps the sense of belonging typical of the post-68 new social movements. Expressions of hashtag solidarity, postings of updates and images, datafied emotions and relations, are all part of a social media logic that contribute to an 'always-on' experience of collective action. Although this has multiplied opportunities for experiencing the collective dimension of social action, Milan argues that it has also come to replace the process of meaning-making within a movement through which collective identity is shaped and sustained. Instead, communication as a process has come to be the organizational ritual of these forms of social media protest, in which the very visibility of the content and interactions within these spaces that, as constituted forms of self-presentation, comes to act as symbols or proofs of group membership and even political activism. That is, it is the very publicity of participation rather than the sense of belonging that has become the defining feature of the collective action, serving as a proxy for identity and any collective 'we'. In such circumstances, protest starts and ends with the individual and its mediated self-expression, in a continuous quest for more and more visible forms of participation that simultaneously has unintended consequences for both internal and external dynamics of a social movement.

In addition to promoting visible forms of self-expression, the logic of commercial social media platforms has also contributed to a significant shift in space and time that, again, needs to form part of the debate on contemporary forms of protest. The emphasis on speeded-up communications across vast distances is often taken as a unidirectional narrative of progress and opportunity, said to enable a host of enhanced possibilities for participation and political activism. Undoubtedly, near-instant communication amongst dispersed communities allows for a great number of organizational tasks to be more easily achieved. However, an algorithmic design that encourages the constant production of highly templated content and that values 'real-time', 'immediacy' and 'abundance' over and above meaning and embodiment also diminishes prospects and potentials for longer-term and sustained efforts towards emancipatory ideals. We see this further discussed in the contributions from both Barassi and Kaun. In these, we are introduced to social media as a 'temporalising practice' in which activists who engage with these platforms as part of their repertoires of protest are forced into a temporal rhythm that for all the opportunities of fast and widespread information-sharing is also far from conducive to collective decision making and democratic practice. Again, as Barassi points out, we are confronted with the tension that arises between activists' progressive and collective cultures on the one hand, and the cultural processes reinforced by digital capitalism—of which commercial social media is a fundamental part—on the other. The abundance of individual expressions ('social noise'), the encouragement of quick and short messages and the fast creation of strategic alliances based on emotional or reactive responses rather than a shared political project all come to constitute a form of mutual superficiality and fragile adhesion by distracting from or even replacing the pursuit of collective issues that require time and space for reflection and discussion. This, Kaun illustrates by introducing some historical comparisons, differs from previous protest movements in which slower forms of media practices not only served to spread messages and share information, but also provided time and space through those very practices for collective identity formation and decision making. The media practices of recent protest movements that have relied heavily on social media activity, Kaun argues, stand in stark contrast to the attempts to challenge dominant power relations in a way that follows the principles of participatory democracy which demands time.

POLICING, CENSORSHIP AND SURVEILLANCE

As all our contributions allude to, the continuous production of data on commercial social media platforms has both intended and unintended consequences for activists. It shapes, shifts and structures protest dynamics in contradictory ways and it simultaneously embeds protest practices within a system based on mining and monitoring activity by a number of different actors. Social media platforms are based on a business model that valorizes surveillance (Cohen 2008), both by enticing users through news feeds and updates of each other's activity, as well as through providing and selling data and content produced by users to interested third parties. This has meant that social media platforms have become central spaces for observing and managing activity, especially activity that might be seen to challenge or upset existing social orders. The role of social media platforms in the governance and regulation of protest is made explicit in Hintz's contribution to this book in which he traces the multitude of ways social media companies have become key actors in censoring and restricting forms of dissent. Rather than being the voice of citizens, advocates for democracy and freedom of expression, we have in recent years witnessed a shift in the societal function attributed to social media companies, one that sees them as part of a much more tightly knit partnership with the state in maintaining social order. As Hintz points out, the Snowden leaks in June 2013 and their aftermath have illustrated the extent to which these corporate actors are now relied upon to carry out state functions of governance and control. This is a continuation of forms of surveillance and censorship that have long been enacted through various types of filters and digital infrastructures, and that now have been evidenced to be all-encompassing through programmes such as Prism and Tempora that target all social media use. They highlight the sheer power of social media companies by having concentrated ownership of such volumes of data on citizens and their activities, both in terms of whom they decide or are forced to share that data with, as well as how and when they choose to intervene in those activities.

This power becomes evident when certain groups suddenly become targeted and have pages or content removed without warning or explanation, or when activists find that their personal data and communication about potential activities are held in state intelligence databases and have been used to inform police strategy aimed at repressing any protest activity. As Redden points out in her chapter, contemporary forms of neoliberal governance rely extensively on surveillance as a way to maintain social order. The dependency on surveillance by the state is not a historically new phenomenon (it is, in many respects, part and parcel of the advancement of capitalism), and targeting and repressing political activists is part of a long-standing tradition in Western democracies. However, as Redden highlights, the sheer failings of neoliberalism that we have witnessed particularly with the financial crisis of 2008 and its aftermath has called for ever-extensive and ever-reaching forms of monitoring and intervention in citizens' lives by the state, predominantly carried out in secret, in order to ensure the continuation of social control. Neoliberalism requires ignorance, Redden argues, and this increasingly entails finding ways to curb knowledge, information and activity, before it reaches the wider public.

One of the most prominent manifestations of such forms of governance in recent years is the development of predictive policing as a core tactic in managing protest. Central to this form of policing is its reliance upon social media data as a way to inform police so as to devise strategies that will limit the size, length and impact of protests through intercepting communications infrastructures, forcing people into contained spaces, intimidating participants with imposing vehicles or horses or other forms of threatening and controlling practices. In Elmer's chapter we are introduced to this tactic in the context of the Toronto G20 protests in 2010. What is particularly interesting about this contribution to the book is that it highlights the uses of digital surveillance to manage and curtail protest activity, but also documents the ways in which the recording and sharing of information via social media by the protestors have become a central aspect of the protest activities and tactics as a way to challenge surveillance 'from above', continuing the themes around visibility and the production of content and data as previously mentioned. Indeed, the protestor/witness subject that Elmer engages with in his chapter is emblematic of contemporary protest in an age of social media. However, as Elmer points out, the actual practices of the protestor/witness subject are far less straightforward than simply being a countertactic to the heavy-handedness of police, particularly when examined in the context of the digital media economy. In such a context we are confronted with questions of not only identity and purpose of capturing and sharing data, but also fundamental issues regarding ownership and copyright of digital content. In his account of making a documentary using solely content produced and uploaded by protestors at the Toronto G20 protests under Creative Commons licences, Elmer illustrates how the terms and conditions and political economy of these commercial social media platforms severely limits any potential for using images and films from protestors uploaded on social media for the purposes of genuinely open, collaborative and antisystemic content.

Rather, we are, again, to quote Milan in this volume, 'confronted with the fundamental ambivalence in contemporary collective action, namely its distancing itself from the values and exploitation of digital capitalism, while at the same time overrelying on its products, and social media above all, for the protest's unfolding, diffusion and survival'.

CONTRADICTIONS, CONTEXT AND MYTHS

These contradictions of using commercial social media platforms for the purposes of protest and the pursuit of emancipatory ideals play out, also, in the consciousness and mindsets of activists themselves. The processes of control that saturate social media platforms as we have discussed here—through the politics of their algorithms, the logic that guides them, the culture they promote, their role in governing and policing dissent, and their conditional limitations on collaborative meaning making—can all be seen to increasingly permeate the psyche of social movements and political activists, presenting them with numerous dilemmas. As Treré outlines in his contribution to this book, looking particularly at the #YoSoy132 movement in Mexico, the communication practices around social media by activists are not constitutive of the 'smooth functioning' of counterpower through mass self-communication that we find in Castells's accounts of protest movements, for example, but are constantly plagued by conflicts, clashes, struggles and discord. These conflicts come to manifest themselves in terms of daily interactions and difficulties as activists express concern and discomfort with integrating social media into their protest practices. Issues of ephemerality and weak ties seep through movement interactions by raising questions of authority and belonging in terms of conflicts over who has access and what can be posted on social media platforms in the name of any given protest. Equally, Treré points out, the concern with surveillance on social media platforms prevails within the movements as a 'light paranoia' that, in the case of Mexico, eventually manifested itself after Mexican police carried out several arbitrary detentions and human rights violations during a protest, leading many activists to quit social media entirely.

Indeed, as Treré outlines, the Mexican context illustrates the extent to which (traditional) politics outside the world of social media continues to constrain and control emerging forms of resistance, both in terms of online and offline practices. That is, we need to look at broader social and political developments in order to understand how and to what extent activists engage with social media for the purposes of protest. This is further developed in our contribution from Porto and Brant, looking at the Free Fare movement in Brazil and the protests that erupted in June 2013. In this, we are presented with the benefits of a contextualist approach to social media and protest that emphasizes a number of important political developments leading up to the protests of 2013. In doing so, Porto and Brant do not dismiss the role played by social media in mobilizing the protests, but they do provide a precise and situated framework for understanding the peculiarities of both the social media practices affiliated with the movement as well as the nature of the movement itself. As such, we are shown an illustrative example in this chapter of how the contradictory nature of social media as discussed above plays out in the Brazilian context. In particular, we see here how social media comes to offer an avenue for information-sharing on activists' terms, but simultaneously contributes to a shift in the movement towards a more individualized and fragmented political agenda, largely constituted by instances of self-expression from members of the young and affluent middle classes. The lack of a shared political project and collective identity, and an emphasis instead on visible forms of fast, short emotive responses was in this case played out within a political context that tended to favour nonspecific and vague demands, such as 'better' public education or 'less' corruption, that could receive widespread forms of visible recognition and affirmation on social media in terms of likes, retweets, and so on. This type of activism came to blur and marginalize more traditional forms of political organization with a clearly focused social justice agenda that had been central in the initial phases of the movement.

In emphasizing the contradictory nature of social media for protest in broader context, we are provided with an opportunity to reassess and challenge some of the dominant discourses in public debate on how social media is said to not only enable protest, but to enable a new kind of protest culture that is more spontaneous, more democratic and more horizontal and grassroots-driven. In fact, such discourse has become so commonplace that it has almost been ingrained as a standard news narrative promoted by journalists in reporting on contemporary protest, particularly when they seek to provide sympathetic coverage of events. Indeed, as Dencik argues in her contribution to this book, emphasizing the role of social media in how protests have been organized and mobilized has become a way of granting legitimacy and credibility to protest movements. That is, by making the case that social media has been instrumental in how a protest movement has emerged, an implicit set of assumptions are accompanied by such a narrative with regards to the 'authentic' nature of such a movement, often based around assumptions that the movement has come about 'naturally' and spontaneously, without vested interests or fixed agendas so frequently associated with traditional forms of political organization, and without hierarchy and power-hungry leaders. As we have outlined here, such a narrative is largely based on myth that ignores broader dynamics, and as Dencik points out, it is a narrative that can be used strategically by different groups in order to obscure or avert focus on the political economy, internal architecture and organizational structure of a movement. Instead, protests become abstracted from context, appearing deinstitutionalized and organization-less, and are largely applauded for it.

WHERE DO WE GO FROM HERE?

So where does this leave the debate on social media and protest? One aspect that we hope to contribute to with the publication of this volume is of course to try and debunk some of these myths that prevail dominant discourses on the relationship between social media and protest. As we want to highlight with the collection of chapters in this book, key critical issues are fundamentally neglected in many of such discourses and by ignoring these, provide only very limited, and largely disingenuous, analysis of the nature and possibilities of contemporary protest. This, we would argue, contributes to maintaining status quo and strengthens the ability for institutions of power to harness social control by promoting a technology-centred illusion of citizen empowerment and opportunity for realizing genuinely emancipatory ideals. These opportunities exist, of course, but commercial social media platforms are unlikely to pave their paths. The political economy, architecture and algorithmic design of these platforms introduce a plethora of contradictory forces in relying on these technologies for long-term antisystemic resistance and social change. As the chapters in this book also illustrate, activists are continuously confronted and forced to negotiate with these limitations, challenges and risks of incorporating commercial social media practices into their repertoires of protest activity. On this alienated pathway, they are in danger of losing critical energies and momentum, that otherwise might have supported their cause.

The other aspect that the collection of contributions in this volume highlight is the question of what this means for contemporary forms of protest. The use of social media, and digital technologies more broadly, is part and parcel of everyday life and the social and political developments of today's society. Activism and protest necessarily entail a digital dimension in such a context, as it most certainly should. This book is not a call to analogue politics or a nostalgic fetishization of 'asphalt' activism. However, there is room to negotiate what such a digital dimension in contemporary protest might look like. Here, our collection of chapters takes us beyond a discussion of merely the nature of digital tools that activists might engage with. Certainly, as Leistert remarks in his chapter, in previous decades of internet communications, grassroots movements built their own services and tools for dissemination and in the luring appeal of abundant 'free' platforms, remembering this heritage of control over the means of production is particularly important. Beyond that, however, our contributions also raise crucial questions about the very character of movements themselves in an age of social media. The nature of protests said to be supported by social media are of a certain kind, often celebrated and endorsed particularly because they are seen to make away with the shackles of traditional forms of political organization claimed to no longer be relevant for the political orientations and concerns amongst ordinary people. Instead, activism becomes possible without the dilemmas and constraints of such organization.

However, is this really the case? And, if so, what is the nature of such political form? In our final chapter, from Lovink and Rossiter, this debate is developed by looking at what happens to the nexus of organization and digital networks. Advancing their concept of organized networks or 'orgnets', we are provided here with a discussion of the inadequacies of the different organizational forms that have constituted much of what we have seen in recent mobilizations of protest, and presented instead with 'orgnets' as a way to formulate an alternative political form that may come closer to realizing emancipatory ideals. In such political form, the question of organization must be coupled with technical and infrastructural issues related to social media use and focused very clearly on the network architectures at the centre of power. It must do so because we have arrived at a stage where the digital has become so omnipresent that it has been pushed to the background and been naturalized, what might be referred to as a postdigital society. A politics of the postdigital must, therefore, according to Lovink and Rossiter, confront and make visible 'the submersion of communication into the vaults of secret data centres scattered about the globe'. As such, the future of protest in a postdigital world is not about making away with organization, or about replacing organization with digital communication networks, but rather about finding ways to create collaborative forms of resistance with more sustainable organizational tools that allow for longer-term (human, not algorithm-centred) decision making.

In putting together the contributions in this book, therefore, we wish to further ignite the debate on the relationship between social media and protest, but we wish to do so on terms that provide a more critical and nuanced perspective on how different aspects of this debate are related to each other. What is more, in so doing, we wish to contribute to a more considered discussion on the nature and future of protest and possibilities for resistance against dominant institutions of power that is able to take account of the multitude of contradictions and paradoxes that surround activism in a digital world. The fact that within the closed walls of corporate data mining platforms the call for social justice becomes attractive and viable for selling advertisements, this we believe, must irritate us all, and needs to be faced, in theory as in practice.

REFERENCES

Cohen, Nicole. (2008). The valorization of surveillance: Towards a political economy of Facebook. *Democratic Communiqué 22*(1), 5–22.
Curran, J. (2010). Technology foretold. In N. Fenton (Ed.), *New media, old news: Journalism and democracy in the digital age*, 19–34. London and Thousand Oaks: Sage.

Chapter One

Promise and Practice in Studies of Social Media and Movements

Sebastian Haunss

The recent protests during the 'Arab Spring' and in the wave of 'Occupy' movements have renewed interest in the use of the internet and especially social media by social movements. Digital social media technologies offer a low-cost way to reach out to large constituencies and to communicate in many-to-many settings. In addition, with the spread of mobile- and smart-phones, this technology is ubiquitously available. These characteristics have led to a widespread adoption of social media in protest mobilizations. Social movements now regularly use social media to communicate and to mobilize for their actions. Are social media, when it comes to social movements and protest, thus the leaflets and political posters of the early twenty-first century? Or do they, as some authors have claimed, fundamentally alter the conditions for the emergence of protest and social movements? May they even cause social movements, as the notion of 'Twitter' or 'Facebook' revolutions suggests?

In this chapter I address these questions by discussing the findings of existing studies on social movements and social media. I assess to which extent some authors' claims about the fundamental importance of social media technologies in recent protests and uprisings (e.g., Howard and Hussain 2013) can be substantiated in empirical studies of protest mobilizations or whether the results lend more support for the claim that social media did not fundamentally influence the mobilization dynamics (e.g., Brym et al. 2014). The aim is not to explore all aspects of the quickly growing research literature, but to discuss some of the more prominent recurring findings along with the literature questioning them, and to offer some structuring elements for relating the various studies to each other.

To do this, this chapter starts with a quick overview over the use of internet technologies by social movements since the 1990s, and discusses four general claims about the relationship between the internet and social media on the one hand, and social movements and protest on the other. It then proceeds to a closer look at recent empirical studies of protest and social media, closing with an evaluation of the current knowledge and remaining research gaps in this field. Special attention is paid to the question how current digital communication tools interact with more established elements in social movements' repertoires of action.

A VERY SHORT HISTORY OF SOCIAL MOVEMENTS AND THE INTERNET

Social movements have been quick to adopt digital computer networks as communication tools for internal planning and deliberation and to reach out to the general public. Long before the invention of the World Wide Web led to the development of the internet as we know it today, already by the end of the 1980s social movement activists created—linked through the Association for Progressive Communications (APC)—mailbox-based computer networks to facilitate communication and information exchange among geographically dispersed activists (Harasim 1993; Lokk 2008). But these early uses of computer networks among movement activists have hardly been noticed by social scientists, and within their movements those activists who were using the networks were clearly a small minority.

This has changed dramatically when the Zapatistas on 1 January 1994 began their struggle against neoliberalism and for the rights of indigenous people in the Mexican state of Chiapas. The Zapatistas, with their charismatic leader Subcommandante Marcos, skillfully used the internet to spread their message across the world. Their 'insurrection by internet' (Knudson 1998) led for the first time to speculations that the internet would facilitate new forms of transnational or even global mobilization, provide social movements with 'historically new organizational capabilities' (Cleaver 1998, 631) and provide the tools and a virtual public sphere for wide participation in direct democratic processes.

After this initial euphoria about the potential the internet would offer to social movements, the protests against the WTO meeting in Seattle in 1999 sparked the next round of scholarly interest in the relation between social movements, protest and the internet (Van Aelst and Walgrave 2002; della Porta and Mosca 2005; Juris 2005). The internet seemed to perfectly fit to this 'movement of movements' with its nonhierarchical, dispersed and global structure. Special attention was paid to the creation of Indymedia, a network of independent media centres where everybody was able to publish news and commentary (Kidd 2003). During the protests in Seattle, and during subsequent protests and mobilizations of various social movements, Indymedia has provided a partisan news channel where activists publish their interpretation of the events while the events are happening. To some degree, Indymedia was the digital pendant to the foundation of alternative leftist newspapers in the early (Libération, France 1973) or late (die tageszeitung, Germany 1978) 1970s. In both cases, movement activists or sympathizers saw a need to create an alternative to the established mainstream press that—in the eyes of the activists—disregarded or misinterpreted the movement and its activities. For the traditional paper-based newspapers, the notorious problem was running them as profitable enterprises and over time they evolved into moderately left daily newspapers written by professional journalists. For Indymedia, financial sustainability also emerged as a problem and resulted in the closure of several Indymedia sites (Giraud 2014), even though the costs for running the web servers on open source software are extremely low in comparison to the production of a traditional newspaper. But in hindsight, Indymedia's more serious problem is that it never managed to reach a similarly broad audience beyond the movements that are using it. Many Indymedia sites have evolved into websites where movement activities are announced and discussed among activists. This has led some authors to claim that Indymedia has failed (Ippolita, Lovink and Rossiter 2009), whereas others interpret the prevalence of debates as a positive sign for the development of alternative democratic online counterpublics (Milioni 2009).

With internet use becoming an integral part of everyday life, its use in protest campaigns and by social movements has meanwhile lost the air of the spectacular. And consequently, since the early 2000s research has branched out and now covers a broad variety of online activism. In an overview of research findings, Jennifer Earl and her collaborators have categorized social movements' internet use into four types of usage patterns: brochure-ware, online facilitation of offline activism, online participation and online organizing (Earl et al. 2010, 428), where brochure-ware stands for internet use that basically replaces flyers, leaflets and brochures with websites and mailing lists. Online facilitation of offline activism adds simple interactive elements to facilitate coordination between activists, online participation provides tools to interact with the addressees of the protest (e.g., online petitions) and online organizing shifts the main mobilizing activities to the internet.

More recently, a new series of massive protest mobilizations that began with the Arab Spring in December 2010 and included the 15-M protests in Spain (March 2011), the Occupy protests in the United States and in several European countries (September 2011), and the protests in Istanbul's Taksim Gezi Park (May 2013) has refocused public and scholarly attention on the specific interaction between large-scale mass protests and social media

(Castañeda 2012; Costanza-Chock 2012; Tufekci and Wilson 2012; Gamson and Sifry 2013; Howard and Hussain 2013; Tremayne 2014). This last wave of scholarly interest concentrated heavily on social movements' use of commercial global social networking and social media sites like Facebook and Twitter, thus shifting the attention from social movements' attempts to create alternative online publics with their own tools and technologies, to social movements' use of existing corporate-provided and corporate-controlled social media tools to facilitate or enable mobilization.

Looking back on twenty years of research on social movements and social media, we can see public and scholarly attention shifting with the evolution of the technology, focusing always on social movements' and protesters' adoption of the most recent technological tools. This focus on the newest internet technologies goes along with the recurring question whether these new technological tools may offer new opportunities for collective action unavailable to previous generations of activists. In addition, this dynamic is also driven by the various social movements' ability to mobilize large-scale protests which have again and again surprised established news media and many social scientists. For most pundits, the insurrection of the Zapatistas, the Global Justice Movement's protests in Seattle, the Arab Spring and Occupy Wall Street were completely unexpected events in times where social movements were often seen as relatively weak and marginal political actors. In this pessimist frame, technology seemed to offer an explanation for the surprise about these unforeseen mobilizations, leading then to a rather optimistic interpretation of the role of technology.

CYBER-OPTIMISTS, PESSIMISTS AND REALISTS?

These technology-focused and often enthusiastic interpretations of recent social movements have usually been complemented by more pessimistic or even dystopian interpretations of the new technological developments. Previous overviews on research about social movements and the internet have identified three general perspectives which have been labeled cyber-optimists and cyber-pessimists, with a large group of realists in between (Earl et al. 2010; Gerbaudo 2012; Torres Soriano 2013; Lutz and Hoffmann 2014). Cyber-optimists assume that the new technology would not only facilitate, but genuinely enable, protest. Cyber-pessimists, on the other hand, either argue that the internet would not have a substantial effect on social movements' ability to mobilize, or that it would even have a negative effect. Between these poles, the largest group of scholars acknowledges effects of new internet technologies but argues that these effects 'tend to be in degree and do not require new theoretical explanations, or even substantial alteration to existing theories' (Earl et al. 2010, 427).

Unfortunately, this neat categorization obscures more than it reveals, because it at least implicitly suggests that the group labeled cyber-optimists and the cyber-pessimists each share a distinct set of assumptions and convictions about the internet and social movements. But a closer look at the writings of authors associated with these groups shows that neither camp is in any way homogenous. The optimism of the first group is based on differing and partially competing assumptions, as is the pessimism of the second. Moreover, optimists do not necessarily answer to the qualms of the pessimists and vice versa.

In order to assess the existing research, it is more helpful not to start from the authors' overall evaluations of the internet or of specific internet technologies but to focus on their assumptions about the relationship between internet technologies and social movements. Following this perspective the existing literature on internet and social movements revolves around four general claims about this relationship. Some of these claims are specific to individual authors, some are shared by several. For the sake of convenience, I phrase these claims here as positive relationships, but obviously the pessimists formulate the inverse claims to denote a negative relationship. The four general claims are:

Claim 1: The internet solves the problem of transaction costs
Claim 2: The internet solves the (rational choice) problem of collective action
Claim 3: The internet corresponds to the conflicts of the network society
Claim 4: The internet enables new form of protest/organizing

In the following sections, I discuss each of these claims and evaluate their empirical and theoretical foundations.

The Internet Solves the Problem of Transaction Costs

Clay Shirky, the US writer and academic, and 'king of the techno-optimists' (Gerbaudo 2012, 7), builds his argument about the benefits of modern internet technologies for social movements on the idea of diminishing transaction costs. In his book about organizations and group formation (Shirky 2008), he argues that the key contribution of social media tools is their ability to radically reduce—if not completely remove—transaction costs for collective action. Shirky writes that social media allow ordinary citizens to share information and coordinate their activities on a previously unknown level. Before the internet, it was hard and relatively costly (in terms of time and resources) to inform people about a perceived injustice and to organize them in a collective action against it. Now, Shirky argues, ordinary people can arrange events 'without much advance planning' (Shirky 2008, 175) because they no longer have to rely on slow and costly traditional means of contacting and coordinating dispersed individuals. As a result, '[t]he collapse of transaction costs makes it easier for people to get together—so much easier, in fact, that it is changing the world' (Shirky 2008, 48).

In his argumentation, Shirky draws on Yochai Benkler, who, in his book *The Wealth of Networks* (Benkler 2006), had developed a somewhat similar thesis. Benkler argues that the internet offers the possibility to coordinate distributed collaboration on a previously unknown scale and with minimal costs. It enables what Benkler calls peer production, that is 'effective, large-scale cooperative efforts' (Benkler 2006, 5), on a global scale and under conditions of abundance, by rapidly reducing the transaction costs of creating knowledge. Under these conditions the likelihood of dispersed individuals to cooperate would increase significantly (for a more detailed discussion, see Haunss 2013, 230).

While the argument that the internet would have the potential to radically reduce transaction costs and thus enable forms of collaboration that were previously almost impossible is compelling, it offers a solution for a problem with at least dubious relevancy for social movements. Shirky argues that the most serious obstacle to the 'basic human instinct' (Shirky 2008, 60) to be part of a group was until now too high transaction costs. But social movements are not simply the result of group formation. While Wikipedia—the prime example of peer production—is certainly impressive in terms of enabling cooperation among otherwise unconnected and geographically dispersed individuals, it is not such a good example for a powerful social movement. Precisely because, in order to act collectively as a political actor, social movements have to define a problem, create a shared interpretation, engage in continued interaction with an opponent, find allies and create a collective identity. Radically lowering transaction costs will facilitate some of these tasks, but it will not help much with others. Consequently, in existing social movement research, high transaction costs have usually not been identified as the most pressing problem social movements face. High transaction costs have been acknowledged to pose a significant problem for transnational movements (Tarrow 1998, 235), but even for them the internet lowers only the costs for communication, not the costs for protesting in distant places (Van Laer and Van Aelst 2010, 1161).

While the observation of diminishing transaction costs is in itself convincing, it helps to explain only some forms of internet-based and internet-enabled activism. Low transaction costs promote, for example, mass participation in online petitions and similar forms of 'clicktivism' that reach a very broad audience and require only minimal individual investments in terms of time and resources.

The Internet Solves the (Rational Choice) Problem of Collective Action

A second line of arguments is built around the claim that the internet would solve the collective action problem as it was formulated in the classical works of Mancur Olson (Olson 1971). Starting from the standard rational choice assumption of utility-maximizing individuals, Olson argues that individual participation in collective action would be unlikely as long as the collective action is aimed at generating collective goods. Collective goods are all nonexcludable goods, meaning that individuals cannot be excluded from using them. They can either be common goods if individual use is depleting them (i.e., they are rivalrous), or they can be public goods if one individual's use does not impair everybody else's use of the good (i.e., they are nonrivalrous). In any case, their nonexcludability means that instead of helping to produce the good, each individual can as well decide to free-ride on other persons' efforts, an option that is, from a utility-maximizing perspective, always more attractive because it allows for the enjoyment of the benefits without paying the costs. Since many goods aspired by social movements are collective goods, this problem should be especially virulent for them.

Lance Bennett and Alexandra Segerberg start exactly from this assumption when they argue that 'digitally networked action' would do away with the problems of collective action because it follows a different logic of 'connective action' (Bennett and Segerberg 2012, 743). In their words, the logic of collective action is riddled with the 'organizational dilemma of getting individuals to overcome resistance to joining actions where personal participation costs may outweigh marginal gains' (Bennett and Segerberg 2012, 748). The internet, or more precisely internet-based personal communication technologies, now offers a new option for collective action centred on the personal transmission and sharing of political information. Bennett and Segerberg argue that this 'connective action' is based on weak tie networks, does not require strong organizational control or the construction of collective identities, but is nevertheless able to react effectively to given opportunities (Bennett and Segerberg 2012, 750).

Bennett and Segerberg thus offer a 'solution' for the classical collective action problem not by providing a new mechanism for selective incentives (which was Olson's solution) but by offering a new logic of connective action built around digital media as organizing agents that supplements and possibly substitutes the logic of collective action.

This optimistic vision is countered by Evgeny Morozov's pessimistic judgement of online activism as 'slacktivism' (Morozov 2011, 220). He argues that the availability of tools for online activism might actually distract activists from those forms of engagement that are needed to achieve significant political change or even overthrow oppressive regimes: activism that embraces the risk of being arrested, intimidated and tortured (Morozov 2011, 218). For him, connective action is less a promise than a threat to conventional activism, because it would create the false illusion of meaningful engagement while actually restricting activism to mostly low-risk and symbolic forms of engagement.

But even if Morozov's pessimistic evaluation of the new social media tools' negative consequences for social movements and protest may be a bit overblown, Bennett's optimistic evaluation suffers from a problem similar to the transaction costs perspective. Since Olson first formulated his collective action problem in the 1960s, a large body of research has accumulated showing that Olson's claim rests on a very narrow assumption, namely that individual participation in collective action should meaningfully be conceptualized as a rational choice cost-benefit-calculation.

A simple empirical observation shows that in contemporary societies there is usually neither a lack of protest and social movements nor of collective action in general. The reason for this is, that collective action and especially participation in protests and social movements is motivated by many things and individual cost-benefit-calculations are only one element among others. Olson's *homo economicus* model is thus not well suited to explain collective action or its obstacles. Consequently social movement research has largely abandoned a pure resource mobilization approach (McCarthy and Zald 1977) that rests on similar epistemological assumptions.

But if the emergence and development of social movements depends on (among others) the availability of resources, of political and discursive opportunities, on successful framing strategies, and the creation of collective identities, then the easily created weak-tie networks of connected action are at most one factor and probably not the most important to facilitate protest and other forms of contentious politics. It thus makes more sense to interpret connective action as one additional element in the repertoires of collective action social movements can draw on, an element that will not replace forms of engagement which require more commitment and sometimes even the risk of bodily harm and incarceration.

The Internet Corresponds to the Conflicts of the Network Society

A more theoretical perspective that is not claiming that the internet or social media would offer a solution to collective action problems can be found in the writings of Manuel Castells (2009, 2012) and his former student Jeffrey Juris (2005, 2014), who argue that the networking logic of current social movements, and especially of the Global Justice Movement, correspond to the more general assertion of networking logics in network societies.

Juris argues that in the global justice movement 'networks as computer-supported infrastructure (technology), networks as organizational structure (form), and networks as political model (norm)' (Juris 2008, 11) are combined in new cultural practices of the digital age developed in the movement. The internet's reticulate structure would correspond to the organizational networks of the movement and also structure the activists' ideals of cooperation and social coordination. Whereas the claims that the internet would solve the problem of transaction costs and of collective action are mainly based on a notion of superior effectiveness of internet-based communication and social media tools, Juris's idea of a cultural logic of networking locates the importance of the internet for social movements on a different level. Here, the focus lies not so much on the technical efficiency but rather on the promise of nonhierarchical social collaboration.

Castells picks up this idea of a cultural logic of networking and integrates it into his theory of the network society, in which the internet represents one instance of a networking logic that replaces the centralized and hierarchical command-and-control logic of the industrial society (Castells 2000, 2009). The emergence of the internet is thus embedded in more far-reaching social transformations. Mobile phones and the internet, or more general modern networked communication infrastructures, are for Castells not only more or less new technologies but technological developments that correspond to more general social changes associated with the emergence of the network society. A similar thought has been developed by Bennett and Segerberg when they argue that today's flexible social weak-tie networks represent a 'shift from group-based to individualized societies' (Bennett and Segerberg 2012, 744).

The internet as a communication infrastructure becomes so important, because in Castells' perspective communication is at the centre of protest mobilizations and social movements 'are formed by communicating messages of rage and hope' (Castells 2009, 301). As a consequence, changes in the communication environment alter social movements' chances to reach an audience and mobilize for protest. He points especially to the strong parallels between the viral logic of social media and the mobilization processes in what he calls 'networked social movements', and in a more far-reaching interpretation, he argues that the internet and networked social movements 'share a specific culture, the culture of autonomy, the fundamental cultural matrix of contemporary societies' (Castells 2012, 230).

To some extent, Castells oscillates between his almost dystopian depiction of the network society as undermining democratic processes and structured by powerful economic actors—a perspective that reminds us that unequal power relations do not vanish with the demise of hierarchical command-and-control systems as the dominant model for social and economic relations—and his very optimistic interpretation of networked social movements as utopian attempts to reprogramme the network and to 'regain autonomy of the subject vis-à-vis the institutions of society' (Castells 2012, 228).

The important contribution of Juris and Castells is their insistence that the networking logic is more important than the concrete technical tools that are used and which enable networked communication and collaboration. But whether the networked structure of current 'networked' social movements differentiates them from earlier social movements is at least disputable. In the literature on social movements, a relatively long tradition exists arguing that social movements in general—and not just current movements that rely strongly on the internet—should be interpreted as networks (Diani 1992, 13; Rucht 1994, 76–77), and not as special forms of organizations (e.g., McAdam 1982, 25) or as relatively unstructured phenomena of collective behaviour (e.g., Blumer 1949, 199). This doesn't contradict the importance of networking logics for social movements but questions that it would be something new and specific to the networked social movements of the network society.

The Internet Enables New Forms of Protest/Organizing

A weaker version of the networking logic is contained in claim that the internet would enable new forms of protest and protest organization. The most prominent idea in this respect is that the internet and/or digital communication technologies would enable leaderless movements. This claim comes in two flavors. The first is what I call the weak-tie version. Its core argument is that new technologies enable multiple and flexible direct connections between (potential) activists. Instead of creating connections through strong organizational ties, they are now directly connected in decentralized weak-tie networks. This makes organizations and leadership superfluous, or at least much less important than before. Bennett calls these weak-tie based mobilizations 'permanent campaigns' (Bennett 2003, 150), sustained by the networking and mobilizing capabilities of digital communication technologies. Howard and Hussain argue that the uprising in Egypt that toppled the Mubarak regime was such an instance of leaderless mobilization (Howard and Hussain 2013, 32).

The second, strong-tie version is put forward by Juris when he argues that the internet enabled the activists of the Global Justice Movement to build alternative, nonhierarchical networks with a strong focus on grassroots democracy. The activists use digital communication networks to build horizontal ties between autonomous elements, to facilitate the free circulation of information, and to collaborate in decentralized consensus-based decision making (Juris 2008, 11). But the links between activists that are created in these networks are not weak ties between otherwise unconnected individuals and existing only for short periods. Instead, Juris shows in his anthropological field study within the Global Justice Movement that activists still establish strong interpersonal links and friendships, that digital communication creates only one layer in a multiplex network connecting the activists and that these different layers are connected. This view is strongly supported by Gerbaudo's research in which he highlights the interconnectedness of online and offline protests and reports activists' claims that their 'Facebook friends' were actually also real friends and thus did not represent only weak ties (Gerbaudo 2012, 146).

Both notions of technology-enabled leaderlessness have been criticized from three perspectives. The first (e.g., Leach 2013) argues that the movements' attempts to create structures without stable and formal hierarchies are not particularly new but have been practiced with more or less success in various social movements at least since the 1980s. Relating leaderless structures and horizontal communication to the internet, to social media or more generally to digital communication tools would thus exaggerate the role of technology.

The second line of criticism does not deny that social media would be effective to coordinate huge weak-tie networks in leaderless protest activities. But it claims—similar to Morozov's criticism of slacktivism—that these forms of activism should not be uncritically applauded and instead seen as weaker and more ephemeral forms of protest. As a result, Geert Lovink argues—or actually rather demands—that 'strong organizational forms, firmly rooted in real life and capable of mobilizing (financial) resources, will eventually overrule weak online commitments (I "like" your insurrection)' (Lovink 2012, 170).

A third line of criticism argues that the communication and cooperation structures which can be observed in current social movements are actually less leaderless and horizontal than asserted in the literature. This position is put forward by Paolo Gerbaudo, who argues that the practices of current movements (his research is based on the Egyptian uprising, the Spanish indignados and Occupy) 'are ridden with a deep contradiction between the discourse of leaderlessness and horizontality and organizational practices in which leadership continues to exist, though in a dialogical or interactive form' (Gerbaudo 2012, 157). Instead of leaderless movements, he observes new forms of leadership based on differential use of social media tools and linked to the still important 'street-level leadership' structures in current social movements. Gerbaudo does not deny that social media play an important role and even structure the practices of current social movements. But he sees their role as one element in a more complex 'choreography of assembly' (Gerbaudo 2012, 11) in which the construction of virtual public spaces interacts with the appropriation of physical public spaces. This echoes to some extent Dieter Rucht's earlier claim that the internet would not replace but complement established media practices of social movements (Rucht 2004). Social media are well suited to reach sympathizers and activists. But social movements usually can only be successful if they reach and get support from a broader audience. And this general public still can only be reached reliably through mass media. Internet and social media tools can thus only complement and not replace other media strategies.

In sum, this discussion of the four most prominent claims about the relation of the internet and social media on the one hand, and protest and social movements on the other, offers a rather ambivalent picture. Overall, the far-reaching claims about fundamental transformations of mobilizing structures and processes generally rest either on weak empirical grounds or they offer solutions for collective-action problems that do not exist or are not among the most pressing problems for current social movements. But even if the internet and social media have not changed everything for protest and social movements, they undeniably have altered the conditions and possibilities for protest mobilizations in numerous aspects. In the following section I therefore discuss the most interesting findings of the growing empirical research literature on internet and social media use in protests and social movements.

SOCIAL MEDIA USE IN CONTEMPORARY PROTESTS

Empirical studies about the use of social media and the internet in contemporary protests are generally based on two types of data sources: on the one hand, authors have directly analysed the content of digital media and the networks that are created between their users. On the other hand, digital media use has been investigated with more general research tools like surveys and (participant) observation.

In the first line of investigation, one way to analyse online activism is to assess the hyperlink structures that connect activist (and other) websites. Researchers quickly have started to collect this readily available information in order to identify important organizations and websites in various protest mobilizations. The results show that organizations which are important in the offline mobilization process (e.g., most visible in news reports about the protests) usually also show up as central and strongly connected nodes in the link networks (Van Aelst and Walgrave 2002; Badouard and Monnoyer-Smith 2013). Hyperlink networks thus seem to replicate relationships among organizations that also exist in the offline world. Some studies find more diversity in online compared to offline networks (Gillan 2009), but generally research points to strong signs of homophily in hyperlink networks, meaning that like-minded (Pilny and Shumate 2012) and/or geographically close (Vicari 2014) organizations are more strongly linked than ideologically or geographically diverse organizations. Unfortunately, only a few studies have systematically compared offline cooperation links and hyperlinks between organizations, but where this is done, strong correlations between both levels are found (Pilny and Shumate 2012, 276).

More recently, researchers have started to look at Twitter communication networks instead of hyperlink networks (Gerbaudo 2012; Conover et al. 2013; Howard and Hussain 2013; Tremayne 2014). Twitter networks constructed from shared hashtags or retweets are promising data sources because they potentially allow analysing connections not only between organizations but at the individual level, and analysing the content of Twitter messages can qualify the nature of the relationships. But Twitter data is also highly problematic because it is often impossible to say whether the originator of a tweet is actually an actively involved protester or only an interested commentator. Robert Brym and his collaborators show, for example, that in the Egyptian uprising in 2011 most tweets (nine out of ten) originated from outside Egypt (Brym et al. 2014, 270). One thing that the analyses of Twitter data consistently show is the highly skewed nature of social media use. Networks of several thousand nodes are usually dominated by a handful of highly connected nodes through which a large part of the information flows. This power law distribution (Gerbaudo 2012, 135) contradicts the notion of social media as tools for more egalitarian participation.

Research that builds on participant observation, surveys of protest participants and general-population polls complements and qualifies the findings of studies based on a direct analysis of internet and social media networks. Beyond explaining specific mobilization and protest dynamics, this research provides insights about at least four general aspects of the relation between internet/social media and social movements/protest: it highlights differences between social media tools, it enhances our understanding of the complex relation between online and offline protest, it points to new and emerging forms and repertoires of protest and it addresses the often problematic relationship between state and corporate interests and social movement use of social media tools, pointing especially to the aspect of censorship and surveillance.

While the more general claims about the effects of the internet and/or social media on social movements and protest often do not differentiate between different technological tools, empirical research on recent protests points to strong *differences between social media tools*: Brym and his collaborators, for example, show that in the Egyptian uprising Twitter has been used 'more like a megaphone broadcasting information about the uprising to the outside world than an internal informational and organizing tool' (Brym et al. 2014, 270). Instead of building networks among protesters, it thus has functioned as a partial replacement of traditional forms of alternative media, aimed at sympathizers, the general public and especially at journalists who then publish the information obtained via Twitter in traditional mass media. The movement activists' differentiated view on Twitter and Facebook is supported by Gerbaudo's study, who argues that in the activists' practices Twitter has replaced mailing lists, while Facebook is seen as a modern equivalent to Indymedia (Gerbaudo 2012, 145).

The second aspect that many empirical analyses address is the complex *relation between offline and online activism*. Studies of all current protests, especially those of the Arab Spring, insist that these mobilizations relied heavily on preexisting strong social ties. The internet and social media played an important role because they were difficult to control and to censor, but neither for coordination among core activists nor for reaching and mobilizing a wider public did they function as primary coordination and information tools (Brym et al. 2014, 282). Preexisting offline social networks were central and indispensable for the core activists. And according to a survey among protesters on Cairo's Tahrir Square, nearly half (48.4 percent) of those interviewed 'reported that they had first heard about the Tahrir Square demonstrations through face-to-face communication' (Tufekci and Wilson 2012, 370), thus making direct personal contacts and foreign mass media the most important avenue to reach out to and mobilize sympathetic populations under conditions of a state-controlled and censored press. The specific contribution of social media could then be providing a tool to broker between different organizations and populations (Lim 2012, 244). And with regard to core activists, Stefaan Walgrave and his collaborators argue that digital communication tools enable them to connect their different activities and stay in touch with different organizations they belong to (Walgrave et al. 2011, 344).

Thus, instead of supporting Howard and Hussain's far-reaching claim that 'digital media has . . . become a necessary and sometimes sufficient cause of democratization' (2013, 39), many empirical studies of internet and social media use in current protests show that in order to understand protest and mobilization dynamics one has to look at the interaction between traditional mass media (and in oppressive regimes, especially foreign mass media), social media and other forms of digital communication and face-to-face communication. One of the most promising frameworks for understanding the specific structure of these interactions in repressive regimes has been developed based on an analysis of movements that were active long before digital communication tools were available for almost everyone. It is Karol Jakubowicz's study of the role of media in the social transition processes in Eastern Europe, in which he analyses the interaction between official mass media as propaganda tools, foreign mass media as sources for alternative views and moral support of local opposition and underground media as providers of alternative information and interpretation as well as connecting nodes in clandestine social networks (Jakubowicz 1995). To which extent the availability of digital communication tools has changed this relationship has still not been systematically analysed, but research on the Arab Spring suggests that social media tend to replace the role underground media and to some extent also foreign mass media have played in the protests leading to the transformations in Eastern Europe.

A third general aspect to which empirical studies on current social movements and protest point is the emergence of new media practices as *new forms and repertoires of protest*. On the one hand, this means the emergence of new internet-specific protest forms like website hacking, email bombing, distributed denial of service (DDoS) attacks or virtual demonstrations in the form of website blackouts or coordinated banner campaigns. These internet-specific forms add to existing protest repertoires and complement established offline action forms (Van Laer and Van Aelst 2010, 1150), and are used to mutually enhance their visibility in the general public (Haunss 2013, 108). On the other hand, studies highlight especially the innovative use of video platforms like YouTube. While social movement activists have used videos in their mobilizations already for a long time, the ubiquitous availability of video-recording hardware in the form of mobile phones and the ease of distributing them via video-sharing websites like YouTube has profoundly changed the role videos can play in current protests. Zeynep Tufekci and Christopher Wilson report that 'almost half (48.2 percent) the respondents [in their survey among protest participants at Cairo's Tahrir Square] had produced and disseminated video or pictures from political protest in the streets' (Tufekci and Wilson 2012, 373). This creates new possibilities to reach out to distant publics and adds a very emotional element to social movements' mobilization tools.

Finally, some studies also address the issue of *censorship and surveillance*. While in the Arab Spring social media have been hailed as being outside state control and thus have enabled communication under conditions of severe state repression, some authors have pointed out that electronic communication comes with its own fallacies. Two problems have been noted, one concerning the contradictions between the commercial goals of the companies that run social media services and activists who use them for protest purposes, and another one that concerns the enhanced surveillance capabilities of states.

With regard to the first problem, William Lafi Youmans and Jillian York have shown how the uses of social media by protesters in Egypt clashed with corporate rules prohibiting anonymous use of Facebook and governing the deletion of 'inappropriate' content on YouTube (Youmans and York 2012). Concerning the second problem, Morozov has presented an account on how Iranian authorities have used information gathered on social media sites to prosecute activists of the failed 'Green Revolution' (Morozov 2011, 11). But it is not only repressive regimes in the Arab world but also democratic regimes like Germany that rely increasingly on digital communication data to persecute protesters (Dix 2012). Connecting the two aspects, Oliver Leistert has argued more generally that corporate interests in extensive data collection and their willingness to disclose this data to state agencies creates a serious risk for oppositional activists (Leistert 2013).

CONCLUSION

Overall, this critical review of the literature on the relationship between internet and social media on the one side and protest and social movements on the other highlights three aspects.

First, the internet and social media do not completely reconfigure the conditions and options for protest and social movements. This is mainly because, in most cases, protest remains place-based and still relies to a very important amount on preexisting and face-to-face social networks. Thus, upon closer inspection, the far-reaching assumptions from cyber-optimists and pessimists often lack sound empirical foundations. Social media neither solve existing collective action problems nor does their use by protesters indicate the emergence of new forms of protest specific to the network society. Cyber-optimists and pessimists alike tend to overestimate the importance of social media for current protests.

Second, empirical studies consistently show that current social movements have quickly adopted new internet and social media technologies and integrate them into their toolbox of more traditional communication and media practices. Research especially shows that core activists tend to be the most intense users of new digital communication technologies for protest and political information purposes, whereas more distant sympathizers and onlookers still rely for their political information mainly on traditional mass media and—especially in repressive regimes—on face-to-face social networks. How exactly internet technologies and social media interact with traditional media and communication technologies and with direct forms of personal interaction is still underresearched. The general pattern is clearly additive—new technologies and communication practices do not replace older ones, they rather complement them and are used alongside established repertoires. But few studies (e.g., Gerbaudo 2012) have really systematically tried to investigate how they add up.

Finally, several issues emerge which have not or only very superficially been addressed, but which are important for understanding the relationship between social media and protest. One such issue is the existence of differences between movements with regard to the use of internet and social media. Research generally focuses on movements in which internet and social media play a prominent role, and often also on movements which have only recently emerged. Whether or not the findings for these movements represent a more general pattern can only be said on the basis of more comparative studies looking on a broader population of movements. Related to this is a lack of knowledge about the changing role of specific digital communication technologies within one and/or across several movements. Research tends to focus on the newest technological developments and their adoption in current social movements and protest. But some technologies stay and social movements continue to use them. Although with changing circumstances and with the emergence of new technologies, the use of existing tools (e.g., Indymedia, SMS, etc.) may change as well.

What is therefore needed to expand the knowledge about the function and use of social media and other digital communication technologies and to overcome the limits of existing research is more longitudinal and more comparative studies that go beyond the most recent and the most prominent uses of these technologies, as well as studies that pay closer attention to the interaction between states, corporations and protesters when it comes to the use of social media.

REFERENCES

Badouard, Romain, and Laurence Monnoyer-Smith (2013). "Hyperlinks as political resources: The European Commission confronted with online activism." *Policy & Internet* 5(1): 101–17.

Benkler, Yochai (2006). *The Wealth of Networks: How Social Production Transforms Markets and Freedom.* New Haven, CT: Yale University Press.

Bennett, W. Lance (2003). "Communicating global activism." *Information, Communication & Society* 6(2): 143–68.

Bennett, W. Lance, and Alexandra Segerberg (2012). "The logic of connective action: Digital media and the personalization of contentious politics." *Information, Communication & Society* 15(5): 739–68.

Blumer, Herbert (1949). "Collective behavior." In Alfred McClung Lee (ed.), *New Outline of the Principles of Sociology*, 167–224. New York: Barnes and Noble.

Brym, Robert et al. (2014). "Social media in the 2011 Egyptian uprising." *The British Journal of Sociology* 65(2): 266–92.

Castañeda, Ernesto (2012). "The Indignados of Spain: A precedent to Occupy Wall Street." *Social Movement Studies* 11(3–4): 309–19.

Castells, Manuel (2000). "Materials for an exploratory theory of the network society." *British Journal of Sociology* 51(1): 5–24.

——— (2009). *Communication Power.* Oxford: Oxford University Press.

——— (2012). *Networks of Outrage and Hope.* Cambridge: Policy Press.

Cleaver, Harry M. (1998). "The Zapatista effect: The internet and the rise of an alternative political fabric." *Journal of International Affairs* 51(2): 621–40.

Conover, Michael D. et al. (2013). "The digital evolution of Occupy Wall Street." *PLoS ONE* 8(5): e64679.

Costanza-Chock, Sasha (2012). "Mic check! Media cultures and the Occupy Movement." *Social Movement Studies* 11(3–4): 375–85.

Della Porta, Donatella, and Lorenzo Mosca (2005). "Global-net for global movements? A network of networks for a movement of movements." *Journal of Public Policy* 25(01): 165–90.

Diani, Mario (1992). "The concept of social movement." *The Sociological Review* 40(1): 1–25.

Dix, Alexander (2012). "Funkzellenabfragen auf dem Prüfstand." *Datenschutz und Datensicherheit—DuD* 37(1): 6.

Earl, Jennifer et al. (2010). "Changing the world one webpage at a time: Conceptualizing and explaining internet activism." *Mobilization* 15(4): 425–46.

Gamson, William A., and Micah L. Sifry (2013). "The #Occupy Movement: An introduction." *The Sociological Quarterly* 54(2): 159–63.

Gerbaudo, Paolo (2012). *Tweets and the Streets: Social Media and Contemporary Activism.* London: Pluto Press.

Gillan, Kevin (2009). "The UK anti-war movement online." *Information, Communication & Society* 12(1): 25–43.

Giraud, E. (2014). "Has radical participatory online media really 'failed'? Indymedia and its legacies." *Convergence: The International Journal of Research into New Media Technologies* 20(4): 419–37.

Harasim, Linda Marie (1993). *Global Networks: Computers and International Communication.* Cambridge, MA: MIT Press.

Haunss, Sebastian (2013). *Conflicts in the Knowledge Society: The Contentious Politics of Intellectual Property.* Cambridge: Cambridge University Press.

Howard, Philip N., and Muzammil M. Hussain (2013). *Democracy's Fourth Wave? Digital Media and the Arab Spring.* Oxford and New York: Oxford University Press.

Ippolita, Geert Lovink, and Ned Rossiter (2009). "The digital given: 10 web 2.0 theses." *The Fibreculture Journal*, issue 14. http://fourteen.fibreculturejournal.org/fcj-096-the-digital-given-10-web-2-0-theses/ (accessed 19 December 2014).

Jakubowicz, Karol (1995). "Media as agents of change." In David L. Paletz, Karol Jakubowicz and Pavao Novosel (eds.), *Glasnost and After: Media and Change in Central and Eastern Europe*, 19–47. Cresskill, NJ: Hampton Press.

Juris, Jeffrey S. (2005). "The new digital media and activist networking within anti-corporate globalization movements." *Annals of the American Academy of Political and Social Science* 597:189–208.

——— (2008). *Networking Futures: The Movements Against Corporate Globalization.* Durham, NC: Duke University Press.

——— (2014). "Embodying protest: Culture and performance within social movements." In Britta Baumgarten, Priska Daphi and Peter Ullrich (eds.), *Conceptualizing Culture in Social Movement Research*, 227–47. Houndmills, Basingstoke: Palgrave Macmillan.

Kidd, Dorothy (2003). "Indymedia.org: A new communications commons." In Martha McCaughey and Michael D. Ayers (eds.), *Cyberactivism: Online Activism in Theory and Practice*, 47–69. New York: Routledge.

Knudson, Jerry W. (1998). "Rebellion in Chiapas: Insurrection by internet and public relations." *Media, Culture & Society* 20(3): 507–18.

Leach, Darcy K. (2013). "Culture and the structure of tyrannylessness." *The Sociological Quarterly* 54(2): 181–91.

Leistert, Oliver (2013). "Der Beitrag der Social Media zur Partizipation." *Forschungsjournal Soziale Bewegungen* 26(2): 39–48.

Lim, Merlyna (2012). "Clicks, cabs, and coffee houses: Social media and oppositional movements in Egypt, 2004–2011." *Journal of Communication* 62(2): 231–48.

Lokk, Peter (2008). "Zur Geschichte von CL-Netz und LINK-M: Die ersten zehn Jahre." In Gabriele Hooffacker (ed.), *Wem gehört das internet?* 17–31. München: Verlag Dr. Gabriele Hooffacker.

Lovink, Geert (2012). *Networks Without a Cause: A Critique of Social Media.* Cambridge: Polity.

Lutz, Christoph, and Christian Pieter Hoffmann (2014). *Part of Me Is Online: A Systematic Literature Review of Online Participation.* ID 2399570. Rochester, NY: Social Science Research Network. http://papers.ssrn.com/abstract=2399570 (accessed 20 May 2014).

McAdam, Doug (1982). *Political Process and the Development of Black Insurgency 1930–1970.* Chicago: University of Chicago Press.

McCarthy, John D., and Mayer N. Zald (1977). "Resource mobilization and social movements: A partial theory." *American Journal of Sociology* 82(6): 1212–41.

Milioni, Dimitra L. (2009). "Probing the online counterpublic sphere: The case of Indymedia Athens." *Media, Culture & Society* 31(3): 409–31.

Morozov, Evgeny (2011). *The Net Delusion: The Dark Side of Internet Freedom.* New York: Public Affairs.

Olson, Mancur (1971). *The Logic of Collective Action: Public Goods and the Theory of Groups.* Cambridge, MA: Harvard University Press.

Pilny, Andrew, and Michelle Shumate (2012). "Hyperlinks as extensions of offline instrumental collective action." *Information, Communication & Society* 15(2): 260–86.

Rucht, Dieter (1994). *Modernisierung und neue soziale Bewegungen: Deutschland, Frankreich und USA im Vergleich.* Frankfurt/Main: Campus.

———— (2004). "The quadruple 'A': Media strategies of protest movements since the 1960s." In Wim van de Donk et al. (eds.), *Cyberprotest: New media, citizens and social movements,* 25–48. London: Routledge.

Shirky, Clay (2008) *Here Comes Everybody: The Power of Organizing Without Organizations.* New York: Penguin.

Tarrow, Sidney (1998). "Fishnets, Internets, and Catnets: Globalization and transnational collective action." In Michael P. Hanagan, Leslie Page Moch and Wayne te Brake (eds.), *Challenging Authority: The Historical Study of Contentious Politics,* 228–44. Minneapolis: University of Minnesota Press.

Torres Soriano, Manuel R. (2013). "Internet as a driver of political change: Cyber-pessimists and cyber-optimists." *Journal of the Spanish Institute of Strategic Studies* 1(1): 1–22.

Tremayne, Mark (2014). "Anatomy of protest in the digital era: A network analysis of Twitter and Occupy Wall Street." *Social Movement Studies* 13(1): 110–26.

Tufekci, Zeynep, and Christopher Wilson (2012). "Social media and the decision to participate in political protest: Observations from Tahrir Square." *Journal of Communication* 62(2): 363–79.

Van Aelst, Peter, and Stefaan Walgrave (2002). "New media, new movements? The role of the internet in shaping the 'anti-globalization' movement." *Information, Communication & Society* 5(4): 465–93.

Van Laer, Jeroen, and Peter Van Aelst (2010). "Cyber-protest and civil society: The internet and action repertoires in social movements." In Yvonne Jewkes and Majid Yar (eds.), *Handbook of Internet Crime,* 230–54. Cullompton: Willan Publishing.

Vicari, Stefania (2014). "Networks of contention: The shape of online transnationalism in early twenty-first-century social movement coalitions." *Social Movement Studies* 13(1): 92–109.

Walgrave, Stefaan et al. (2011). "Multiple engagements and network bridging in contentious politics: Digital media use of protest participants." *Mobilization: An International Quarterly* 16(3): 325–49.

Youmans, William Lafi, and Jillian C. York (2012). "Social media and the activist toolkit: User agreements, corporate interests, and the information infrastructure of modern social movements." *Journal of Communication* 62(2): 315–29.

I

Algorithmic Control and Visibility

Chapter Two

The Revolution Will Not Be Liked

*On the Systemic Constraints of Corporate
Social Media Platforms for Protests*

Oliver Leistert

In an interview that Tiziana Terranova conducts with one of the Occupy LA activists, Joan Donovan, about how commercial social media platforms and other media technologies were used to support the Los Angeles Occupy Movement in 2011–2012, the whole drama we currently witness is articulated in a question by Terranova in a very nonchalant way: 'Corporate social networking platforms are the new mass media; they are giving you access to a potentially mass public and carrying over all of the issues inherent in communicating with a mass public to a new technological interface and protocol' (Terranova and Donovan 2013, 303). For protests against established power structures, against crude social injustice in the twenty-first century and, in very general terms, for a life in dignity, the media technologies of choice are corporate social media platforms *precisely* because they have become what traditional mass media has ceased to be: a way to inform the general population about relevant societal issues, however disputable and flawed this function always has been. Donovan states: 'For Occupy and other networked social movements, the question is not about whether corporate social media is good or bad, but rather how can we leverage all available communication tools and infrastructures to inform the public and bring them into our networks' (Terranova and Donovan 2013, 310).

In this chapter, I want to investigate some of the very interesting contradictions that this constellation offers. At the core is a tension between a business model that can be described as a psychopower whose primary interest is to target affects and cognition with a complex and dynamic set of highly opaque tools for selling advertisements, commodities and data and the inherently contradictory interests of emancipation and self-determination fostered by activists and manifested in protests, camps and occupied places. This tension is comprised of a bundle of heterogeneous, conflated elements. First, the obvious shift in what mass media might be today if Facebook and Twitter can meaningfully be called so. Second, an intrinsic nonoperationability of platforms like Facebook for collective actions that undermines collective decision-making processes that protests and camps are aiming for in order to gain momentum and sustainability. Third, the question of surveillance, and particularly the productivity of surveillance in commercial social media for governments and their agencies. Total digital surveillance can be seen as technique for governments (and corporations alike) to understand intensities, dynamics and possible trajectories of protests and activism in general. Capturing data, mining it and thus producing new relations between data sets is a contemporary mode of government (for a hands-on introduction into the technique of mining social media, see Russell 2011). Using protest data collected from Facebook and Twitter offers very cheap ways to manage protests. Fourth, I want to describe why platforms like Facebook transform control from the question of legality to a question of benevolence. Here I mean a transition from rights to express opinions to the necessity to fit within an often changing and intransparent regime of codes of conduct, terms of services and ownership. Censorship, too, undergoes a transition, because never before has a data-mining company like Facebook been in the position to vastly influence what can be said and what not. Even more so, the regulating mechanisms of legitimate expressions are also exercised by algorithms, thus indicating strongly the performative aspect of automated communication regimes while at the same time remaining opaque to the persons concerned.

In short, this contribution aims at a better understanding of the establishment of corporate social media platforms with mass media powers that at the same time are configured and programmed to attack the very processes of collectivity and emancipation that protests aim to ignite. At the core of these powers are the politics of algorithms and database empires. Thus, each of the following parts discusses the algorithmically imposed regimes in regard to specific mediation processes.

While this chapter is overall very critical about corporate social media platforms as tools for protests, my aim is not to state that they are dysfunctional in toto. Facebook and Twitter have supported protests and activism in many countries (see, e.g., Tufekci and Wilson 2012). My interest here concerns the side effects, or collateral damages that protest movements quite likely encounter on corporate platforms. Putting some of them to the fore has been neglected in many recent accounts of social media and protests (cf.

Gerbaudo 2012). By magnifying these aspects, the diverging trajectories of corporate platforms and protest movements become apparent.

PSYCHOPOWERS OF CORPORATE SOCIAL MEDIA PLATFORMS

Essentially, the differences in goals that corporate social media platforms aim at and those of activists like the Occupy LA movement could not be more drastic: whereas Facebook's and Twitter's primary interest is increase in revenue via targeted advertisements, selling user data and social relations to the highest bidder, emancipatory social movements challenge the commodification of sociality and, in general, commercialization of everyday life. The occupation of places to allow for discursive spaces that are freed from the individualization trajectories of neoliberalism can be understood as a profound anticorporate activity, starting from the almost forgotten demand for a public free from commercial imperatives.

Corporate social media platforms have been described as 'digital enclosures' (Andrejevic 2007b), as training grounds for free labour (Coté and Pybus 2007) and assessment centres to manage one's neoliberal subjectivity (Wiedemann 2011) amongst others (Leistert and Röhle 2011). Much less attention has been paid to the affective capacities and, borrowing a term from Bernard Stiegler (2010), psychotechnologies that corporate social media platforms unleash. It is only recently that we learned how bluntly manipulative Facebook agitates. The newsfeed, the core element of the user's interface, was subjected to a psychological experiment of grand scale by Facebook's own researchers (Kramer, Guillory and Hancock 2014). Seven hundred thousand Facebook users' newsfeeds were 'altered' to present sadder and more negative contents. The aim of the study was to understand how emotional contagion spreads, as it was reported (Meyer 2014).

But this is all hearsay, since the enclosures of Facebook are inaccessible for independent research and it is impossible by design to identify whether such experiments are part of Facebook's daily operations. The obvious aim of the platform to foster positivity and affirmation, a prerequisite for consumption and keeping the users on the platform as long as possible, already indicates inherently calculated affective and emotional interferences. Psyops (psychological operations) in times of Facebook have entered a whole new state (Fuller and Goffey 2012). The current configuration of digital media as a flagship of the commodification of everyday life has tremendously decreased the costs of behavioural sciences and all sorts of psychological research just as the surveillance operations it is based on. The affective grip is tight since there is no escape from it within the enclosure, while at the same time it modulates control in a soft and hardly conceivable manner. It puts the soul to work as it designs the fields of desire (Berardi 2009).

Understanding that Facebook can modulate emotions of its users beyond its interface design, where disliking contents amounts to exile, might come as a surprise to those who assume Facebook (or Twitter) are common websites. This is not the case. The like economy Facebook rests on is running on very different paradigms than the link economy of common websites and search engines (Gerlitz and Helmond 2013).

Psychopowers, the modulation of emotional and affective states, of course are not new to media. Cinema, for example, essentially is built on the production of psychic effects and its function as a substitute for all the experiences that we are devoid of as members of a regulated modern society. Still, the difference is one *in quality* when everyday communication becomes subjected to psychopower operations. Even more so, as it doesn't end after ninety minutes, but becomes integrated into everyday life and as such becomes ubiquitous.

Beyond the displacement of meaning by frequency and proximity (Dean 2010) or the discrepancies between meaning and meaningfulness on such platforms (Langlois 2014) it is the asignifying semiotics (Lazzarato 2006) of corporate social media platforms that present a whole new set of possibilities to modulate the user's state of mind and body. Affective economies are operating on sentiment analysis and behavioural advertisement in the realms of big data (McStay 2011; Andrejevic 2013). Affective capitalism as it is programmed into corporate social media platforms is 'both pre-emptive and productive: to minimize negative sentiment and maximize emotional investment and engagement: not merely to record sentiment as a given but to modulate it as a variable. Modulation means constant adjustment to bring the anticipated consequences of a modelled future into the present in ways that account for the former, and thus alter the latter' (Andrejevic 2011). Or, to put it in the words of Facebook's former Chief Operations Officer Sheryl Sandberg: 'We're demand generation, before you know you want something' (Hof 2011). Users and sociality in general here become preemptive sensors for a programmed future (Clough 2009).

As such, affective capitalism is a time-based operation which aims at a programmed present oriented at some premodelled future. It 'is a parasite on the feelings, movements, and becoming of bodies, tapping into their virtuality by investing preemptively in futurity' (Parisi and Goodman 2011). This investment in futurity by no means is open to negotiation or even perceptible for outsiders. Subjected to business models and their execution, 'participation' on corporate social media platforms transforms into self-indulged flight from self-determination (Leistert 2013a), however shaky, flawed and precarious the concept of self-determination may be.

To highlight the modulations of affective control with reference to a programmed futurity that are exercised silently and imperceptibly is a necessary prelude to grasp the notion that corporate social media platforms have become mass media. If this is the case, then this mass media is operating on entirely new paradigms.

CORPORATE SOCIAL MEDIA PLATFORMS AS ALGORITHMIC MASS MEDIA

Mass media traditionally are portrayed as one-to-many media, being programmed by editors and relying on a mass of recipients, whose main task is to consume the programme (Dutton et al. 1998). The production of visibility has always been at the core of media politics (Thompson 2005), likewise the role of news production should at best be seen as ambiguous, since it plays an important role in 'engineering consent' in complex societies (Bernays 1947). While feedback loops have been built into media dispositifs quite early to understand if there is a mass of recipients *at all* (Andrejevic 2007a), both channels have by and large been separate. This led to a time shift in their operational setup: if recipient numbers dropped, the media industry could only react after the fact. Recent internet-based TV channels, such as Netflix, managed to shorten this gap as viewers are constantly monitored, related to 'same-interest' groups, and this assessment towards the programme is fed back via recommendation systems (Hallinan and Striphas 2014).

For corporate social media platforms, these problems do not exist anymore. All users are individually and constantly measured and followed in the format of a diversity of data points, bundled into data sets. In its fully fledged incarnation, like in the default setup of apps or browsers, even mouse movements have been integrated into the feedback cycle (Rosenbush 2013). In terms of reach, Facebook easily trumps all classic mass-media channels with its user base of around 1.4 billion. But while even the viewers of Netflix productions can be sure that what they watch is the same that their neighbours watch, Facebook users are isolated within their 'individual' newsfeed whose 'programme editors' are algorithms. The visibility here is of algorithmic kind instigated in the case of Facebook by its edge rank algorithm (Bucher 2012). Facebook as mass media has no common public but a mass of individuals who are being served different media contents, designed as feeds from their social relations, paid feeds (openly or disguised as friends' recommendations), depending on their own activity and the platform's current algorithmic operations. This has been termed 'Filter Bubble' (Pariser 2011), highlighting the dangers of a reproduction of homogeneous contents for each individual (Dahlberg 2007).

For messages from grassroots movements like Occupy LA, such a drift towards computed homogenization becomes an algorithmic barrier. Under no circumstance can a reliable signalling path towards possible fellow activists or even larger publics be guaranteed. Even less likely stand the chances for a sufficient ranking to catch attention. For Facebook, contents from grass-roots movements amount to a question of unconscious benevolence. 'Political activism, in this context, becomes a side-note that is tolerated as long as it does not threaten the broader commercial goal' (Hintz in this volume).

How such a production of a public differs from one that gets their information from an old-fashioned news desk becomes comprehensible when Twitter Trends is taken into account.

Members of Occupy accused Twitter of censorship when tweets related to the protests were not represented by Twitter Trends as a trending topic. But it is quite likely that Twitter did not interfere. Besides its high-speed flows and lack of long-term archives, Twitter Trends often is understood as an authority precisely because it lacks editorial control. This lack emits a sense of objectivity regularly attributed to algorithmic sorting. But noninterference by humans into machinic sorting does not alter the fact that sorting always rests on criteria. Even more so, the perceived objectivity is an effect of its opaqueness; a problem that society more and more is confronted with in the 'age of big data', as the integration of data sources poses serious problems for the user's agency (Peacock 2014). Confronted with outcomes of complex calculations that seem to rest on objective precision, users, and in other contexts, citizens, lose the ability to criticize or even question their algorithmic doubles. At the same time, these doubles gain considerable powers over determinations of insurance tarifs or credit scores, to give just two examples. It is this powerlessness vis-à-vis algorithmic sorting that the Occupy movement experienced.

Twitter Trends measures activity on Twitter and does not present public concerns as such. Twitter Trends 'claims to know the public through an algorithmic assessment of their complete traces, [. . .] these indices are rendered in an instant and built immediately back into the service itself' (Gillespie 2012). It is well possible that no semantic analysis is at work here. In addition, this platform-specific public is solely Twitter related. Not trending can therefore have many reasons, but most importantly, they are to be seen in the design of the algorithms, which is kept secret to avoid manipulation by third parties. 'Despite what Twitter is willing to make known, any effort to discover the Trends criteria can only amount to sophisticated guesswork' (Gillespie 2012).

Twitter Trends is just one example of a very different and new kind of constructed public in the corporate social media platform ecology. Even if common newspapers and other mass media have failed to report on what concerns social movements historically, or even have inflicted damage on them by uncritically copying and pasting police press releases about protest actions without being interested in the nature of the clashes, the submission under an algorithmically produced public aligns protest media with an order that cannot be addressed in informed ways because of the de facto unaccountability of privatized machine intelligence. Criticizing algorithms which affect millions of people's idea of what is currently important for public discourse amounts to the impossible since we still lack tools and concepts to understand their workings properly. Algorithms have become key agents in the 'distribution of the sensible' (Langlois 2013 with reference to Ranciere 2006). Despite their inaccessibility, I agree with Gillespie that 'we must firmly resist putting the technology in the driver's seat' (Gillespie 2014). Algorithms are products of human, corporate and institutional choices, and thus are in principle open to contestation and negotiation (McKelvey 2014).

Algorithmically driven corporate social media platforms have become authorities in news delivery and as such turned into news corporations. More and more people receive their news from such platforms. This has tremendous effects on the public sphere since for the platforms their becoming news corporations is just a side effect they instrumentalize to keep users on the platforms as long as possible.[1] They have no explicit mandate and thus cannot be held accountable for their power within this critical societal function. For them, the public sphere is an historically elapsed phase from the twentieth century they now exploit for their own interests by simulating it.

THE GRANULAR COLLECTIVE IN THE MACHINE

To successfully gather attention on corporate platforms is actually an easy task: just pay for it. This is what these platforms are made for and it works fine to gain attention of and produce favoured effects within an exactly discriminated group of consumers/users. And while larger nongovernmental organizations (NGOs), unions, presidential campaigns and corporate bedfellows in the fields of activism have embraced this official model (Dauvergne and LeBaron 2014; see also Dencik in this volume), grassroots activists, besides their notorious lack of financial resources, shy away from this privileged route to the algorithmically produced individuated masses. This is where the often-cited cheapness for information dissemination on these platforms finds its nemesis: if you pay for it and become a regular customer you are invested with rights (as laid out in the contract). The success of your campaign can be measured and refined if outcomes are not meeting the goals you have set. On the other hand, submission to the advertising machine involves techniques and finesse from marketing and PR. This implies a very different view of users, in essence a targeting as consumers, than what grassroots movements envision, at least in the predominant cases when they want to convince subjects as political agents and appeal to their agency beyond what they may want or should consume.

In the previous decades of internet communications, grassroots movements built their own services and tools for dissemination (Milan 2013). This effort to have control over one's own means of communication has been overrun by the abundance and success of 'free' platforms by and large and it is only now, after the Snowden revelations (Greenwald 2014), that activists remember their heritage of control over the means of production. And it is crucial to explain the difference between autonomous decentralized server infrastructures and the centralized corporate empires, not only in terms of surveillance and resilience over censorship: the difference between traditional services such as websites, blogs, email and chat and centralized corporate platforms is one of *kind*, because the former lack almost all functionalities in the back end the latter provide: a database containing all signals that any user had ever sent back to the platform.[2] Not only that corporate platforms offer services that formerly had been distributed and decentralized, and as such hard to control; effectively they use the established communication forms and convert them into a simulation because their primary interest is to capture all data. To achieve this, corporate platforms include forms of communication that had been established in earlier phases of the internet. It is precisely here that the difference in kind materializes and a different order emerges, as Lazzarato explains: 'Not only is the dividual of a piece with the machinic assemblage, but he is also torn to pieces by it: the component parts of subjectivity [. . .] are no longer unified in an "I", they no longer have an individuated subject as referent. Intelligence, affects, sensations, cognition, memory, and physical force are now components whose synthesis no longer lies in the person but in the assemblage or process' (Lazzarato 2014, 27). Corporate platforms perform their very own diagrammatization by constantly de- and recomposing the dividuated data points of the user into data sets that their customers, the advertising industry and data brokers, ask for. At the same time, the back end also modifies the categories of identity formation (Cheney-Lippold 2011) since the categories themselves (such as 'football fan') do not have any independent meaningful ontological base but to be linked with data points generated by the users. It is the users who effectively describe what the categories 'mean' while the categories are used to identify suitable users for targeting.

This reciprocity of cybernetic models indicates the pure immanence of its ontology where any outside or transcendence has vanished (Rosenblueth, Wiener and Bigelow 1943). In particular, cybernetic machines lack capacities for change while favouring system stability. Categories are thus not meaningful, independent values that can be implemented. Their realization depends on the data points referenced. Or to put it drastically: for such complex machines there is no outside, only input and output, whose comparabilities and computabilities are its base and regime. Such machinic assemblages act out their ontology of immance and system stability into all connected parts. In a sense, the interaction via Facebook is delusional if it is understood as anything but an interaction with the platform itself. The process of mediation, or better, feeding the machine with data and receiving data from the machine lacks true kinship with mass media. Its only resemblance with mass media is in terms of a simulation. In this sense, such platforms are platforms of alienation, because they pretend to be or have essential characteristics of common mass media while all they do is compute a look-alike.

The consequences of this shift in quality can be observed regularly when it becomes apparent that Facebook or Twitter lack sufficient knowledge about their users' activities in regard to content because the algorithmic order of these platforms is beyond contents and is run by asignifying semiotics: programmed instructions. This is why such platforms are a success in any region of the world (be it Qzone in China or VKontake in Russia): their operations are basically independent from the norms, values or ideas that drive their users. These machinic regimes are self-sufficient, detached from any particular interests (besides profit). 'The creators of Facebook probably didn't plan on designing platforms that would encourage parents to spy on their children, employers to fire their employees, FBI agents to track suspects, insurance companies to deny medical benefits, gay people to be involuntarily outed or corporations to humiliate the families of litigants. That the systems are being used for these purposes means that we have to include both intended and unintended outcomes in our analysis' (Monahan and Gilliom 2013, 55). Clearly, it would be too simple to state only the negative effects of corporate platforms. Nonetheless, my argument is that their success is based very much on this operational void and it is precisely this that makes them powerful.

For protest movements that seek mobilization of larger publics and dissemination of debates on contested societal and economic issues, this granularization of a public into databases has severe consequences. Corporate social media platforms are aiming at subjectivities produced in and on the individual and its body which the platform then granulates into flexible, meaningless and dynamic categories. The production of masses or collectives that these platforms are inherently prescribing therefore relies on parts and parcels of descriptions which can be assembled in any possible way. Such a mass, or better, set of data on precisely discriminated groups, stands in stark contrast to the envisioned formation of a collective body which relies on some unity in composition, while at the same time becomes only a promising candidate for political discourse if it is also composed of heterogeneous subjectivities which through discussion and action become a temporary collective. This cannot be produced from within the database. It transcends the immanence of cybernetic systems. Contemporary corporate platforms, governed by a politics of algorithms and database empires, systemically fail to meet such human aspirations, as they remain indifferent towards collective politics. Again, their only possible reaction towards such aspirations rests on simulations. They are incapable of addressing beyond individuals. Their ontology is based on data snippets. Collective processes are unintelligible, incompatible and finally nonexistent.

In addition, the swirl of social media, its speed and ultimately systemic indifference in values of what matters and what does not undermines the establishment of sustained and equal participation (see Kaun and Barassi in this volume). Corporate social media platforms favour not only the individual over the collective (Fenton and Barassi 2011), but favour tech savvy, high-speed, crowd-assembling info junkies over those who actually endure debates amongst fully present subjects. Here they radicalize a trend that has started with mass online culture before platforms took over. Occupy LA, again, as being narrated by Donovan, experienced this difference between online and offline cultures: 'I have witnessed a lot of online "drama" play out where the argument hinges on someone's ability to mobilize more support online for their position. It's like an online version of tyranny of the majority, where some people are scared to voice their opinions online. The tone of the speech online seems to be much more divisive than that of the assemblies too' (Terranova and Donovan 2013, 307).

FACEBOOK AND TWITTER AS SENSORS OF UNREST

The imposition of group productions through granulated database technologies is without doubt an attempt of governance, or an 'engineering the public' (Tufekci 2014). This technique can be observed similarly in a variety of societal fields, usually referred to as big data mining (Crawford, Gray and Miltner 2014; Struijs, Braaksma and Daas 2014). In many ways it can be understood as an organized and institutionalized *function creep*, the mining and relating of data collected for independent and nonrelated purposes (Andrejevic and Gates 2014; Lyon 2014).

For protests that are displayed, intensified and reproduced on corporate platforms, very specific aspects come into play in terms of governance. Being subjected to platforms that are constantly capturing, storing, mining and analysing data points in their back end, protests, as antagonists of established power structures, are naturally monitored by state agencies, police and secret services (Pieri 2013). Access to private data repositories for state agencies has been 'liberalised' after 9/11 and since then, not only substantial parts of the agencies' budgets have been used to build software that captures and produces without significant delay the dynamics on corporate platforms (Greenwald 2014; Ericson and Haggerty 2006), but since the 'financial crisis' of 2008 the securitization dispositif has been shifted to include protests and unrests into the antiterrorism framework (cf. Redden in this volume).

Measuring protest, finding relations between key actors, understanding patterns of time and place are amongst the default tasks of watchful police units (Trottier 2012; Lieberman, Koetzle and Sakiyama 2013; Lipp 2013) and the growing security apparatus. If further analysed, the integration of data sets easily provides insights into social status and personal data of participants. Assessments about risks, dynamics, durations, growth are amongst the analytical tasks that are performed on corporate media platforms, let alone if other data sources like mobile phone data (Green and Smith 2002), weather data, any kind of communications meta data (Leistert 2008) or assessments about parallel events such as sport events (Boyle and Haggerty 2009) are integrated into the surveillance assemblage (Haggerty and Ericson 2000). Corporate social media platforms operate on the identical logic that policing operations are striving for. Again, this should not come as a surprise, because if their overall global success resides in their indifference towards meaning and signification, asignifying machines are tools for a variety of goals.

Albeit, this indifference towards meaning comes with a price tag for all parties concerned: while protests that are supported on corporate platforms consequently become transparent and archived as never before, activists who do not try to instrumentalize digital surveilled means actually increase their agency for surprises and successful street actions, as the belief in the adequate representation of public concerns via algorithmically produced publics obstructs also the organization of surveillance and repression. The simulation of meaningful media perpetuates in the same way a simulation of meaningful surveillance and if this shift is ignored, the delusion of the almighty overseer of societal dynamics starts to haunt police and security agencies. The extension of digital surveillance technologies has not necessarily made potential threats more transparent. Nonetheless, this belief in transparency transforms governance and control into a project that relies on simulations. Data mining, to give just one example, only correlates and never gives reasons as to what the produced outcomes mean or its causal relation. This alienates governance and control from understanding the inherent motivations of unrests and protests and weakens a society's means to mediate interests.

It should be stressed that simulation does not at all mean a nonrelation to what is 'real'. Effectively, simulations produce their own realities, which unfold their own effects on reality once they are integrated into corporate and government activities (Bogard 1996).

It is in this sense that grassroots movements that are indulging in digital abstinence are actively challenging the neoliberal dispositif of productivity and intensified flows of communications. 'A radical passivity would definitely threaten the ethos of relentless productivity that neoliberal politics has imposed' (Berardi 2011, 138). The allurement of global reach induces all the forces of neoliberalism, such as competition, control and surveillance. Local grassroots activities on a small scale, acting in context and with slow deliberation, certainly escape to large degrees the giga infrastructures of corporate surveillance platforms. For Occupy LA, the strategy seemed to have been somewhere in between centralization and decentralization: 'The most important way to guard against the Occupy network becoming too centralized or effacing the promise of horizontalism is to maintain the way our communication infrastructure is spread out across many different corporate and non-corporate networks. So, the only recourse for police is to attempt to pluck the nodes of the rhizome, one by one, but where one is squashed another sprouts' (Terranova and Donovan 2013, 308). Grassroots movements' media use should be anchored within the fields of their own practice and develop from there. The fetishism of coverage and reach appears to be one of the prevailing obstacles towards a situated concept of tactical media.

CENSORSHIP AS A NORMALIZATION TOOL

In the early spring of internet-supported activism, during the 1990s, when regulations and surveillance were unable to catch up with the growth and speed of the new infrastructure and gross idealisms such as the well-known proclamation of independence in cyberspace from state interference by John Perry Barlow were expressed, censorship, too, was by and large a failing strategy. At that time, HTML was written directly into simple editors and uploaded via the file transfer protocol (ftp) onto servers. Back then, primarily universities and research facilities provided access to both the internet and hosting capacities. The first wave of commercialization was only beginning, and its first crash, known as the dot-com crash of 2000, reminds us how shaky the prospects for e-commerce have been.

The technological simplicity of HTML 2, which was standardized in 1995 by the Internet Engineering Task Force (IETF) without participation from commercial software producers, was also ideal for mirroring websites all around the internet. In addition, the topological structure of the net had its decentralized heydays in the 1990s, while afterwards it got recentralized to relevant degrees, putting larger corporations in the driver's seat and allowing for the NSA to capture data on a grand scale (Oram 2015). Statements such as the following echo the spirit of that time: 'People who use these new entry points into the Net may be in for a shock. Unlike the family-oriented commercial services, which censor messages they find offensive, the internet imposes no restrictions. Anybody can start a discussion on any topic and say anything' (Elmer-Dewitt 1993). Mirroring websites was a nifty and usually sufficient strategy against coerced deletion of contents.

Today, the tools, techniques and regulations to control contents on the net have reached a level of a whole different quality (and it is beyond the scope of this chapter to discuss this in detail). An important element in the process of internet regulation and governance has been to shift responsibilities towards the providers of internet services (Braman 2004; 2009), followed by the terms of services that corporate platforms impose on their users. While the former had been seen by the providers themselves as a burden they only reluctantly accepted, the latter is a product of the corporations themselves which often goes beyond what the laws prescribe. In addition, corporate platforms behave rigorously Janus-faced vis-à-vis laws. Facebook continues to violate privacy laws in Europe since its inception but relentlessly enforces their own regimes on their platforms. This double face in terms of policy and regulation remains a cornerstone of contemporary business models and intrinsically bears clashes with grassroots activist movements.

Corporate platform users effectively have lost all control over their freedoms of expression after their acceptance of corporate terms of services. This weak position and diminishment of agency in the corporate algorithm machines becomes apparent when all of a sudden accounts are deleted (Dencik 2014). There is no accountability on the side of the platform providers in these matters and the archives of what has been lost is inaccessible except for those that have been granted the right to access the back ends of the database empires.

Besides the dependency on a benevolent dictatorship on corporate platforms, it remains a conundrum how the imposition of specific norms and values on online content on a global scale would not resemble what might be called 'value imperialism', making all the more visible that corporate platforms are actively shaping globally cultural values and norms. The Californian White Anglo-Saxon Protestant's pursuit of happiness, its puritanism and cowboy libertarianism becomes the role model for all users, no matter how implicitly and softly the shaping of subjectivity on corporate platform proliferates.

Protest movements rely on their ability to criticize established power structure and the emancipation via values and norms by subjects. It is apparent that within corporate platforms only a self-imposed censorship can limit the risks of a loss of communication means. This inherently contradicts any practice of emancipation. In addition, the corporate speech regimes indicate a double functionality since the deletion of contents and accounts at the same time might trigger interests by surveillance agencies.

The more societies convert to algorithmic control and production, censorship, just as the public, undergoes a major transition. In the 1990s, one had the possibility to go to court when faced with coerced deletion of contents. In the digital enclosures, a simulation of that functionality is still a gaping abyss.

CONCLUSION

For the concluding remarks, I want to return to the rather abstract notion of programmed futurity on corporate platforms. To design the present along the lines of a corporately desired futurity has important consequences on possible action in the present, since the limitation and channelling of actions are a necessary means to bridge the uncertainty of the future into the present condition. Neoliberalism, contrary to its ideological proclamation of freedom, heavily invests in such channelling practices, limiting agency towards economic motifs (Foucault 2008; see also Redden in this volume). The subjection under semiotic regimes, temporalities and mediated crippled memories structures the fields of desires and invests into affects that sustain power structures. For protests and grassroots movements such as Occupy, the most important task then is to break with these powers of subjectivation and challenge the laid out futurity of neoliberal governance. 'In order for political subjectivation to occur, it must necessarily traverse moments in which dominant significations are suspended and the hold of machinic enslavements is thrown off. Strikes, struggles, revolts, and riots constitute moments of rupture with and suspension of chronological time, of the neutralization of subjections and dominant significations' (Lazzarato 2014, 19).

Corporate platforms that target individuals fragmented into data points by asignifying semiotics suppress such a rupture in signification by design. The imposed regimes of what is euphemistically called 'community rules' or terms of services allow for automated or manual removal of radical signals. Further, the ersatz public that corporate platforms constantly compute adheres to the asignifying semiotics of secret algorithms. Tinkering with this regime falls into the same category as optimizing search results (Search Engine Optimization). On top of all that, the platforms are monitored by government agencies to detect signs of unrest immediately and act upon it.

For protests and grassroots movements, the inadequacy of corporate platforms poses then serious issues. A shift towards other, independent, noncommercial services would single out these contrary effects and prevent or increase costs of targeted surveillance and analysis of dynamics. Of course, the loss of the algorithmically produced larger public would be the price to pay. On the other hand, this would be the first moment of a rupture and the admittance into new political significations and subjectivations including a self-determined field of desire. Since such a change depends solely on first-hand experiences, the empires of social media platforms are of no use. The absurdity to click 'like' in such a context is apparent. And there is not such a tweet to follow. Emancipatory media practice must relate to other forms of political practice. If protest movements externalize this question from their common practice, soon the price they pay is a programmed, neoliberal attack on their core values.

NOTES

1. Since the 1990s, a larger discourse about how the internet changes debates and influences the public has been established. This chapter cannot reproduce all arguments brought to the fore. For an early problematization of the academic discourse see Dahlberg (2004).

2. The move from single sites and independent services to integrated platforms for large parts of internet and mobile data traffic is a subject of its own. For an overview of the platformization of networked communication, see Hands (2013). I have discussed the penetration of poorer countries by Facebook's mobile strategy and the caveats of a shift from internet to mobile phone providers as data delivery infrastructures in Leistert (2013b).

REFERENCES

Andrejevic, Mark. 2007a. *ISpy: Surveillance and Power in the Interactive Era*. Lawrence: University Press of Kansas.

———. 2007b. "Surveillance in the Digital Enclosure." *The Communication Review* 10 (4): 295–317.

———. 2011. "The Work That Affective Economics Does." *Cultural Studies* 25 (4-5): 604–20.

———. 2013. *Infoglut: How Too Much Information Is Changing the Way We Think and Know*. New York: Routledge.

Andrejevic, Mark, and Kelly Gates. 2014. "Big Data Surveillance: Introduction." *Surveillance & Society* 12 (2): 185–96.

Berardi, Franco. 2009. *The Soul at Work: From Alienation to Autonomy*. Los Angeles, CA: Semiotext.

———. 2011. *After the Future*. Oakland, CA: AK Press.

Bernays, Edward. 1947. "The Engineering of Consent." *ANNALS of the American Academy of Political and Social Science* 250 (1): 113–20.

Bogard, William. 1996. *The Simulation of Surveillance: Hypercontrol in Telematic Societies*. Cambridge: Cambridge University Press.

Boyle, Philip, and Kevin D. Haggerty. 2009. "Spectacular Security: Mega-Events and the Security Complex." *International Political Sociology* 3 (3): 257–74.

Braman, Sandra. 2004. *The Emergent Global Information Policy Regime*. Basingstoke: Palgrave Macmillan.

———. 2009. *Change of State: Information, Policy, and Power*. Cambridge, MA: MIT Press.

Bucher, Taina. 2012. "Want to Be on the Top? Algorithmic Power and the Threat of Invisibility on Facebook." *New Media & Society* 14 (7): 1164–80.

Cheney-Lippold, J. 2011. "A New Algorithmic Identity: Soft Biopolitics and the Modulation of Control." *Theory, Culture & Society* 28 (6): 164–81.

Clough, Patricia Ticineto. 2009. "The New Empiricism: Affect and Sociological Method." *European Journal of Social Theory* 12 (1): 43–61.

Coté, Mark, and Jennifer Pybus. 2007. "Learning to Immaterial Labour 2.0: MySpace and Social Networks." *Ephemera: Theory and Politics in Organization* 7 (1): 88–106.

Crawford, Kate, Mary L. Gray, and Kate Miltner. 2014. "Critiquing Big Data: Politics, Ethics, Epistemology | Special Section Introduction." *International Journal of Communication* 8: 1663–72.

Dahlberg, Lincoln. 2007. "Rethinking the Fragmentation of the Cyberpublic: From Consensus to Contestation." *New Media & Society* 9 (5): 827–47.

———. 2004. "Net-Public Sphere Research: Beyond the 'First Phase.'" *Javnost—The Public* 11 (1): 27–43.

Dauvergne, Peter, and Genevieve LeBaron. 2014. *Protest Inc. The Corporatization of Activism*. Cambridge: Polity.

Dean, Jodi. 2010. *Blog Theory: Feedback and Capture in the Circuits of Drive*. Cambridge, UK; Malden, MA: Polity.

Dencik, Lina. 2015. "Why Facebook Censorship Matters." http://www.jomec.co.uk/blog/why-facebook-censorship-matters/ (accessed 19 March 2015).

Elmer-Dewitt, Philip. 1993. "First Nation in Cyberspace Twenty Million Strong and Adding a Million New Users a Month, the Internet Is Suddenly the Place to Be." *TIME International*, December 6. http://www.chemie.fu-berlin.de/outerspace/internet-article.html (archived version).

Ericson, Richard Victor, and Kevin D. Haggerty. 2006. *The New Politics of Surveillance and Visibility*. Toronto: University of Toronto Press.

Fenton, Natalie, and Veronica Barassi. 2011. "Alternative Media and Social Networking Sites: The Politics of Individuation and Political Participation." *The Communication Review* 14 (3): 179–96.

Foucault, Michel. 2008. *The Birth of Biopolitics: Lectures at the Collège de France, 1978–79*. Basingstoke and New York: Palgrave Macmillan.

Fuller, Matthew, and Andrew Goffey. 2012. *Evil Media*. Cambridge, MA: MIT Press.

Gerbaudo, Paolo. 2012. *Tweets and the Streets: Social Media and Contemporary Activism*. London: Pluto Press.

Gerlitz, Carolin, and Anne Helmond. 2013. "The Like Economy: Social Buttons and the Data-Intensive Web." *New Media & Society* 15 (8): 1348–65.

Gillespie, Tarleton. 2012. "Can an Algorithm Be Wrong?" *Limn*, no. 2 (March). http://limn.it/can-an-algorithm-be-wrong/.

———. 2014. "The Relevance of Algorithms." In *Media Technologies: Essays on Communication, Materiality, and Society*, edited by Tarleton Gillespie, Pablo J. Boczkowski and Kirsten A. Foot, 167–95. Cambridge, MA: MIT Press.

Green, Nicola, and Sean Smith. 2002. "'A Spy in Your Pocket'? The Regulation of Mobile Data in the UK." *Surveillance & Society* 1 (4): 573–87.

Greenwald, Glenn. 2014. *No Place to Hide: Edward Snowden, the NSA and the Surveillance State*. London: Penguin.

Haggerty, Kevin D., and Richard Ericson. 2000. "The Surveillant Assemblage." *British Journal of Sociology* 51 (4): 605–22.

Hallinan, Blake, and Ted Striphas. 2014. "Recommended for You: The Netflix Prize and the Production of Algorithmic Culture." *New Media & Society*, first published on June 23.

Hands, Joss. 2013. "Introduction: Politics, Power and 'platformativity.'" *Culture Machine* 14. http://svr91.edns1.com/~culturem/index.php/cm/article/viewArticle/504.

Hof, Robert D. 2011. "You Are the Ad." *MIT Technology Review*. April 19. http://www.technologyreview.com/featuredstory/423721/you-are-the-ad/.

Kramer, Adam D. I., Jamie E. Guillory and Jeffrey T. Hancock. 2014. "Experimental Evidence of Massive-Scale Emotional Contagion through Social Networks." *Proceedings of the National Academy of Sciences* 111 (24): 8788–90.

Langlois, Ganaele. 2013. "Participatory Culture and the New Governance of Communication: The Paradox of Participatory Media." *Television & New Media* 14 (2): 91–105.

———. 2014. *Meaning in the Age of Social Media*. Basingstoke: Palgrave Macmillan.

Lazzarato, Maurizio. 2006. "'Semiotic Pluralism' and the New Government of Signs. Homage to Félix Guattari." *Transversal Texts*. http://eipcp.net/transversal/0107/lazzarato/en.

———. 2014. *Signs and Machines: Capitalism and the Production of Subjectivity*. Translated by Joshua David Jordan. Los Angeles: Semiotexte.

Leistert, Oliver. 2008. "Data Retention in the European Union: When a Call Returns." *International Journal of Communication* 11(2): 925–935.

———. 2013a. "Der Beitrag der Social Media zur Partizipation." *Forschungsjournal Soziale Bewegungen* 26:39–47.

———. 2013b. "Smell the Fish: Digital Disneyland and the Right to Oblivion." *First Monday* 18 (3).

Leistert, Oliver, and Theo Röhle, eds. 2011. *Generation Facebook. Über das Leben im Social Net*. Bielefeld: transcript.

Lieberman, Joel D., Deborah Koetzle and Mari Sakiyama. 2013. "Police Departments' Use of Facebook Patterns and Policy Issues." *Police Quarterly* 16 (4): 438–62.

Lipp, Kenneth. 2013. "Police Departments Work to Expand Capability to 'Shut Down' Social Media." October 24. https://kennethlipp.wordpress.com/2013/10/24/police-departments-work-to-expand-capability-to-shut-down-social media/.

Lyon, David. 2014. "Surveillance, Snowden, and Big Data: Capacities, Consequences, Critique." *Big Data & Society* 1 (2): 1–13.

McKelvey, Fenwick Robert. 2014. "Algorithmic Media Need Algorithmic Methods: Why Publics Matter." *Canadian Journal of Communication* 39 (4).

McStay, Andrew. 2011. *The Mood of Information: A Critique of Online Behavioural Advertising*. New York: Continuum.

Meyer, Robinson. 2014. "Everything We Know About Facebook's Secret Mood Manipulation Experiment." *The Atlantic*. June 28. http://www.theatlantic.com/technology/archive/2014/06/everything-we-know-about-facebooks-secret-mood-manipulation-experiment/373648/.

Milan, Stefania. 2013. *Social Movements and Their Technologies: Wiring Social Change*. Basingstoke: Palgrave Macmillan.

Monahan, Torin, and John Gilliom. 2013. *SuperVision: An Introduction to the Surveillance Society*. Chicago: The University of Chicago Press.

Oram, Andy. 2015. "How Did We End up with a Centralized Internet for the NSA to Mine? O'Reilly Radar." http://radar.oreilly.com/2014/01/how-did-we-end-up-with-a-centralized-internet-for-the-nsa-to-mine.html (accessed 19 March 2015).

Pariser, Eli. 2011. *The Filter Bubble*. London: Penguin.

Parisi, Luciana, and Steve Goodman. 2011. "Mnemonic Control." In *Beyond Biopolitics: Essays on the Governance of Life and Death*, edited by Patricia Ticineto Clough and Craig Willse, 163–76. Durham, NC: Duke University Press.

Peacock, Sylvia E. 2014. "How Web Tracking Changes User Agency in the Age of Big Data: The Used User." *Big Data & Society* 1 (2): 1–11.

Pieri, Elisa. 2013. "Emergent Policing Practices: Urban Space Securitisation in the Aftermath of the Manchester 2011 Riots." *Surveillance & Society* 12 (1): 38–54.

Ranciere, Jacques. 2006. *The Politics of Aesthetics: The Distribution of the Sensible*. London and New York: Bloomsbury.

Rosenblueth, Arturo, Norbert Wiener and Julian Bigelow. 1943. "Behavior, Purpose and Teleology." *Philosophy of Science* 10 (1): 18–24.

Rosenbush, Steve. 2013. "Facebook Tests Software to Track Your Cursor on Screen." October 30. http://blogs.wsj.com/cio/2013/10/30/facebook-considers-vast-increase-in-data-collection/?mod=e2tw.

Russell, Matthew. 2011. *Mining the Social Web: Analyzing Data From Facebook, Twitter, LinkedIn, and Other Social Media Sites*. Sebastopol: O'Reilly Media.

Stiegler, Bernard. 2010. *Taking Care of Youth and the Generations*. Stanford, CA: Stanford University Press.

Struijs, Peter, Barteld Braaksma and Piet Daas. 2014. "Official Statistics and Big Data." *Big Data & Society* 1 (1): 1–6.

Terranova, Tiziana, and Joan Donovan. 2013. "Occupy Social Networks: The Paradoxes of Using Corporate Social Media in Networked Movements." In *Unlike Us Reader: Social Media Monopolies and Their Alternatives*, edited by Geert Lovink and Miriam Rasch, 296–311. Amsterdam: Institute of Network Cultures.

Thompson, John B. 2005. "The New Visibility." *Theory, Culture & Society* 22 (6): 31–51.

Trottier, Daniel. 2012. *Social Media as Surveillance: Rethinking Visibility in a Converging World*. Farnham: Ashgate.

Tufekci, Zeynep. 2014. "Engineering the Public: Big Data, Surveillance and Computational Politics." *First Monday* 19 (7). http://firstmonday.org/ojs/index.php/fm/article/view/4901.

Tufekci, Zeynep, and Christopher Wilson. 2012. "Social Media and the Decision to Participate in Political Protest: Observations From Tahrir Square." *Journal of Communication* 62 (2): 363–79.

Wiedemann, Carolin. 2011. "Facebook: Das Assessment-Center der alltäglichen Lebensführung." In *Generation Facebook*, edited by Oliver Leistert and Theo Röhle, 161–81. Bielefeld: transcript.

Chapter Three

Mobilizing in Times of Social Media

From a Politics of Identity to a Politics of Visibility

Stefania Milan

7 January 2015: the hashtag #JeSuisCharlie ('I am Charlie') became a trending topic on the microblogging platform Twitter. In about a half hour, over twenty-one thousand tweets commemorated the victims of the attack against the French satirical magazine *Charlie Hebdo*, which left twelve people dead (BBC 2015). In the weeks that followed, thousands of people took to the streets in various European cities, holding up signs with the same slogan. But the hashtag, which is simply a keyword that assigns information to categories to help users retrieve it, did not just express support for those killed. It also signaled the ultimate adhesion to the core values of Western democracy, freedom of the press above all. Similarly, other hashtags emerged, in support of diverse viewpoints on the same events: for example, #JeNeSuisPasCharlie questioned the contradictory 'neo-liberal nod of solidarity' (Vigo 2015) that reduced the Paris killings to a mere attack on freedom of speech, ignoring the socio-historical background that nurtured the conflict; #JeSuisAhmed honored Ahmed Merabet, the Muslim policeman of Algerian descent fallen in the attack.

25 February 2015: the hashtag #Maagdenhuisbezet ('Maagdenhuis occupied') rapidly went trending on Twitter. It referred to the 'appropriation' by students and staff of the central building of the University of Amsterdam, the biggest in the Netherlands. They protested against the proposed budget cuts to the School of Humanities, and called for 'a new university' not ruled by profit (Vrousalis et al. 2015). However, the hashtag was also a reference to the 1969 occupation of the same building—an event that triggered a reform process that resulted in 1971 in a new law affirming the involvement of both faculty and students in the governance of the university. In other words, the

hashtag was evocative of perceived commonalities between the 1969 movement and today's, as well as an omen for radical change to come.

Twitter 'trending topics', that is to say terms or combinations of words
that are tagged at a greater rate than others, can be seen as discursive waves
that shake and shape contemporary digital activism. Typically they are
ephemeral and erratic; sometimes they get rapidly viral. Yet often they contribute to set the agenda of the public debate at the local, national and transnational level. As the above examples show, social media posts—and their
baggage of symbolic conventions such as hashtags, shortened links and the
'lingo' of abbreviations—are not just slogans. They signal solidarity, and
reclaim a sense of belonging and commonality. In other words, they communicate and create identity.

Social media have become a relentless presence in our life. At the end of
2014, there were two billion active social media accounts out of a total three
billion internet users, corresponding respectively to the 29 percent and the 42
percent of the world population (Kemp 2015). Developing countries are expected to account for most growth from 2016 on (Kemp 2015). Five hundred
million 'tweets' of maximum 140 characters are sent per day, in thirty-three
languages, and 77 percent of Twitter accounts are outside the United States
(Twitter, Inc. 2015)—yet Twitter is not the most popular platform. Facebook
leads the way, with QZone (available in Chinese only) and Google+ following on the distance (Kemp 2014).

Social networking platforms are deeply interwoven into the fabric of
daily life. By subverting familiar dichotomies between the individual and the
collective, the intimate and the public, copresence and distance, they have
spawned a fundamental cultural shift in the 'process of inscribing meaning
into our contemporary social and spatial interactions' (Farman 2012, 1).
Protest and organized collective action have been reformatted, too. Organizing has become easier and quicker, and relatively inexpensive. Organizational patterns of social movements have changed under the pressure of networked collective action, and digital media increasingly function 'as organizing agents' (Bennett and Segerberg 2012, 752). Individualized action has
become more prominent to the detriment of traditional movement groupings.
The identities of both protests and protesters come to life in the myriad of
individual and collective narratives that unfold on social media platforms as
much as they do in real life, and often simultaneously. I have termed this
novel mobilization dynamic 'cloud protesting', in reference to the digital
backbone that upholds it.

In what follows, I focus on the level of micro-interactions to explore
different aspects of cloud protesting seen in relation to the technical properties of social media, paying attention to organizational patterns, the creation
and reproduction of a collective identity and the consequences of social
media use on protest and group dynamics. The chapter combines critical

technology studies and social movement research in view of offering a theoretical approach to understand protest in relation to its digital support. It explores the idea that social media identify a discursive space where identities are incrementally built through the engagement of multiple individuals acting on their own accord, and to a degree superseding organizations. Any given collective identity, thus, results from the complex interplay between a 'politics of identity', typical of the so-called new social movements,[1] and the 'politics of visibility' fostered by social media. Moreover, the notion of visibility of people, their doings and whereabouts, translates in surveillance and self-surveillance. These are so entrenched in social media use to have become integral to contemporary protests.

The chapter is organized as follows. The first section explores social media from a critical technology perspective, linking their features to the logics they contribute to enforce on collective action. The second presents the dynamics of cloud protesting, shedding light on organizational patterns in their interplay within social and mobile media. The third part posits communication as the ritual at the core of cloud protesting, and explores the politics of visibility promoted by social media in relation to identity building. The last section looks at the consequences of the politics of visibility for contemporary mobilizations, focusing on surveillance and self-surveillance dynamics.

IN THE MAZE OF SOCIAL MEDIA

Contemporary organized collective action is deeply affected by a pervasive 'social media logic' determined by 'the strategies, mechanisms, and economies underpinning these platforms' (van Dijck and Poell 2013, 3). Does this social media logic change the nature of contemporary collective action, and if so, how?

In earlier writings (Milan 2015a; Milan 2015b), I argued that the primary, fundamental change that social media introduce to the realm of organized collective action is *at the material level*. By materiality, I mean both the online platforms people increasingly depend on for interpersonal communication and organizing, but also the messages, images and 'datafied' (c.f., Cukier and Mayer-Schoenberger 2013, 29) emotions and relations that come to life on these online platforms. This materiality has two main consequences: first, it offers a (digital) embodiment to user contents and feelings, and, second, it supports the enactment of social interactions and online collective action. Overall, it alters the 'discursive terrain in which meaning contests occur' (Snow 2004, 405).

Social movements history is awash with excellent examples of entanglement of the symbolic and the material dimensions. Think, for instance, of protest slogans and banners, but also occupations, encampments and performances like flashmobs. These manifestations of the protesters' grievances, values and feelings—in other words, the cultural and symbolic production of a movement—are the result of the 'interactive process of constructing meaning' (Gamson 1992, xii) enacted by social actors in the making of collective action. However, by altering the relation between the symbolic and the material of meaning-making processes, the layer of materiality introduced by social media contributes to transform both the content and the process of the aforementioned 'meaning work'. More specifically, by becoming a ubiquitous presence in our portable, always-on personal devices, the 'material' powered by, and enshrined in social media, has *multiplied the opportunities for experiencing the collective dimension of social action* beyond sporadic events like protest marches or strikes. In so doing, the 'material' of social media has developed into the primary vehicle of meaning work, adding to (and somewhat substituting) other traditional mediators like mass and movement media but also face-to-face exchanges. In other words, this materiality is not only the support or the mere physical and/or virtual representation of the symbolic, but also the *process* through which the symbolic takes shape.

Nowadays social media play a unique *broker* role in the protesters' meaning construction processes. In this 'semiotic-material co-presence' (Leistert 2013, 4), content and infrastructure are utterly linked: the latter shapes and orders the former. Furthermore, content is to some extent immanent to the infrastructure, as it cannot manifest itself in the same form outside the specific structure of a given social media platform (e.g., the tweet, the hashtag, the shortened link). Hence, we ought to take a closer look at the specific 'regimes of the production and circulation of meaning' (Langlois 2011, 3) typical of commercial social media, for they bear important consequences on the way meanings are reproduced and circulated.

Social media are algorithmic media. With some exceptions, they are sustained by proprietary and opaque machine languages that function as 'control technologies [. . .] dynamically modifying content and function through [. . .] programmed routines' (McKelvey 2014). By continuously collecting data from consumer preferences and interactions, they profile users in view of offering a customized service but also of monetizing user exchanges (see also van Dijck and Poell 2013). This tailored distortion of the ranking, selection and presentation of information intervenes at both the individual and the interpersonal or community level, affecting not only what shows up on one's own interface, but also the prominence of users' content in relation to one another. Algorithms, however, are invisible to end-users: their outcome is visible (e.g., the manipulated content that shows up on one's customized interface), but it bears no indication of having been manipulated. They leave no trace, because they exist only when operational in the micro-temporalities of computing (McKelvey 2014). Nevertheless, they do create rules for social interaction, and as such deeply affect the meaning work of contemporary movements. What is more, and contrary to what seems to be a widespread perception among users, social media are not neutral platforms devoid of politics, but embody specific power relations built within (c.f., Gómez García and Treré 2014). By subscribing to commercial platforms and agreeing to the 'Terms of Service', which are in fact actual legal contracts between platform owners and their customers, users become involved in a complex socio-technical environment characterized by specific algorithmic, socio-legal and normative conditions. As many observers have pointed out (see, among others, Andrejevic 2005; Dean, Anderson and Lovink 2006; Fuchs and Sandoval 2014; Leistert 2013), the core tenets of this socio-technical environment are exploitation and surveillance of user contents and relationships, in a sort of 'digital enclosure' where private information is expropriated to enable tailored interactivity (Andrejevic 2007). Customers have only very limited awareness of the *modus operandi* of most social media platforms, as technical and policy arrangements, including collaboration with law enforcement agencies, are deliberately kept away from user oversight (Beer 2009).

We can identify a number of patterns within the current social media regimes, which result in the redefinition of, amongst others, the priority, visibility and popularity of content. These patterns include *publicity* (content and interactions are usually public and traceable, albeit sometimes within the 'walled gardens' of user communities); *mobility* (77 percent of users access social media via mobile devices [Kemp 2014], which results in the modification of the temporality, spatiality and frequency of content production and fruition); *real-timeness* (the content uploaded online usually appears on-screen in nearly real time, allowing for a quasi-simultaneity of the action or emotion and its representation); *datafication* (platforms quantify exchanges and interactions, ultimately turning users into profiles and data entries); *virtual/real copresence* (the blurring of the boundaries between virtual and real promotes the superimposition of the two dimensions); *automated disruption* (whereby fake accounts and social bots, that is to say virtual agents performing automated tasks, operate alongside with regular users, potentially distorting their activities and perceptions).[2] All told, social media impose severe material constraints on their social affordances. They do not simply 'enable but not determine' (Bennett and Segerberg 2013, Kindle lo 923–26); they significantly contribute to structure modes of interactions and relationships.

In this context, my notion of cloud protesting, which takes inspiration from cloud computing (Milan 2015a; Milan 2013a), might sound woefully contradictory. The centralized and privatized nature of the cloud (Mosco 2014) might not be the best metaphor to indicate the distributed efforts of contemporary mobilizations. The reference to cloud computing, however, points to a fundamental ambivalence in contemporary collective action, namely its distancing itself from the values and exploitation of digital capitalism, while at the same time overrelying on its products, and social media above all, for the protest's unfolding, diffusion and survival. In what follows, I explore the main features of cloud protesting, investigating what social dynamics the logic of commercial social media contributes to trigger, why and how.

THE MOBILIZATION TRAJECTORIES OF CLOUD PROTESTING

Popular wisdom and scholarly production are abound of enthusiastic recollections of how social media have multiplied the opportunities and the venues for self-expression and political intervention (see, among others, Castells 2012; della Porta and Mattoni 2015; Gerbaudo 2012; Juris 2012). 'Connective action' (Bennett and Segerberg 2013), 'networked individuals' (Rainie and Wellman 2014) and 'crowds of individuals' (Juris 2012) have emerged alongside with 'traditional' movements, their organizations and 'entrepreneurs' (c.f., McCarthy and Zald 1977). Digital and seemingly spontaneous manifestations of rage or solidarity, and the corresponding exercise in identity building, intersect the dynamics of postindustrial 'new' social movements. By the same token, over the last few years, observers of social mobilizations have triumphantly announced the death of organizations and traditional groupings, which have supposedly surrendered to spontaneous, inexpensive mobilizing via social media. There is some truth in these analyses, as they recognize that digital protest and resistance has partially inverted the logic of collective action. Instead of creating an oppositional mass, social media celebrate the role of decentralized units and individual action in disrupting the system (Milan 2013a). But there is also a normative argument embedded in these views, whereby 'natural' protest is purported as intrinsically more authentic and 'pure' in intentions and goals. Expressive and cultural forms of protest, as they are facilitated by the immediacy of social media, are believed to be unaffected by the vested interests of consolidated organizations (see also Dencik in this volume). Furthermore, policy makers and mainstream media alike tend to explicitly link these expressive forms of protest to youth and/or internet cultures, in an implicit attempt to belittle protest outbursts. Being decoupled from the dynamics of traditional party and interest politics, accused of merely aiming at conquering power or advancing the needs of the few, 'social media protests' are increasingly seen as a temporary phenomenon that is likely to die out with the same speed at which it emerged. It is a process that brings contemporary protest closer to last century's definition of forms of irrational collective behaviour like crowds, mobilized by shared emotions, and masses (c.f., Park and Burgess 1921; Smelser 1962), rather than to a coordinated, sustainable social movement, expression of a democratic citizenry that policy makers cannot ignore.

This chapter argues against the precipitous dismissal of organizations in social movements, which might ultimately play in the hands of the socioeconomic system contemporary movements intend to fight. Social media regimes certainly focus on the individual, rather than the collective, and thus tend to empower (and give visibility to) single actors rather than collectivities, enabling loose temporal connections and affect-based decisions rather than consensus-based (democratic) processes. Organizations are indeed elusive, increasingly volatile and even occasionally amorphous. But the fact that they appear opaque to external observers should not be sufficient to announce their passing. Rather, social and mobile media *transform* organizations. The idea, not at all new in the sociology of the web (Castells 1998; Bennett 2003), is that social media serve as a metaphor for a specific type of social interactions, which results in distinctive groupings. More specifically, social media identify discursive arenas of interaction able to sustain idiosyncratic cultures of relation building, which differ from but also augment face-to-face exchanges. In doing so, they promote specific trajectories of mobilization that are functional to the development of new practices, tactics and identities. What is more, these trajectories and cultures of relation building spill over to face-to-face exchanges, altering the experience of individuals as they engage in collective action. In this section, I explore organizational patterns of cloud protesting, positioning organizational dynamics in relation to social media.

Organizations have historically been the engine of social movements and organized collective action. However, if we look back to the last half dozen decades, we can identify a trajectory that sees the progressive enfranchising of informal groupings, small clusters and individuals. Oversimplifying, this evolution can be seen as a function of the technology that became progressively available over time, and of the communication dynamics such technology enabled. We can distinguish three phases, characterized respectively by social movement organizations, by clusters of networked individuals and by what I have termed the 'cloud'. The first phase was dominated by the textbook social movement organization, which offered straightforward membership on the basis of gender, religion or life cycle (see, for example, Tilly 2009). Its leaders controlled the cultural, ideological and normative production of the movement, and served as a point of contact for mass media and journalists. Movement media (see Downing 2011), increasingly popular in the form of free and pirate radio stations, alternative magazines and home-printed pamphlets, remained on the fringes of society, and in the hands of a few 'expert' activists. In the second phase, which corresponded to the diffusion of the internet in the late 1990s, internal and external communication became diffused and to a degree unfiltered, as so did the cultural and symbolic production of social movements. Identities and values were produced and reproduced through networked digital communication and increasingly cheap camcorders and computers, in a myriad of self-produced media like websites and autonomous video productions. As a metaphor, the network inspired innovative experiments in horizontal organizing, which resulted in flexible coalitions such as affinity groups, temporary clusters oriented to action and rooted on shared values and objectives (see McDonald 2002). They existed and operated in the context of broader networks, which often spilled over national borders. They emphasized the role of individuals, their needs, preferences and experiences, as well as their acting together. They gave rise to 'experience movements', which stressed the experiential dimension of individuals and their relationship with others (McDonald 2004). But the advent and mass diffusion of social media in the mid-2000s has paved the way for a third dynamic to emerge, that of cloud protesting, of which social media are an integral part.

If we compare the internet era of experience movements with present-day 'spontaneous' groupings coalesced around social media communities, we can see how the focus on the micro-interactional level of collective action is not new within social movements. Scholars have acknowledged the importance of the micro level of interaction (Melucci 1996), and of personal and collective emotions (Jasper 1997; Goodwin, Jasper and Polletta 2001). There is consensus in the field around the understanding of social movement organizations as 'arenas of interactions' able to 'sustain distinctive cultures of interaction and shared trajectories of mobilization' (Clemens and Minkoff 2004, 157–58). What have changed in the time of social media are the magnitude of individual direct interactions (more people can potentially communicate with one another), their frequency (social media are accessed through always-on personal mobile devices) and their breadth (as the boundary between the private quotidian and the political has lost relevance). In addition, the publicity and visibility of this micro-interactional level to both external observers and the participants themselves fosters solidarity and protest diffusion, and facilitates media coverage.

Social media and mobile devices have provided the organizational principle for cloud protesting. Groupings approach 'dispersed and individualized constituenc[ies]' (Gerbaudo 2012, 5) rooted on flexible individual engagement in the first person. They take the form of *micro-organizations* with variable geometry, clustered around magmatic constellations of preexisting interpersonal connections, interactions and networks. Precisely because the quotidian can hardly be distinguished from the political, these groupings, here labeled 'clouds', increasingly resemble familiar assemblages like groups of friends or communities of interest, where various kinds of nonpolitical content are also occasionally exchanged. Similarly to experience movements, participants do not seek to manifest a group identity (a cohesive, univocal 'we') through action. Instead, they are after 'other grammars of action: healing, touching, hearing, feeling, seeing, moving'—'grammars of embodiment' (McDonald 2006, 37).

The mobilization trajectory identified by cloud protesting, and by the cloud as a group, is one that starts and ends with the individual and its mediated self (and self-representation). In what follows, I explore the dynamics of identity building within cloud protesting, and investigate the interplay between the individual and the collective dimension as they are filtered by social media.

VISIBILITY RELOADED: PRESENCE AS IDENTITY AND COMMUNICATION AS RITUAL

Identity has been defined as the process through which 'a collective becomes a collective' (Melucci 1996, 84): a sort of 'esprit de corps' (Blumer 1939) that holds people together. Adopting Melucci's interactionist perspective, I see identity building as an 'interactive and shared' process, in which 'elements are constructed and negotiated through a recurrent process of activation of the relations that bind actors together' (Melucci 1996, 70). Communicative action, according to Habermas (1984), enables people to form their identity. Hence the question: how is identity building rewritten by the invasive mediation of social media?

At the core of the cloud as an organizational paradigm lies communication as a process, seen as the ritual that supports and sustains micro-organizations. Following Melucci, I maintain that social, micro-level interaction has generative qualities, and that 'communicative channels and technologies of communication are constitutive parts' of the social relationships that make a movement (Melucci 1996, 71). Furthermore, the publicity and materiality inherent in the social media regime, whereby user content and interactions are to a large extent public and observable, drives communication to take place into the open, in a sort of recursive 'front stage' where self-presentation is played out (c.f., Goffman 1959). Interpersonal communication on social media can therefore be considered a quintessential interaction ritual (Collins 2004), whereby participation in the online discussion and social networking becomes a symbol, proof and fetish of group membership. According to Collins's interaction ritual theory, a ritual can be seen as 'a mechanism of mutually focused emotion and attention producing a *momentarily shared reality*, which thereby generates solidarity and symbols of group membership' (Collins 2004, 7; emphasis added). Continuously reenacting the protest as well as shared emotions and beliefs (c.f., Goffman 1959), the ritual of social media communication contributes to pump up individuals with positive emotional energy, which in turn fuels action in a spiral mechanism of reinforcement of both belonging and action. Indeed rituals, which are naturally 'stylized and dramatized', contribute to pass on crucial information about social relationships (della Porta and Diani 2006, 109). If we look at the meso or group level, we see how communication becomes a ritual at the meta level too, whereby exchanges on social media are reinforced by the consistent inclusion of 'metacommunication' elements (e.g., who contributes, when, how and so on—visible for example in the 'tagging', when individuals are directly called into question). This way, presence and interactions on social media turn into a substitute for the group. Social media rituals are then instrumental in regenerating interpersonal bonds, thus strengthening collective identity. They promote inter-group solidarity, but also support, reproduce and reinforce hierarchies. To say it with Collins, social media rituals support *ad infinitum* 'momentary encounters among human bodies charged up with emotions and consciousness because they have gone through chains of previous encounters' (Collins 2004, 3). Furthermore, social media contribute to enlarge the discursive terrain/contest of a social movement by including bystanders and potential supporters: the immediacy of communication afforded by social media allows protesters to recursively celebrate their rituals with and within the public in an existential time which is concurrent and shared.

How is the 'collective we' created in this process, and what is its function? Contrary to earlier assumptions in classical social movements scholarship (see, for example, Snow 2001), in cloud protesting the identification of the individual in a 'collective we' is no longer the final stage of a process that starts with the individual and ends with different selves 'merged' in an indistinct, harmonious 'we'. Rather, the 'collective we' has become an intermediary stage, a *filter* that merely provides a flexible context to individual selves. On social media, the 'collective we' is called into being by the incremental juxtaposition of individual contributions, which would otherwise risk to go unnoticed if taken in isolation. Porous but viscous at the same time, this 'collective we' allows for individuals to stay true to themselves, while being incrementally and imperceptibly altered by the experience of joint action, both real and virtual, or imagined.

All told, social media redesign the process of identity building, but also the notion of what is collective in collective identity—that is to say, the experience rather than the belonging. I call this transposed identity building process 'visibility'. Visibility is taken to mean the virtual embodiment of individuals and groups and their respective meanings, as these are relentlessly negotiated, reinvigorated and updated in online platforms. Visibility communicates urgency and inexorable interpersonal exchange on the 'front stage'. It is the results of two elements introduced by social media into organized collective action, namely materiality and publicity of users, their actions and interactions, and the related symbolic dimension. But it also intersects another crucial element of identity building, specifically recognition. Recognition is a central tenet of a 'collective we', as it entails the 'ability to recognize and be recognized' as part of a group (Melucci 1996,

71). Social media make this recognition tangible in the form of, for example, 'likes' and 'shares'. They boost it, by magnifying the number of others that are potentially reached, but also by introducing an element of repetition and continuity in the message. In addition, they enhance the exercise of reciprocity, by means of 'friending', returned 'likes' and 'favourites' typical of the datafication they promote. This process has spectacular consequences for organized collective action. Not only has this emerging 'politics of visibility' in some measure replaced the 'politics of identity' typical of social movements (c.f., Melucci 1989), it has also turned into a proxy for collective identity. To paraphrase McDonald, this 'grammar of action [. . .] lead[s] to an ethic and forms of action underlining presence' (McDonald 2004, 590) rather than belonging and joint action. Moreover, the politics of visibility is the result of a process that originates and ends with and within the individual, which reproduces exactly the trajectory of cloud protesting illustrated above: the coalescing of a group is a necessary intermediary stage, functional to peer recognition, but is no longer the end in itself. In what follows, I explore what the politics of visibility means for contemporary organization collective action and protest.

THE CONSEQUENCES OF VISIBILITY

The shift to a politics of visibility promoted by social media brings about both intentional and unintentional forms of presence and publicity, which can have significant consequences on collective action. These consequences affect the relations between movements and the state, but also the internal and external dynamics of a social movement. Both speak to the ambivalent attitude towards publicity, visibility and surveillance which characterizes the contemporary social movement ecology (see, for example, Leistert 2013). This section explores three such consequences. First, visibility in an online environment that discloses relationships makes a movement transparent to its opponents, facilitating surveillance and repression. Second, the visibility afforded by social media fosters mechanisms of self-surveillance, which can alter the internal cohesion of a movement. Third, the quest to capture and record action may be turned into an opportunity for activism; for example, enacting 'sousveillance' (or inverse surveillance) tactics (c.f., Mann, Nolan and Wellman 2003). Digital surveillance, sousveillance and self-surveillance are three facets of the same phenomenon, which has ubiquitous interactivity at its core. The three have become constitutive elements of protest identities in the time of social media, but they have different outcomes on protest emergence, its development and sustainability over time. Moreover, the politics of visibility bears also consequences on the mobilization dynamics per se. On the one hand, the evaporation of the group as the necessary precondition for collective action alters crucial interpersonal dynamics typical of social movements, like internal solidarity. On the other, the pursuit of visibility at all costs may override action itself, emphasizing a media-centred definition of the impact and effectiveness of a social movement.

First of all, the exercise of visibility makes movements visible to their opponents, including the state, law enforcement and the secret services. In so doing, it dramatically eases both surveillance and repression. Surveillance is made possible by the collaboration of corporations acting as 'regulatory agents, turning private centres of power to state purposes' (Braman 2009, 34; see also MacKinnon 2012 and Hintz in this volume), but counts also on users volunteering their information while trading privacy for 'better', more convenient services. Although movements have historically been subject to protest policing and repression (della Porta and Reiter 1998; della Porta, Peterson and Reiter 2006), surveillance has now reached new frontiers and the costs of mass scrutiny have decreased substantially (Bankston and Soltani 2014). 'Connective surveillance', as Libert (2015) labeled the surveillance logic enabled by commercial social-networking services, allows authorities to take advantage of this ready-made 'surveillant assemblage' of state and nonstate actors (Haggerty and Ericson 2000). Rather than creating a surveillance infrastructure *ex novo*, the state can simply 'bring these systems together into a whole' (Libert 2015, 9). On social media, law enforcement can exercise preemptive monitoring, and infiltrate groups by polluting communications (see, for example, Elmer and Redden in this volume). Connective surveillance even makes it possible for authorities to watch and potentially repress movements even before they appear (Libert 2015, 10).

Although surveillance has historically been the bugbear of social movements in authoritarian and democratic regimes alike, it seems that nowadays the habit to social media has cleared the activist sphere from this concern. It has also given it an aura of inevitability that is met by a resignation that grazes into indifference. Protesters expose themselves to digital surveillance by merely relying on commercial services or 'tethered devices' (c.f., Zittrain 2008); they run location services on their appliances, contributing to expand the reach of the surveillance machine. In doing so, they dramatically increase the information available to police forces, secret services and beyond, amplifying the discrepancy in (information) resources between movements and their opponents. But the digital surveillance prompted by the exercise of visibility has also an effect on a movement's identity, and one that is rarely productive. If on the one hand, surveillance is perceived as inscribed in the medium and thus goes largely unnoticed, on the other hand, the easiness at which one can create a digital persona and the activity of bots hinders the collegiality of the group. And while repression normally reinforces the 'collective we' (Milan 2013b; Koopmans 1992), the more subtle surveillance generates suspicion in the long run. It is detrimental to internal deliberation and political participation more in general, and may foster self-censorship.

In the second instance, the emphasis on visibility contributes to create internal boundaries and identify insiders and outsiders through citizen-initiated unmasking based on presence and publicity, possibly subverting the internal cohesion of a movement. Social media, in fact, enable novel forms of self-surveillance, whereby a movement can watch its borders and engage in a game of inclusion and exclusion that ultimately contributes to reinforce the 'collective we'. But it is a double-edge sword: while self-surveillance contributes to define the 'we', it paves the way to unhealthy collaborations between a movement and those in charge of watching and repressing it. Self-surveillance becomes particularly dangerous when it intersects a tactic widely used by law enforcement, namely the attempt to take advantage of internal divisions to break a movement. Not surprisingly, authorities increasingly sponsor self-surveillance asking activists to collaborate in unmasking fringes that are considered violent or subversive. As such, self-surveillance functions as a Trojan horse: used by both activists and law enforcement, it is enacted by the former to the benefit of the latter. It allows police forces to outsource some of their prerequisites and tasks and take advantage of the activists' insider knowledge. It also breaks the traditional separation between protesters and the state, subverting the rules and the roles of the protest game; it may even have deep consequences on internal solidarity.

The third facet of the regime of surveillance of social media can be traced in the possibility of subversion and tactical appropriation it offers to activists, and sousveillance above all. It is not uncommon nowadays to find protesters filming officers on duty as they police demonstrations and encampments (see also Elmer in this volume). Thanks to smartphones and digital cameras 're-cording police has never been easier . . . neither has publicizing these record-ings' (The Economist 2011). Dedicated applications such as Sukey have been developed to 'keep protesters safe during demonstrations' by exchanging information about police whereabouts and doings (Sukey 2011). Investigating Twitter use during the protests against the 2009 G20 meeting in Pittsburgh, United States, Earl et al. (2013) have shown how the microblogging service was extensively used to broadcast information about police action, including particular units, weapons or equipment, as well as about interactions with protesters.[3] Other examples of tactical use of the politics of visibility include using surveillance on social media to the advantage of movements, deliberately misrepresenting actions, plans and motives to mislead authorities. On the whole, engaging in sousveillance and subverting state surveillance can have a productive effect on movements. As the creation of a shared identity implies also the identification of a 'them' in opposition to the 'we', monitoring practices to 'police the police' and other tactical uses of surveillance are likely to reinforce a group's identity and cohesion.

Finally, it is worth looking briefly at the consequences that the transition to a politics of visibility has on movement dynamics, both internal (between members) and external (between activists and bystanders). Visibility becomes a proxy for the 'collective we' at the expenses of critical group dynamics such as commitment, internal solidarity and responsibility towards fellow activists (c.f., Hunt and Benford 2004). While the cloud supplants traditional assemblages in providing activists with a (loose, wavering) sense of belonging, it demands less responsibility towards the collective component: in other words, it offers identification but comes with no strings attached. The somewhat marginal role of the group in a process that starts and ends with the individual and posits the 'collective we' as a mere intermediary stage, might in the long run have dramatic effects on the sustainability of movements, as well as on their internal cohesion. But the politics of visibility affects also movement tactics and the very definition of what constitutes impact and effectiveness. The quest to capture and record protests and other forms of joint as well as individual action in order to render presence visible ('I was there because I have content to show I was there') results in presence being ranked well above actual action. Self-expression might be privileged over self-organization, and presence may well remain exclusively digital. In turn, impact and effectiveness might be defined solely in terms of media visibility, without this necessarily reflecting a growing attention by policy makers. And while the current fascination of mainstream media for anything social media-related plays in the hands of these distorted dynamics, movements might have to reinvent themselves when media attention is over, or otherwise disappear.

CONCLUSION

This chapter held micro-organizations and the small-scale, here-and-now rituals of interpersonal communication mediated by social media as constitutive of the symbolic and cultural dimensions of collective action, as well as of the construction and reproduction of the 'collective we' that stands for collective action. It argued that there is a certain type of mobilization and collective action 'built into' social media, which is the direct consequence of the specific regime of materiality brought about by social networking services. Social and mobile media have offered the organizational principle for the emergence of a novel mobilization dynamic, which I have termed cloud protesting. They reshape the process of identity building, promoting a politics of visibility that builds on materiality, publicity and reputation as they are enhanced by social media, and emphasizes experience over belonging. The mobilization trajectory identified by cloud protesting starts and ends with the individual and its mediated self-representation. The 'collective we' is reduced to an intermediary stage, a filter that offers a flexible context to self-contained selves. Visibility has become a proxy for collective identity.

It is undeniable that social media have some merits, too. They have enlarged the normative debate to sectors of the population difficult to reach otherwise; they have brought protest under the spotlight of mainstream media with a minimum outflow of human resources. Yet, the protesters' overreliance on commercial platforms is a harbinger of the lack of a much-needed critique of shifting power dynamics in the capitalist internet. Not only is it contradictory vis-à-vis the values progressive activists profess; it is also a missed opportunity to exercise reflexivity and self-organization in the communications realm, rather than solely self-expression. The German radical tech collective Nadir has pled with fellow activists to abandon the 'Trojan horse' of Facebook, 'the most subtle, cheapest and best surveillance technology available' and a true 'political enemy'. 'The chatter on Facebook reproduces political structures for the authorities and for companies', Nadir wrote. 'Activist Facebook users feed the machine and thereby reveal our structures—without any need, without any court orders, without any pressure. [. . .] They expose structures and individuals who themselves have little or nothing to do with Facebook. We see Facebook users as a real danger for our struggles.' It is a plea worth listening to.

NOTES

1. New social movements have symbolic production, identity-processes and cultural and lifestyle claims at their core (Melucci 1989).

2. For an extensive and detailed explanation of the main patterns within the current social media regimes, please refer to Milan 2015b.

3. However, during the same protest, two people were allegedly arrested for using Twitter to relay information about police planned actions; their houses were raided (Citizen Media Law Project 2011).

REFERENCES

Andrejevic, Mark. 2005. "The Work of Watching One Another: Lateral Surveillance, Risk, and Governance." *Surveillance & Society* 2 (4): 479–97.
———. 2007. "Surveillance in the Digital Enclosure." *The Communication Review* 10: 295–317.
Bankston, Kevin S., and Ashkan Soltani. 2014. "Tiny Constables and the Cost of Surveillance: Making Cents Out of United States v. Jones" 123 (January). http://www.yalelawjournal.org/forum/tiny-constables-and-the-cost-of-surveillance-making-cents-out-of-united-states-v-jones.
BBC. 2015. *Now, Thousands Are Expressing Their Feelings on Today's Events in France with Pictures Like This #JeSuisCharlie.* https://twitter.com/BBCtrending/status/552819936343883776.
Beer, David. 2009. "Power through the Algorithm? Participatory Web Cultures and the Technological Unconsciousness." *New Media & Society* 11 (6): 985–1002.

Bennett, Lance W. 2003. "Communicating Global Activism." *Information, Communication & Society* 6 (2): 143–68.

Bennett, Lance W., and Alexandra Segerberg. 2012. "The Logic of Connective Action: Digital Media and the Personalization of Contentious Politics." *Information, Communication & Society* 15 (5): 739–68.

———. 2013. *The Logic of Connective Action: Digital Media and the Personalization of Contentious Politics*. Cambridge: Cambridge University Press.

Blumer, Herbert G. 1939. "Collective Behavior." In *An Outline of the Principles of Sociology*, edited by R. E. Park, 221–80. New York: Barnes & Noble.

Braman, Sandra. 2009. *Change of State: Information, Policy, and Power*. Cambridge, MA: MIT Press.

Castells, Manuel. 1998. *The Information Age: Economy, Society and Culture*. Cambridge, MA: Blackwell.

———. 2012. *Networks of Outrage and Hope: Social Movements in the Internet Age*. Cambridge: Polity Press.

Citizen Media Law Project. 2011. *United States v. Madison*. http://www.citmedialaw.org/threats/united-states-v-madison.

Clemens, Elizabeth S., and Debra C. Minkoff. 2004. "Beyond the Iron Law: Rethinking the Place of Organizations in Social Movements Research." In *The Blackwell Companion to Social Movements*, edited by David A. Snow, Sarah A. Soule and Hanspeter Kriesi, 155–70. Oxford: Blackwell.

Collins, Randall. 2004. *Interaction Ritual Chains*. Princeton, NJ: Princeton University Press.

Cukier, Kenneth, and Viktor Mayer-Schoenberger. 2013. "The Rise of Big Data: How It's Changing the Way We Think about the World." *Foreign Affairs* 92 (3): 28–40.

Dean, Jodi, Jon W. Anderson and Geert Lovink, eds. 2006. *Reformatting Politics: Information Technology and Global Civil Society*. New York: Routledge.

Della Porta, Donatella, and Mario Diani. 2006. *Social Movements: An Introduction*. Malden, MA and Oxford: Blackwell.

Della Porta, Donatella, and Alice Mattoni. 2015. "Social Networking Sites in Pro-Democracy and Anti-Austerity Protests. Some Thoughts from a Social Movement Perspective." In *Social Media, Politics and the State: Protests, Revolutions, Riots, Crime and Policing in the Age of Facebook, Twitter and YouTube*, edited by Daniel Trottier and Christian Fuchs, 39–62. New York: Routledge.

Della Porta, Donatella, Abby Peterson, and Herbert Reiter, eds. 2006. *The Policing of Transnational Protest*. Farnham, UK: Ashgate.

Della Porta, Donatella, and Herbert Reiter. 1998. *Policing Protest: The Control of Mass Demonstrations in Western Democracies*. Minneapolis: University of Minneapolis Press.

Downing, John D. H., ed. 2011. *Encyclopedia of Social Movement Media*. Thousand Oaks, CA: Sage.

Earl, Jennifer, Heather McKee Hurwitzb, Analicia Meija Mesinasc, Margaret Toland and Ashely Arlottie. 2013. "This Protest Will Be Tweeted. Twitter and Protest Policing during the Pittsburgh G20." *Information, Communication & Society* 16 (4): 459–78.

Farman, Jason. 2012. *Mobile Interface Theory: Embodied Space and Locative Media*. London and New York: Routledge.

Fuchs, Christian, and Marisol Sandoval, eds. 2014. *Critique, Social Media and the Information Society*. London and New York: Routledge.

Gamson, William A. 1992. *Talking Politics*. Cambridge, MA: Cambridge University Press.

Gerbaudo, Paolo. 2012. *Tweets and the Streets: Social Media and Contemporary Activism*. London: Pluto Press.

Goffman, Erving. 1959. *The Presentation of Self in Everyday Life*. New York: Anchor Books.

Gómez García, Rodrigo, and Emiliano Treré. 2014. "The #YoSoy132 Movement and the Struggle for Media Democratization in Mexico." *Convergence: The International Journal of Research into New Media Technologies* 20 (4): 496–510.

Goodwin, J., J. M. Jasper and F. Polletta, eds. 2001. *Passionate Politics: Emotions and Social Movements*. Chicago: University of Chicago Press.

Habermas, Jürgen. 1984. *Theory of Communicative Action, Volume One: Reason and the Rationalization of Society.* Boston: Beacon Press.

Haggerty, Kevin D., and Richard V. Ericson. 2000. "The Surveillance Assemblage." *British Journal of Sociology* 51 (4): 605–22.

Hunt, Scott A., and Robert D. Benford. 2004. "Collective Identity, Solidarity, and Commitment." In *The Blackwell Companion to Social Movements*, edited by David A. Snow, Sarah A. Soule and Hanspeter Kriesi, 443–547. Oxford: Blackwell.

Jasper, James. 1997. *The Art of Moral Protest: Culture, Biography, and Creativity in Social Movements.* Chicago: Chicago University Press.

Juris, Jeffrey S. 2012. "Reflections on #Occupy Everywhere: Social Media, Public Space, and Emerging Logics of Aggregation." *American Ethnologist* 39 (2): 259–79.

Kemp, Simon. 2014. "Global Social Media Users Pass 2 Billion." *We Are Social.* August 8. http://wearesocial.net/blog/2014/08/global-social media-users-pass-2-billion/.

———. 2015. "Digital, Social & Mobile Worldwide in 2015." http://wearesocial.net/blog/2015/01/digital-social-mobile-worldwide-2015/.

Koopmans, R. 1992. *Democracy from Below: New Social Movements and the Political System in West Germany.* Boulder, CO: Westview.

Langlois, Ganaele. 2011. "Meaning, Semiotechnologies and Participatory Media." *Culture Machine* 12.

Leistert, Oliver. 2013. *From Protest to Surveillance—The Political Rationality of Mobile Media. Modalities of Neoliberalism.* Frankfurt am Main: Peter Lang.

Libert, Timothy. 2015. "The Logic of Connective Surveillance: Distributed Social Movements and the Surveillance State." Unpublished manuscript. Annenberg School for Communication, University of Pennsylvania.

MacKinnon, Rebecca. 2012. *Consent of the Networked: The Worldwide Struggle for Internet Freedom.* New York: Basic Books.

Mann, Steve, Jason Nolan and Barry Wellman. 2003. "Sousveillance: Inventing and Using Wearable Computing Devices for Data Collection in Surveillance Environments." *Surveillance & Society* 1 (3): 331–55.

McCarthy, J. D., and M. N. Zald. 1977. "Resource Mobilization and Social Movements: A Partial Theory." *American Journal of Sociology* 82: 1212–41.

McDonald, Kevin. 2002. "From Solidarity to Fluidarity: Social Movements Beyond 'Collective Identity'—The Case of Globalization Conflicts." *Social Movement Studies* 1: 109–28.

———. 2004. "One as Another: From Social Movement to Experience Movement." *Current Sociology* 52 (4): 575–93.

———. 2006. *Global Movements: Action and Culture.* Maldena, MA and Oxford: Blackwell.

McKelvey, Fenwick Robert. 2014. "Algorithmic Media Need Algorithmic Methods: Why Publics Matter." *Canadian Journal of Communication* 39 (4): 597–613.

Melucci, Alberto. 1989. *Nomads of the Present. Social Movements and Individual Needs in Contemporary Society.* London: Hutchinson Radius.

———. 1996. *Challenging Codes: Collective Action in the Information Age.* Cambridge: Cambridge University Press.

Milan, Stefania. 2013a. "WikiLeaks, Anonymous, and the Exercise of Individuality: Protesting in the Cloud." In *Beyond WikiLeaks: Implications for the Future of Communications, Journalism and Society*, edited by Benedetta Brevini, Arne Hintz and Patrick McCurdy, 191–208. Basingstoke, UK: Palgrave Macmillan.

———. 2013b. *Social Movements and Their Technologies: Wiring Social Change.* Basingstoke, UK: Palgrave Macmillan.

———. 2015a. "From Social Movements to Cloud Protesting: The Evolution of Identity." *Information, Communication & Society* 18(8): 887–900.

———. 2015b. "When Algorithms Shape Collective Action: Social Media and the Dynamics of Cloud Protesting." *Social Media and Society.*

Mosco, Vincent. 2014. *To the Cloud: Big Data in a Turbulent World.* New York: Paradigm Publishers.

Park, Robert E., and Ernest W. Burgess. 1921. *Introduction to the Science of Sociology.* Chicago: University of Chicago Press.

Rainie, Lee, and Barry Wellman. 2014. *Networked: The New Social Operating System*. Cambridge, MA: MIT Press.

Smelser, Neil J. 1962. *Theory of Collective Behavior*. Glencoe, IL: Free Press.

Snow, David A. 2001. "Collective Identity and Expressive Forms." In *International Encyclopedia of the Social and Behavioral Sciences*, edited by Neil J. Smelser and Paul B. Baltes, 2212–19. London: Elsevier.

———. 2004. "Framing Process, Ideology, and Discursive Fields." In *The Blackwell Companion to Social Movements*, edited by David A. Snow, Sarah A. Soule and Hanspeter Kriesi, 380–412. Oxford: Blackwell.

Sukey. 2011. "Open Invitation to Police Chiefs: Prove It." February 9. https://docs.google.com/document/pub?id=1ShIYL9ridlokTXAlmq5FCx3nLhZvJsJXAzirCIkfiyw.

The Economist. 2011. "Don't Shoot. Police May Not Like Being Filmed, but They Had Better Get Used to It," December 10. http://www.economist.com/node/21541467.

Tilly, Charles. 2009. *Social Movements, 1768–2008*. 2nd ed. New York: Paradigm Publishers.

Twitter, Inc. 2015. "Company. Our Mission." https://about.twitter.com/company.

Van Dijck, José, and Thomas Poell. 2013. "Understanding Social Media Logic." *Media and Communication* 1 (1): 2–14.

Vigo, Julian. 2015. "#JeNeSuisPasCharlie: Why I Can't Support the Original Hashtag." *Huffington Post*. January 9. http://www.huffingtonpost.ca/julian-vigo/jesuischarlie-racism_b_6435038.html.

Vrousalis, Nicholas, Robin Celikates, Joan Hartle and Enzo Rossi. 2015. "Why We Occupy: Dutch Universities at the Crossroads." *openDemocracy*. March 2. https://www.opendemocracy.net/can-europe-make-it/nicholas-vrousalis-robin-celikates-johan-hartle-enzo-rossi/why-we-occupy-dutch-un.

Zittrain, Jonathan L. 2008. *The Future of the Internet—And How to Stop It*. New Haven, CT: Yale University Press.

II

Temporal Alienation
and Redefining Spaces

Chapter Four

Social Media, Immediacy and the Time for Democracy

Critical Reflections on Social Media as 'Temporalizing Practices'

Veronica Barassi

On 10 September 2014, different tech firms including Netflix, FourSquare, KickStarter, Mozilla, Reddit and Vimeo installed a widget which slowed down their sites as a sign of protest (Rushe 2014). The 'slow down' day was meant to demonstrate what the internet would look like if the Federal Communications Commission (FCC) allowed internet service providers to offer fast lanes to higher paying customers. All the tech firms which joined the 'slow down day' wanted to highlight the fact that creating fast lanes of information flows would overturn 'net neutrality' rules and break the principle that all traffic is treated equally online (Nunziato 2009; Marsden 2010).

These growing concerns about the fairness of the 'speed' of our internet communications, and their repercussion on social equality and justice, mark the very beginning of a critical reconsideration of the relationship between internet technologies and social time.

The relationship between media technologies and the social construction of time has long been a topic of academic debate within communication studies and beyond, especially if we consider debates around the role of media in the creation of a feeling of simultaneity (Anderson 1991; Scannell 1996; Mattelart 1996) or if we look at discussions on technological developments and social acceleration (Tomlinson 2007; Hassan 2007, 2009; Rosa 2013; Rosa and Scheuerman 2009). In this chapter, I want to focus on the relationship between media technologies and social time by looking at the temporality of social media and by considering its impact on social protest.

As Keightley (2013) has rightly argued, mediated time is not character-ized by a singular speed but it's defined by the juncture of different temporal modes and rhythms (Keightley 2013, 67), and this is particularly true if we consider the temporality of social media. As different scholars have shown, there are many different and interconnected ways in which we can start to understand the mediation of time on social media. We can look at the con-struction of new understandings of copresence and temporal consciousness (Leong et al. 2009; Petranker 2007); we can investigate the relationship between the temporality of internet networks and capitalism (Hassan 2007, 2009; Lovink 2007; Fuchs 2013) or we can reflect on the relationship be-tween social media use, time and collective memory (Kaun and Stiernstedt 2014).

Although I recognize the fact that there are multiple ways in which we can understand the temporal context of social media, in this chapter I focus on the notion of 'immediacy'. In contrast to Keightley (2013), who believes that the concept of immediacy can only lead to techno-deterministic under-standings of mediated time, I propose that we need to understand 'immedia-cy' by looking at the relationship between hegemonic constructions of social time on the one hand, and everyday social media practices on the other.

The argument is structured as follows. In the first part of the chapter, I argue that there are three different—albeit interconnected—ways in which we can understand the temporality of 'immediacy'. The first is by focusing on its *political economic* dimension, namely on the analysis of the complex relationship between internet technologies, changing modes of production and the establishment of a specific 'hegemonic time consciousness' (Thompson 1967; Thrift 1990; Hassan 2007; Leccardi 2007; Fuchs 2013). The sec-ond way in which we can analyse immediacy is by looking at its *cultural dimension*, and exploring the relationship between Western cultural narra-tives of speed/progress and new technologies (Tomlinson 2007; Virilio 1986; Rosa and Scheuerman 2009; Rosa 2013). The third way is by analysing *everyday practice* and by appreciating how temporal contexts are created and reproduced through human practice (Bourdieu 1964; Elias 1993; Munn 1992; Keightley 2012, 2013).

In the second part of the chapter, the argument shifts to an analysis of the way in which immediacy is shaping and defining activists' everyday experi-ence of social media. Drawing on an extensive anthropological and ethno-graphic research amongst three political groups in Europe, I argue that imme-diacy is a double-edged sword for social media protest. Although this tempo-ral context is beneficial for political and democratic processes, by accelerat-ing information sharing, and mobilizing political participation and support in fast and effective ways, it also represents a challenge for processes of politi-cal participation, reflection and elaboration. Appreciating the challenges im-mediacy poses to political activists is of central importance, if we want to develop a more critical understanding of the democratic opportunities and constraints of social media protest.

THE DIFFERENT DIMENSIONS OF SOCIAL MEDIA IMMEDIACY

The Political Economic Dimension of Immediacy

We cannot fully understand the temporal context created by social media technologies, and in particular the temporality of immediacy, without considering broader political economic factors. This implies that we need to take into account the bound relationship between capitalism and the social construction of time, and consider the role media technologies play in the construction of a 'hegemonic time-consciousness'.

The relationship between capitalism and the social construction of time has long been a topic of academic debate. In *Capital*, Marx discusses the notion of 'labour time' as a fundamental aspect of the political economy of capitalism (Marx 1990, 302–14), and he was one of the first to highlight the intrinsic value of time under capitalism. It is because 'time is money' that— as Thompson (1967) argued—between the fourteenth century and the nineteenth century, we have seen a gradual synchronization of human activities in Europe and the establishment of what we understand today as 'clock-time' (Thompson 1967, 70–71). This transformation was largely made possible by the combination of technical developments on the one side and an institutionally driven organization of people's behaviours on the other. In fact, while in the Middle Ages, time was still organized around specific agricultural or social activities, and there were only a few areas of exact time keeping such as the 'church bells' of towns, from the fourteenth century onwards, we have witnessed clocks entering households and organizing the everyday lives of people (Thompson 1967, 82–86). The early history of capitalism, as Thrift (1990) has argued, was therefore defined by a gradual diffusion of a new type of 'time-consciousness', where 'clock time' was established as the *hegemonic* form of time measurement through a process of propaganda aimed at 'civilizing' the working classes. This process was made possible through institutions such as 'the factory' or 'the school', which used incentives, fines and other strategies to transform people's behaviours (Thompson 1967, 90–95).

In the last decades, we have seen a major shift in our forms of 'collective time consciousness', and this shift has been shaped by both an economic transformation in modes of production (i.e., the globalization of markets, and the reliance on new forms of flexible, casual and immaterial labour) and a technological transformation (i.e., the development of internet technologies). As the work of the Autonomous Marxists has shown, the very extension of internet technologies has facilitated the emergence of a new type of capitalist accumulation and exploitation, which is based on new forms of immaterial labour, casual work, and exploitation of 'digital labour' (Lazzarato 1996; Dyer-Witheford 1999; Hardt and Negri 2000, 2001; Terranova 2004). This transformation needs to be understood largely in terms of our changing relationship to time, where the temporality of life has now become governed by work (Gill and Pratt 2008, 27; Agger 2004; Rosa 2013). Today, working routines are no longer dictated by 'clock-time' like in the factory, but by a self-regulating flexibility and by the deconstruction of the boundary between labour-time and leisure time. This self-regulating flexibility is made possible by the increased pervasiveness of internet technologies in our lives (Hassan 2007; Leccardi 2007; Beck 2005), which are not only changing our perceptions of notions of intimacy, domesticity and production (Gregg 2011), but are also altering our sense of 'temporality' (Adkins 2009).

The understanding that there is a bound relationship between internet technologies, capitalism and our changing time consciousness has been, therefore, a key theme in the social and critical theory of the last decade (Agger 2004; Rosa 2003, 2013; Hassan 2007, 2009; Rosa and Scheuerman 2009). This is because, as Fuchs (2013) has argued, internet technologies are key to the acceleration of capitalist accumulation. Fuchs's contribution is particularly interesting here because he focuses specifically on social media, and argues that the very structure of social media technologies is a vivid expression of the changing time regimes imposed by capitalism today.

Our analyses therefore cannot overlook the fact that the architecture of social media facilitates instantaneous forms of communication, and is based on a type of mediation that valorizes 'real-time' and constant productivity. This type of mediation, as Fuchs (2013) has shown, is largely shaped by broader political economic factors, and by the economic needs of capitalism.

As Hassan (2007) has argued, it is important to appreciate the fact that this form of mediation is directed at producing and reproducing the temporal context of 'immediacy', in other words a shared perception that the internet offers 'real time' connection with events and people (Hassan 2007, 44). This is of course an ideological perception, because nothing really happens in real time, yet immediacy creates the shared impression that we live in a continuous present, a *hyper now*, where past and future are subservient to the logic of the present (Hassan 2009, 103). The temporality of immediacy, which defines the technological architecture of social media, therefore has strengthened people's appreciation of the value of continuous connectivity (Van Dijck 2013; Agger 2007) and triggered the ideological belief that we need to constantly keep up with the pace of information flows.

Therefore, in conclusion to this part of the chapter, one of the first steps that we need to take when understanding the temporality of immediacy is to consider the fact that it operates as an ideological force, which is determined by broader political economic factors. The next step, however, as we shall see here below, is to look at how this ideology has been constructed upon Western cultural narratives of speed and progress.

The Western Narrative of Speed and the Cultural Dimension of Immediacy

In order to shed light on the ideological power of immediacy, we need to consider how this temporal context is constructed and largely legitimized by Western cultural thought. According to Tomlinson (2007), in fact, the notion of immediacy carries two different yet interconnected cultural understandings. On the one hand, it serves to indicate the compression of space and a sense of 'proximity' (from the Latin, immediate). On the other hand, it serves to specify the compression of time and the notion of 'instantaneity'. Drawing on the work of Bauman (2005), Tomlinson, therefore, concludes that 'immediacy' is built on a notion of instantaneous contact and immediate fulfilment (Tomlinson 2007, 91), and he argues that this is a cultural value that finds its roots in twentieth-century thought.

Departing from Marinetti and the futurist avant-garde, Tomlinson (2007) explores the way in which technological narratives in the West are largely shaped around the cultural understanding that technologies act as accelerators, and that there is a causal relationship between technological developments, speed and progress. Rosa (2009, 2013) traces the origins of such cultural narratives to the very early stages of modernity. He argued that the very promise of modernity needed to be found in the eighteenth-century belief that scientific and technological progress would enhance human freedom, and he contended that this constituted the very basis for modern acceleration.

We cannot understand these Western cultural narratives of speed and technological development without considering their political dimension. This latter aspect emerges very well in the work of Virilio (1986, 1995, 2000). In fact, according to Virilio (1986, 46), Western cultural narratives of speed cannot be detached from the understanding that technical superiority can be translated into supremacy over other people. This is particularly evident if we deconstruct the discourses of the futurist avant-garde during and just after the First World War, which coincided with the birth of Fascist thought in Italy. Virilio (1986), therefore, argued that cultural narratives of speed are tightly connected to politics.

In his later work, Virilio (1995, 2000) expanded his analysis of speed and politics to an investigation of the relationship between information technologies and social acceleration. He argued that globalization had made possible a new 'instantaneity' of time, and that this coupled with the extension of new information technologies has created a 'dictatorship of speed' (Virilio 1995, para 7). According to Virilio (2000, 127), new technologies have created a temporality defined by the 'incessant telepresence of events', and he contends that this temporality is based on the 'relief of instantaneity', which is winning on the depth of historical successivity.

Different scholars in the last decade have been profoundly inspired by Virilio's work (Hassan 2007, 2009; Tomlinson 2007; Leccardi 2007; Rosa 2009, 2013). What emerges well from these works is the understanding that cultural narratives of speed and progress define people's perception of technologies, and as Tomlinson (2007) has argued, this includes our very Western perception of the internet and of the importance of 'instantaneous communication'. He thus concluded that 'Immediacy stands as a cultural principle in relation to the technological—and particularly the communicational—bases of our particular modernity' (Tomlinson 2007, 74).

Thus, as argued here, we cannot really understand the ideological force of immediacy, without considering the way in which immediacy is grounded on Western cultural narratives of speed, progress and technological proficiency. Although it is important that we acknowledge the relationship between immediacy, capitalism and Western cultural narratives of speed and progress, we need to be aware of the fact that as Keightley (2012, 2013) has argued, we cannot emphasize speed and acceleration without a careful consideration of people's everyday practices. The next part of the chapter focuses on the notion of 'temporalizing practice', and explores the lived dimension of social media immediacy.

Immediacy and Social Media as Temporalizing Practices

In order to understand social media immediacy, as mentioned above, we need to consider the way in which this temporality is reproduced and experienced through everyday social media practices. Within the emerging literature on internet time, very little attention has been paid to human practices and experience. As Keightley (2012, 2013) has argued, in order to understand the relationship between media technologies and the social construction of time we need to appreciate the fact that there are multiple and often contradicting ways in which time is experienced and mediated. Influenced by Bergson (1898), Keightley believed that the temporal experience of time is defined by a great deal of uncertainty, and in contrast to scholars like Virilio (1986, 1995, 2000), she argued that it is essential that we move beyond the idea that cultural immediacy is delivered to the subject through the media, and we instead consider the active role of the subject in creating his or her temporal experience of mediated time.

Keightley's (2012) understanding that we need to focus on the complexity of people's temporal experience is of fundamental importance to unravelling the different dimensions of social media and the construction of social time. However, in this chapter I distance myself from her approach, as I do not believe that we need to disregard the notion of immediacy. On the contrary, I believe that the notion of immediacy enables us to appreciate the tension between hegemonic constructions of social time, media technologies and everyday practices.

One particularly interesting element that emerges in the literature on social time is the understanding that the social construction of time is tightly connected to the notion of social practice. This latter understanding emerges particularly well in the sociology and anthropology of time. While anthropologists have focused on the relationship between the construction of time and the coordination of human activities, and have considered how 'other' cultures constructed their time systems (Malinowski 1927; Evans-Pritchard 1939; Leach 1971; Bourdieu 1964; Munn 1992; Gell 1992), sociologists have looked at the construction of hegemonic time consciousness and social practices (Bourdieu 1964; Elias 1993; Thompson 1967; Thrift 1990).

All these works show that the collective understanding of time is made possible through the synchronization (and control) of people's behaviours. Here I want to focus in particular on the work of Elias (1993). Elias strongly criticized those approaches to time that understood the making of social time through the use of binary oppositions such as 'nature'/'culture', 'individual'/'society', 'structure'/'agency'. In contrast to these approaches, and somehow similarly to Thrift (1990), Elias (1993) shows that social time—especially in Europe—operated as a form of social *habitus* that was linked to broader processes of 'civilization' and manners, which developed with the rise of the 'merchant' society and the earlier forms of capitalism. According to Elias (1993), social time is tightly connected to forms of self-regulation, and is perceived subjectively as part of everyday human experience.

The understanding that there is a bound connection between hegemonic constructions of social time and people's practices is essential in the analysis of the temporality of media technologies. This is because it enables us to look at how people and cultures internalize and negotiate with hegemonic understandings of mediated time, through everyday media practice. In theorizing the relationship between social media and time, therefore, here I want to argue that it is *through everyday human practices that we construct specific temporalities*. My understanding is that immediacy is constantly produced and reproduced through everyday social media practices. Consequently we need to understand social media use as 'temporalizing practice' (Munn 1992; Adkins 2011), in other words, as a form of human practice that produces specific temporalities.

Of course, as Keightley (2012, 2013) has argued, the social construction and social experience of time through media technologies is a matter of great complexity and uncertainty. Nevertheless, we need to appreciate that the social experience of mediated time is often influenced by hegemonic temporalities, which shape the architecture of specific technologies and define people's practices. This latter point is particularly evident if we consider how the need to reproduce immediacy—to be constantly connected and keep up with the flow of information—leads people to technological dependency and compulsion (Rosa 2013).

Therefore we need to consider how people internalize the hegemonic temporality of immediacy and negotiate with it. This understanding, as we shall see below, is essential if we want to appreciate how immediacy as hegemonic temporality is reproduced through everyday social media practices and how these temporalizing practices are impacting on political activism.

SOCIAL MEDIA IMMEDIACY
BETWEEN OPPORTUNITY AND CHALLENGE

A Cross-Cultural Ethnographic Research

In the last five years, I carried out a cross-cultural anthropological research amongst three different political collectives in Europe (Barassi 2015). The premise behind the project was to analyse from an anthropological and ethnographic perspective how three very different political groups used internet technologies for political action, and how they negotiated with the technological constraints created by the increased commercialization and corporatization of web platforms.

The three organizations were chosen for their diverse historical and social contexts as well as for their difference in political ideologies, structures and understandings of political action (Labour Movement, Environmental Movement, Autonomous Movement). Methodologically, this research project drew on the insights of the new social movement theory (Touraine 1985; Melucci 1996) and the work of those scholars who looked at the 'newest movements' of the late 1990s (Holloway 2002; Day 2005; Juris 2008). The first organization studied is the *Cuba Solidarity Campaign*, a British international campaigning group that was created in 1978 and is attached to the 'old' left political ideologies of the British Trade Union movement. The second organization is *Ecologistas en Acción*, an environmental activist group that was founded in 1998 during the global justice movements, and is based on a political culture that combines radical left ideals with environmental awareness and direct action. The third organization is called the *Corsari*. It was created in 2008 and is embedded in the Italian autonomous movement, which is based on self-management, anarchist and autonomous discourses.

My research highlighted that activists are not only critically aware of the fact that the main social media (Facebook, Twitter, YouTube) platforms are largely shaped by the digital discourses and practices of corporate power but also that their everyday internet uses are largely defined by processes of negotiation with digital capitalism. These processes of negotiation are giving rise to a series of different 'ethnographic tensions', or in other words, a series of collective experiences which are defined by the tension between activists' progressive and collective cultures on the one side, and the cultural processes reinforced by digital capitalism on the other. Among the different tensions that activists need to come to terms with, the issue of the temporality of internet technologies is certainly a pressing concern for political activists. This is particularly true if we consider social media activism and the reproduction of immediacy.

Political Activism and Social Media as Temporalizing Practices

During fieldwork, I came to the conclusion that activists' social media practices are a form of 'temporalizing practice' which enabled them to reproduce the temporality of immediacy. At crucial protest events, activists posted images, comments and newsfeeds on social media and other online platforms in 'real time'. In the day-to-day life, they replied to social media posts and messages immediately, or at least as fast as they could; most of the time by interrupting face-to-face conversations or activities in order to focus on social media communication. Immediacy was thus reproduced through their online practices while they lived their everyday lives, as they engaged in political demonstrations and amidst tear-gases and clashes.

The temporality of immediacy was of fundamental importance to activists. This is because immediacy implied that images and information spread at an incredible pace, creating the ground for the establishment of networks of solidarity and affinity and for the creation of mass movements. This understanding emerged particularly well within the context of *Ecologistas en Acción* during the 2011 movements in Spain (Gerbaudo 2012; Castells 2012).

In the summer of 2011, I was sitting in a coffee shop near the metro station of Bilbao in Madrid chatting to Javier, the web developer of *Ecologistas en Acción*. During our chat, Javier reflected on the role of social media platforms in the creation and organization of political action. He argued that, during the 15M movements, social media technologies acted as 'accelerators' and made the organization of the protest much more effective, because activists were able to rapidly establish networks of solidarity and action. A few days later, I was talking to Mariola, a freelance journalist and activist. Like Javier had done, during her interview Mariola talked about the 'speed' and 'efficiency of connection' of the 15M movement and she argued that such efficiency could not have been possible ten years ago.

Activists' understanding of the importance of instantaneous communication shares many lines of similarity with the work of digital activism scholars like Castells (2012) and Gerbaudo (2012), who have argued that social media enable processes of 'emotional contagion' and the rapid organization of collective action. However, my research revealed that, within the everyday contexts of political activism, immediacy can be particularly problematic as it challenges political and democratic processes in a substantial number of ways. Here below I will be focusing on three problems: the problem of *visibility*; the problem of *political elaboration*; the problem of *weak ties*.

SOCIAL MEDIA PROTEST AND THE PROBLEM OF IMMEDIACY

Instantaneous Communication and the Issue of Visibility

The temporality of immediacy presupposes that mediation occurs in 'real-time', and thus on social media, 'unproductive communicators' are literally buried under the sheer abundance of individual messages. To be visible, activists have to adapt to the pace of information and constantly produce content. During my research within the three political collectives, activists expressed a profound sense of anguish because many felt that they simply could not respond to the pace of technology. Within the three political collectives, I collected a variety of testimonies on the personal difficulties encountered in the reproduction of immediacy. Activists recognized that social media were central to their work, yet they also expressed a profound anxiety when talking about instantaneous communication because they believed that they were simply not doing it the 'right way'.

As argued elsewhere (Barassi 2009), the problem of immediacy and instantaneous communication on social media is that it produces 'information overload', or as David[1]—from *Ecologistas en Acción*—once told me, it produces a type of 'social noise' that has serious social and political implications for the flow of information. In fact, as he explained:

> **D**: Everybody says that there is no censorship on the internet, or at least only in part. But that is not true. Online censorship is applied through the excess of banal content that distracts people from serious or collective issues.

David's critique is important, as it shows that the immediacy of information flows leads to information overload and this impacts upon the visibility and reach of collective messages. To achieve visibility and reach, activists must ensure that they become productive communicators and that they keep up with the pace of information flows. In a society where, as Rosa (2013) has argued, people are always short of time, it is difficult for activists to ensure that they are always productive communicators on social media, and this leads to a great deal of anxiety which affects their everyday practices.

While the anguish for managing immediacy can be found in many different social contexts (e.g., Gregg 2011), this anguish is particularly problematic in the context of political activism. This is because not only do activists struggle with the fact that they have to keep up with the everyday reproduction of immediacy, but they also feel that social media activism is 'too time consuming' and is distracting them from other forms of political action, such as demonstrations, lobbying and political organization on the ground. Immediacy therefore is impacting on the organization of activists' strategies and political priorities, and this is creating a great deal of tension in the everyday life of social groups.

Immediacy and the Impossibility of Political Reflection and Elaboration

The second problem that activists faced is a problem of *political elaboration.* Information on social media needs to be quick, short and immediate. It also has to be catchy. This means that activists do not have the space and time to articulate their political reflections. During my research, across the different organizations I was constantly asked to understand the fact that social media were not a space for political discussion and elaboration, because the communication was too fast, too quick and too short.

Within the *Corsari,* many different activists told me that they did not believe that social media could be considered a space for political discussion and elaboration, because activists do not have the time on these platforms to construct alternative ideologies. Many other activists who were involved with the other two organizations shared a similar understanding. One day, for instance, as I was interviewing Max[2] of *Ecologistas en Acción,* he argued that on social media, activists did not have the space or time to communicate their message, and especially to express a more thorough explanation of their reflections and propositions, and added:

> **M:** If we look at the nuclear energy issues, it is not about whether we should have nuclear energy or not, it's much more. It is about how the production of nuclear energy relates to the diminishing of carbon fossils and a life based on consumption. Yet it is also about explaining the importance of our degrowth model and to contextualize it for people, without having people think that we want to return to the caves. We also need to propose our alternatives. The problem is that these complex analyses need to be developed properly; we need time and space to do that.

The temporality of immediacy, therefore, is perceived by activists as problematic because it challenges processes of political elaboration. However, processes of political reflection and the articulation of alternative ideologies are essential to the life of political groups. Yet these processes require the creation of thorough texts that explore issues at length. This thoroughness—that cannot be achieved through social media activism—is often achieved through the production of alternative media, and in particular activist magazines or through group discussion.

Immediacy and the Problem of Weak Ties

The temporality of immediacy is problematic for political activism for another reason, which is the problem of the 'temporality' of activist networks. During my research, it quickly became evident that the reproduction of immediacy through social media enabled the coming together of different networked singularities and political realities in fast and effective ways. Yet the strengthening of these activist networks was only conceivable through the process of assembly and face-to-face political elaboration and confrontation.

This latter point emerged very vividly amongst the activists of the *Corsari*, who were involved in a variety of different struggles against Berlusconi's government in Italy and amongst the activists of *Ecologistas en Acción* who were involved with the 15M Movement. In both instances, activists argued that one problem of the networks that they build on social media was represented by the fact that strategic alliances can be also problematic, in the sense that they are often based on a common reaction/emotion and not on a shared political project and neither on a shared understanding of social conflict.

It is for this reason that we need to be aware of the fact that those activist networks that are born on social media more often than not are 'weak ties' (Granovetter 1973), which do not translate into long-term political projects. The possibility for translation into stronger ties and concrete political projects comes from the action on the ground, from face-to-face interaction, discussion, deliberation and confrontation. This latter point was highlighted well by Patricia[3] from *Ecologistas en Acción*, when she said:

> **P**: One thing that really surprised me about the 15M was that all the tweeting, all the social media messages and internet campaigns effectively had a unique effect: they made people come together in a single square, sit on the floor and start to talk [. . .] So technologies have made people come together but what made the movement so powerful was the physical space, the process of discussion, and reflection and the availability of the people to sit down and discuss without the pressure of time.

Although the possibility for translation into proper political projects comes from the interaction on the ground, what I realized during fieldwork was that once the momentum of the protest event passed, activist networks often dissipated. In July 2011, when I returned to Madrid to continue my fieldwork, for instance, the tents of the 15M movement were still up in Puerta del Sol, yet during the daily assembly not many people participated, and the few tents remaining had to struggle with a variety of different day-to-day issues as well as the lack of resources and participation. This was a very different scenario from the mass mobilization, which took place only two months earlier. Understanding the temporality of networks, therefore, can shed some light on some of the challenges of social media protest.

CONCLUSION

The aim of this chapter was to critically address the pressing, yet neglected question of the temporality of social media and to investigate its (often) negative effects on political practice and social protest. I have argued that social media technologies have created a temporal context, which—as different scholars have shown—cannot be understood without considering broader political economic factors, such as the changing modes of capitalist accumulation or without appreciating how social media immediacy is embedded in broader cultural narratives of technological progress and speed. Yet, as this chapter has argued, in the understanding of immediacy we also have much to gain if we focus on the anthropology and sociology of time, and appreciate the fact that it is through our everyday practices that we reproduce temporal contexts.

This understanding, I have argued, is particularly important in the study of social media protest. This is because it enables us to highlight the fact that, within the everyday realities of social movements, social media use needs to be understood as a 'temporalizing practice' that enables activists to reproduce the logic of immediacy. While immediacy can be of fundamental importance for the organization of social protest, it also has profoundly problematic effects on political action. This is not only because social media communication tends to simplify complex reflections and discourses, but also because the pace of information exchange reduces the political visibility of activists and creates a type of 'political participation' which relies on weak affinities.

In conclusion, the issue concerning the temporality of social media highlights some of the complexities involved in the relationship between these technologies and democratic processes. As Riechmann (2004) has argued, the time necessary for democratic process is slow. This is because democracy requires time, much time: the time necessary for confrontation, elaboration and collective decision making. The very structure of social media reinforces a type of mediation that is based on the immediacy of instantaneous communication. Yet we need to be aware of the fact that, as Tomlinson (2007, 118) argued, 'instantaneity' leads to immediate fulfilment but also, immediate exhaustion. This implies that social media leave little possibility for political discussion and elaboration, or for the articulation of alternatives.

Laux (2011) argued that it is important to understand the fact that in contemporary societies, the time of politics is often challenged by the time of other social institutions which are based on speed and social acceleration (e.g., science and the media). In the understanding of the relationship between social media and social protest we need to take into consideration this tension. Activists in the field were usually critically aware of it, and were looking for different ways in which they could negotiate with the logic of immediacy. In some instances, this process of negotiation leads to the establishment of an ethos of real-time resistance (Adams 2013) on the ground, where immediacy is scrutinized and critically understood. In other instances, this process of negotiation leads to active resistance against the time of fast capitalism and to the articulation of different alternatives (Leccardi 2007; Barassi 2015). Acknowledging these processes of negotiation is of central importance, as it enables us to shed light on the nuances and complexities of social media protest, and realize that it is in the way in which people imagine and negotiate with social and technological structures that social change can happen.

NOTES

1. Fictional name to protect the activist's choice of anonymity.
2. Fictional name to protect the activist's choice of anonymity.
3. Fictional name to protect the activist's choice of anonymity.

REFERENCES

Adams, Jason M. 2013. *Occupy Time: Technoculture, Immediacy, and Resistance After Occupy Wall Street*. New York: Palgrave Pivot US.

Adkins, Lisa. 2009. "Sociological Futures: From Clock Time to Event Time." *Online Sociological Research* 14 (4) (8). https://www.academia.edu/653438/Sociological_Futures_From_Clock_Time_to_Event_Time.

———. 2011. "Practice as Temporalisation: Bourdieu and the Economic Crisis." In *The Legacy of Pierre Bourdieu: Critical Essays*, edited by Simon Susen and Bryan S. Turner, 1st edition, 347–65. London and New York: Anthem Press.

Agger, Ben. 1989. *Fast Capitalism: A Critical Theory of Significance*. Chicago: University of Illinois Press.

———. 2004. *Speeding Up Fast Capitalism: Cultures, Jobs, Families, Schools, Bodies*. St. Paul, MN: Paradigm.

———. 2007. "Time Robbers, Time Rebels: Limits to Fast Capital." In *24/7: Time and Temporality in the Network Society*, edited by Robert Hassan and Ronald Purser, 1st edition, 195–219. Stanford, CA: Stanford Business Books.

Anderson, Benedict. 1991. *Imagined Communities: Reflections on the Origin and Spread of Nationalism*. 2nd revised edition. London and New York: Verso Books.

Bauman, Zygmunt. 2005. *Liquid Life*. Hoboken, NJ: Wiley.

Barassi, Veronica. 2009. "Mediated Resistance: Alternative Media Imagination and Political Action in Britain." PhD, Goldsmiths College (University of London). http://ethos.bl.uk/OrderDetails.do?uin=uk.bl.ethos.514228.

———. 2015. *Activism on the Web: Everyday Struggles Against Digital Capitalism*. New York: Routledge.

Beck, Andrew. 2005. *Cultural Work: Understanding the Cultural Industries*. New York: Routledge.

Bergson, Henri. 1898. *Essai sur les données immédiates de la conscience*. F. Alcan. http://archive.org/details/essaisurlesdonn00berggoog.

Bourdieu, Pierre. 1964. "The Attitude of the Algerian Peasant toward Time." In *Mediterranean Countrymen: Essays in the Social Anthropology of the Mediterranean*, edited by Julian Alfred Pitt-Rivers, 55–72. Paris and The Hague: Mouton.

Castells, Manuel. 2000. "Materials for an Exploratory Theory of the Network Society." *The British Journal of Sociology* 51 (1): 5–24. doi:10.1111/j.1468-4446.2000.00005.x.

———. 2009. *Communication Power*. Oxford: Oxford University Press.

———. 2012. *Networks of Outrage and Hope: Social Movements in the Internet Age*. 1st edition. Cambridge, UK and Malden, MA: Polity Press.

Day, Richard J. F. 2005. *Gramsci Is Dead: Anarchist Currents in the Newest Social Movements*. London and Ann Arbor, MI: Pluto Press.

Dyer-Witheford, Nick. 1999. *Cyber-Marx: Cycles and Circuits of Struggle in High-Technology Capitalism*. Chicago: University of Illinois Press.

Elias, Norbert. 1993. *Time: An Essay*. Translated by Edmund Jephcott. Reprint edition. Oxford: Blackwell.

Evans-Pritchard, E. E. 1939. "Nuer Time-Reckoning." *Africa* 12 (2): 189–216. doi:10.2307/1155085.

Fuchs, Christian. 2013. "Digital Prosumption Labour on Social Media in the Context of the Capitalist Regime of Time." *Time & Society*. October. 0961463X13502117. doi:10.1177/0961463X13502117.

Gell, Alfred. 1992. *The Anthropology of Time: Cultural Constructions of Temporal Maps and Images*. Oxford: Berg.

Gerbaudo, Paolo. 2012. *Tweets and the Streets: Social Media and Contemporary Activism*. London: Pluto Press.

Gill, Rosalind, and Andy Pratt. 2008. "In the Social Factory? Immaterial Labour, Precariousness and Cultural Work." *Theory, Culture & Society* 25 (7–8): 1–30. doi:10.1177/0263276408097794.

Granovetter, Mark S. 1973. "The Strength of Weak Ties." *American Journal of Sociology* 78 (6): 1360–80.

Gregg, Melissa. 2011. *Work's Intimacy*. 1st edition. Cambridge, UK and Malden, MA: Polity Press.

Hardt, Michael, and Antonio Negri. 2000. *Multitude: War and Democracy in the Age of Empire*. New York: Penguin.

———. 2001. *Empire*. Cambridge, MA: Harvard University Press.

Hassan, Robert. 2007. "Network Time." In *24/7: Time and Temporality in the Network Society*, edited by Robert Hassan and Roland Purser, 1st edition, 37–62. Stanford, CA: Stanford Business Books.

———. 2009. *Empires of Speed: Time and the Acceleration of Politics and Society*. BRILL.

Holloway, John. 2002. *Change the World without Taking Power: The Meaning of Revolution Today*. London and Sterling, VA: Pluto Press.

Juris, Jeffrey S. 2008. *Networking Futures: The Movements against Corporate Globalization*. Durham, NC: Duke University Press Books.

Kaun, Anne, and Fredrik Stiernstedt. 2014. "Facebook Time: Technological and Institutional Affordances for Media Memories." *New Media & Society* 16 (7): 1154–68. doi:10.1177/1461444814544001.

Keightley, Emily. 2012. "Introduction: Time, Media and Modernity." In *Time, Media and Modernity*, edited by Emily Keightley, 1–25. London: Palgrave Macmillan.

———. 2013. "From Immediacy to Intermediacy: The Mediation of Lived Time." *Time & Society* 22 (1): 55–75. doi:10.1177/0961463X11402045.

Laux, Henning. 2011. "The Time of Politics: Pathological Effects of Social Differentiation." *Time & Society* 20 (2): 224–40. doi:10.1177/0961463X11402439.

Lazzarato, Maurizio. 1996. "Immaterial Labor." In *Radical Thought in Italy: A Potential Politics*, edited by Paolo Virno, 133–51. Minneapolis: University of Minnesota Press.

Leach, Edmund. 1971. "Two Essays Concerning the Symbolic Representation of Time." In *Re-Thinking Anthropology*, 124–36. London: Athlone Press, University of London.

Leccardi, Carmen. 2007. "New Temporal Perspectives in the 'High-Speed Society.'" In *24/7: Time and Temporality in the Network Society*, edited by Robert Hassan and Ronald Purser, 1st edition, 25–37. Stanford, CA: Stanford Business Books.

Leong, Susan, Teodor Mitew, Marta Celletti, and Erika Pearson. 2009. "The Question Concerning (Internet) Time." *New Media & Society*, November. doi:10.1177/1461444809349159.

Lovink, Geert. 2007. "Indifference of the Networked Presence: On Time Management of the Self." In *24/7: Time and Temporality in the Network Society*, edited by Robert Hassan and Ronald Purser, 1st edition, 161–73. Stanford, CA: Stanford Business Books.

Malinowski, Bronislaw. 1927. "Lunar and Seasonal Calendar in the Trobriands." *The Journal of the Royal Anthropological Institute of Great Britain and Ireland* 57 (January): 203. doi:10.2307/2843682.

Marsden, Christopher T. 2010. *Net Neutrality: Towards a Co-Regulatory Solution*. London: A&C Black.

Marx, Karl. 1990. *Capital: Critique of Political Economy, v. 1*. Edited by Ernest Mandel. Translated by Ben Fowkes. New Ed edition. London and New York: Penguin Classics.

Mattelart, Armand. 1996. *The Invention of Communication*. Minneapolis: University of Minnesota Press.

Melucci, Alberto. 1996. *Challenging Codes: Collective Action in the Information Age*. Cambridge and New York: Cambridge University Press.

Munn, Nancy D. 1992. "The Cultural Anthropology of Time: A Critical Essay." *Annual Review of Anthropology* 21 (1): 93–123. doi:10.1146/annurev.an.21.100192.000521.

Nunziato, Dawn C. 2009. *Virtual Freedom: Net Neutrality and Free Speech in the Internet Age*. Stanford, CA: Stanford Law Books.

Petranker, Jack. 2007. "The Presence of Others: Network Experience as an Antidote to the Subjectivity of Time." In *24/7: Time and Temporality in the Network Society*, edited by Robert Hassan and Ronald Purser, 1st edition, 173–95. Stanford, CA: Stanford Business Books.

Riechmann, Jorge. 2004. *Gente que no quiere viajar a Marte: ensayos sobre ecología, ética y autolimitación*. Los Libros de la Catarata.

Rosa, Hartmut. 2003. "Social Acceleration: Ethical and Political Consequences of a Desynchronized High-Speed Society." *Constellations* 10 (3) (March): 3-33.

———. 2013. *Social Acceleration: A New Theory of Modernity*. New York: Columbia University Press.

Rosa, Hartmut, and William E. Scheuerman. 2009. *High-Speed Society: Social Acceleration, Power, and Modernity*. Edited by Hartmut Rosa and William E. Scheuerman. University Park: Penn State University Press.

Rushe, Dominic. 2014. "Large US Tech Firms Plan 'Go Slow' Day in Protest over Net Neutrality Rules." *The Guardian*. http://www.theguardian.com/technology/2014/sep/04/etsy-mozilla-reddit-protest-net-neutrality (accessed 19 January 2015).

Scannell, Paddy. 1996. *Radio, Television and Modern Life*. Oxford, UK and Cambridge, MA: Blackwell Publishers.

Terranova, Tiziana. 2004. *Network Culture: Politics for the Information Age*. London and Ann Arbor, MI: Pluto Press.

Thompson, E. P. 1967. "Time, Work-Discipline, and Industrial Capitalism." *Past & Present*, no. 38 (December): 56–97.

Thrift, Nigel. 1990. "The Making of a Capitalist Time Consciousness." In *The Sociology of Time*, edited by John Hassard. London: Palgrave Macmillan.

Tomlinson, John. 2007. *The Culture of Speed: The Coming of Immediacy*. Los Angeles and London: Sage.

Touraine, Alain. 1985. *Actores sociales y sistemas políticos en América Latina*. PREALC.

Van Dijck, Jose. 2013. *The Culture of Connectivity: A Critical History of Social Media*. Oxford and New York: Oxford University Press.

Virilio, Paul. 1986. *Speed and Politics*. Los Angeles, CA: MIT Press.

———. 1995. "Speed and Information: Cyberspace Alarm!" Edited by Arthur Kroker and Marilouise Kroker. *Ctheory.net*. http://www.ctheory.net/articles.aspx?id=72.

———. 2000. *The Information Bomb*. London: Verso.

Chapter Five

'This Space Belongs to Us!'

Protest Spaces in Times of Accelerating Capitalism

Anne Kaun

> We are here taking up this space because we're saying NO MORE.
> —Speaker at Ferguson solidarity rally in Philadelphia, November 2014

Protest movements are fundamentally about the production and control of space. Whether in a discursive or physical sense, protesters aim to carve out spaces that give room to their political causes. The negotiation and contestation of the production of space has potentially changed in the context of social media that connect activists over vast distances and in real time. In line with that, media scholars, urban geographers and sociologists have attributed changes in the production and perception of space to emerging media technologies that are extending the human body (McLuhan 1964), contributing to deterritorialization (Tomlinson 1999) and space-time compression (Harvey 1990). What are then the strategies of protest movements that are actively challenging the hegemonic logic of the production of space and how are the strategies relating to communication technologies? What are the consequences of changes in the production of protest spaces for activism in terms of temporality? This chapter investigates the changes in the production of space of protest movements in the context of advancing capitalism that is increasingly based on digital communication technologies. In that sense it contributes to the discussion of how contentious politics and the production of space are changing with social media while contextualizing these changes historically by putting current protests into dialogue with previous movements and their media practices.

The questions outlined above are investigated by drawing on an in-depth analysis of Occupy Wall Street and one of its major direct actions, the march on Brooklyn Bridge in October 2011. In order to contextualize the production of space in relation to temporal structures historically, the chapter considers two earlier protest movements that emerged in the United States in the context of the Great Depression in the 1930s and the oil and fiscal crisis in the early 1970s. By way of considering these historical case studies, I aim to complicate the current overemphasis on the role of social media for protest movements. Furthermore, I aim to trace significant changes in organizing and mobilizing protest that are related to media technologies over time specifically when it comes to the production of space.

PROTEST IN SPACE AND TIME

Marches interrupt the daily stream of traffic and the routes of pedestrians (Merrifield 2013), protest camps establish self-organized spatial infrastructures (Feigenbaum, Frenzel and McCurdy 2013), community archives provide a space for the preservation of digital and material representations documenting histories from the margins (Flinn, Stevens and Shepherd 2009), alternative and social media provide a discursive space for radical politics: protest practices are always also practices that are shaping spaces and encounters between people. As Merrifield argues, when people are coming together there is a realization of commonalities 'because bodies and minds take hold in a space that is at once territorial and deterritorial, in a time that isn't clock or calendar time but eternal time' (Merrifield 2013, 34).

Since the 1980s, there has been a strong interest in space and spatial practices in social sciences and humanities. With the growing research interest in different disciplines and fields, the understanding of space was extended and encompasses its physical appearance (Castells 1977), its social character (Bourdieu 1989), discursive formation and mode of production (Lefebvre 1991).

Related to the globalization debate, media technologies came to be understood as annihilating space; for example, shortening distances and connecting remote areas. The fundamental argument is that media technologies are freeing us from the boundaries of space and constitute the end of geography (Mosco 2005). Paul Virilio (1986) suggests that 'space is no longer in geography—it is in electronics'. In that context, politics become less about physical space, but about the time regimes of technologies, which is what he calls a shift from geo- to chrono-politics.

This focus on mobility and space as distance has been critically addressed by Doreen Massey (2005) arguing that space encompasses more than distance and continues to matter. She suggested that proximity is central for human experience, but multiple forms and dimensions are constituting space as a process and social practice. Hence, space is always in the making (Crang and Thrift 2000; Massey 2005). Furthermore, the myth of the end of geography has been debunked by commentators reminding us of the material basis of media technologies that are supposedly substituting space (Jansson 2007). Richard Maxwell and Toby Miller (2013, 90), for example, argue that 'it is as if telecommunications, cell phones, tablets, cameras, computers and so on sprang magically from a green meritocracy of creativity, with by-products of code, not smoke'; however, these media technologies are actively produced and consume large landscapes in the form of server farms and data centres that remain invisible for the majority of their consumers. Hence, I follow André Jansson when he argues that 'the spatial turn must incorporate a material turn as well—a turn towards the conditions and practices (constellations and movements of people and objects) which put communication in (or out of) place, as well as towards the spatial materialities and sensibilities of communication' (Jansson 2007, 186).

The discussion of the end of geography and the annihilation of distance is embedded in a social structure characterized by economic, politico-institutional and ideological configurations (Castells 1977), and while the idea that media technologies help us to overcome the boundaries of space persists, physical public spaces are disappearing as they are turned increasingly into commercial areas and security zones heavily controlled by police forces. Jeremy Nemeth and Justin Hollander (2010), for example, analyse the shrinking of public spaces in New York and discuss the consequences for democratic conduct and society. Paolo Gerbaudo, referring to Mike Davis, argues that 'the public space of the new megastructures and supermalls have supplanted traditional streets and supplanted their spontaneity. Inside malls, office centres, and cultural complexes, public activities are sorted out into strictly functional compartments under the gaze of private police forces' (Gerbaudo 2012, 105).

At the same time, the domination of space by certain actors often intersects with the domination of media technologies and the other way around. In that context, protest movements challenge the hegemonic production and ordering of space. Hence it is pertinent to ask whether radical protest practices challenge the currents of both the dominant logic of spatial production and the role of media technologies for these spatial practices. In this chapter, I aim to engage with these questions and trace changes in the production of space that are related to changes of dominant media technologies since the 1930s. Drawing on Lefebvre's notion of the production of space and three case studies of protest movements of the dispossessed that emerged at critical junctures of capitalism, I follow the change from a space bias to hyper-space bias and mechanical speed to digital immediacy. An ideological move from space-bias to hyper-space bias is based on the assumption that social media 'blur the boundaries not only between perceived and/or conceived spatial categories (public-private, local-global, etc.), but also between the processes (material, symbolic and imaginary) that constitute space itself' (Jansson 2007, 185). The changes in temporality are particularly based on the decrease in circulation time of information with the help of social media towards real time and immediacy in which production and consumption are collapsed. Immediacy is here understood in terms of acceleration of circulation towards direct delivery. Similarly, real time captures access to media content without perceptible delay (Weltevrede, Helmond and Gerlitz 2014). This acceleration, however, often obscures the peculiar process of mediation and mediated meaning production. In that context, media technologies in general and social media in particular have certain properties that allow for particular content production. This is to say that digital immediacy encompasses an acceleration in production, distribution and consumption time, but does not preclude mediation and experiences beyond the immediate (Thompson 1995; Silverstone 2007).

SOCIAL MEDIA AND THE PRODUCTION OF SPACE

Theoretical engagements with the notion of space shifted from questions of the production of objects in space to the production of space itself. Lefebvre could be considered a key figure in this shift of perspective. Lefebvre distinguishes between three forms of producing space: the representation of space (space as conceived), the representational space (space as perceived) and spatial practices (space as lived and experienced). The representation of space is concerned with the physical form of space that is built and used. Representational space considers practices of 'knowing' space, such as maps and mathematics, producing space as a mental construct. Spatial practices, in contrast, are concerned with space as it is produced and changed over time through its specific use at the intersection of the physical appearance of space and its imagined form (Elden 2007).

In his seminal work *The Production of Space*, Lefebvre dwells on a clear link between the production of space and technology as well as knowledge. Technology and knowledge have a particular relevance for the mode of production and every mode of production is linked to its own kind of space (Lefebvre 1991, 31).

> What constitutes the forces of production, according to Marx and Engels? Nature, first of all, plays a part, then labour, hence the organization (or division) of labour, and hence also the instruments of labour, including technology, and, ultimately, knowledge. (Lefebvre 1991, 69)

In Lefebvre's sense technologies are essential to understand any kind of production process, including the production of space. As the current capitalist mode of production is increasingly—but not exclusively—based on communication and information (Fuchs 2010; Castells 2000), technologies such as social media that assist in the production, resources, forms of labour and commodities are of particular importance.

A Historical-Sociological Approach to the Production of Space

This chapter is based on material collected for a larger project entitled *Crisis and Critique* (Kaun forthcoming). The overarching aim of the project is to explore the interconnection between crisis and critique and to ask whether crisis situations can open up new opportunities as well as require new forms of radical critique. This background links to Walter Benjamin and Bertold Brecht's journal project *Krise und Kritik* that they pursued in the 1930s. The journal never actually materialized; however, in several editorial meetings and written exchanges Brecht and Benjamin developed the idea of discussing the interconnections between crisis and critique.

My project traces forms of media participation in different crisis contexts, namely the Great Depression 1929, the crisis of the early 1970s and the Great Recession 2008. These eclipses of crisis moments are understood as nodal points around which avant-garde protest groups formed and participated in public discourse as forms of critique. Empirically, the analysis builds on three case studies that consider the—according to the appearance in main-stream news media and secondary sources—most relevant protest movements that emerged in the context of the three major economic crises: (a) the unemployed workers movement, (b) new urban movements here particularly the rent strike and squatters movement and (c) the Occupy Wall Street (OWS) movement. However, the focus here is on the latter, the OWS movement. The three movements represent very diverse organization structures. While the unemployed workers movement was dominated by the work of political parties such as the Communist Party, a civil society organization called the Metropolitan Council on Housing had major importance for the tenants' movement. The OWS movement in contrast emphasized its leaderless, multivoiced structure. In this context of the movements, structures media technologies established for organization and mobilization have specific temporal and spatial affordances that enable or constrain the movements in reaching their goals.

The chapter draws on a variety of methods ranging from in-depth archival work investigating documents of central organizations that aimed to organize the dispossessed including personal papers' collections of political organizers such as Carl Winter (Chair of the Communist Party of Michigan), Sam Winn (activist and an organizer in District Council 9 of the International Brotherhood of Painters and Allied Trades), Sam Adams Darcy (organizer and leading official in the Communist Party USA) and Jacob Benjamin Salutsky (director of education and cultural activities of the Amalgamated

Clothing Workers of America) and autobiographies of other central figures such as William Z Foster (General Secretary of the Communist Party USA), Sadie van Veen Amter and Israel Amter (founding members of the Communist Party USA) in the 1930s and extensive records of the Metropolitan Council on Housing from the 1970s. The materials for the analysis of the rent strike movement also include project materials of a large-scale study on the tenants' movement led by Ronald Lawson, including interview and observation protocols as well as student essays and master's theses. In order to investigate the Occupy movement, I conducted in-depth interviews with activists being involved in the OWS encampment and more particularly with the work of the media group. Beyond the in-depth interviews in the case of OWS, I also analysed central publications and outlets of the OWS media group, including their websites and the collectively written book *Occupy Wall Street: The Inside Story of an Action That Changed America*, and worked with a hard drive collecting digital materials archived by the OWS archiving working group. These materials were gathered to identify central media practices and their role for the respective movement organization in general to investigate the purpose of the employed practices, and to identify the media technologies that had a prominent place in their media work.

These media technologies were considered in terms of their structuration of time and space of the work of activists and supporters of the movements.

In order to analyse the changes in spatial practices, I am following the tradition of historical sociology of events. Rather than tracing the history of one specific movement, I aim to uncover connections between crisis and critique that find expression in protest movements and their media practices promoting social change. In that sense, I follow what Sewell (2005) has termed an eventful history that considers specific events that transformed or have the potential to transform social structures significantly. Large-scale economic crises and their consequences have this potential for structural changes. The protest movements become in that sense entry points to trace these structural changes. This diachronic comparative approach allows me to disentangle connections between media-related conditions to express critique and large-scale economic crises for social change. Drawing on Sewell's (2005) outline of an eventful temporality, I consider history as being characterized by often contingent events following each other. In this conception events have the potential to accelerate historical developments and transform social relations. In this view, change can only be understood by considering previous events that have led to later occurrences. Sewell is in that context very cautious to point out that an eventful consideration of temporality assumes that events are temporally heterogeneous and not uniform. Hence, structures that emerge from particular events are transformations of previous structures.

The consideration of eventful temporality is helpful here to trace changes in the production of space over time. In the analysis I focus on three major events for each of my case studies to identify the potentially changing role of spatial practices. The first event is the International Unemployment Day that the Communist Party declared and mobilized for on 6 March 1930. This International Unemployment Day culminated in numerous protest marches in many larger US-American cities. The second event is the Housing Crimes Trial organized by the Metropolitan Council on Housing in New York on 6 December 1970. The third event is the OWS March on Brooklyn Bridge on 1 October 2011 which resulted in the arrest of around seven hundred protesters.

The analysis focuses on specific, formative events for the protest movements of interest here while considering them in their broader context. It is not the aim to isolate single events, but to identify turning points in the development of the movements and how spatial practices are played out during those events.

THE PRODUCTION OF SPACE THROUGH EVENTS OF CONTENTION: THE OWS MARCH ON BROOKLYN BRIDGE

The OWS movement emerged in the aftermath of the so-called Great Recession in 2008, criticizing enhanced financial capitalism (Foster and McChesney 2012). In July 2011, AdBusters, the notorious facilitator of anticonsumerism campaigns, launched a call to occupy Wall Street by introducing the hashtag #occupywallstreet on Twitter. After online mobilization, New York–based activists followed the call on 17 September 2011. Since Wall Street was strongly secured by police forces, the occupiers turned to the close-by Zuccotti Park (Bray 2013). The small, privately owned square became the place for camping, campaigning and deliberating for the upcoming weeks until the first eviction in November 2011 (Graeber 2013). Initially there was only a handful of activists. The numbers grew quickly, however, and the encampment developed into a diverse group of occupiers being based on what has been characterized as leaderlessness and nonviolence (Bolton et al. 2013). At the same time, there was a 'division over conventional politics, over reform and revolution' (Gitlin 2012, xv). Although describing themselves as representing a variety of demands, the OWS movement could in general be characterized as a critique of accelerated financial capitalism and the growing inequalities in US society.

The Occupy encampment was initially set up on 17 September 2011. Besides building up an infrastructure that accommodated the everyday needs of the occupiers such as a kitchen tent, a donation tent, a library tent, a medic tent and so on, the activists organized numerous direct actions moving out of the encampment into the streets of New York. One of these events was the March on Brooklyn Bridge on 1 October. Together with a previous incident of three female protesters being maced by the police, the Brooklyn Bridge March marked a turning point for OWS in terms of support and the growing number of people joining the camp and protests organized by OWS.

The march itself remained rather quiet until the activists reached the entrance of Brooklyn Bridge. While some marchers took the pedestrian part, others streamed onto the roadway heading towards Brooklyn, seemingly with the consent of the police. After a few meters however, police officers stopped the marching group on the roadway and blocked the way back. Around seven hundred protesters were entrapped on the Bridge, while their coprotesters live-streamed their arrests with their mobile phones. Live streaming was not only a central feature during protest actions. Early on, the Media Working Group set up a twenty-four-hour live stream from the camp, with programming elements including scheduled interviews with occupiers and passersby, talks, music sessions and so on.

The day after the march, the *New York Times* referred to the unscripted nature of OWS that led to the mass arrests. 'Marchers make on-the-spot alterations in their routes, and Saturday was a prime example: the march across the Brooklyn Bridge seemed as though it would be confined to the pedestrian walkway until a smaller group of protesters decided to march across the roadway, leading to hundreds of arrests' (Baker, Moynihan and Maslin Nir 2011).

The combination of immediate spreading of information and images from the bridge and the police brutality were for Ady—one of my informants—the reason why the support for OWS grew exponentially after the incident.

> The media team or whoever it was got the word out and I have no idea why that protest at that moment, but that story made it. It was after a normal protest, smaller one. And it was different because it was growing; normally protests start big and then get smaller, but this one was growing. And after that it went from huge to mega huge. That was a changing point. Because the cops were doing that and then there was the response. My friends still, they wanted to thank the police, one of my buddies was involved in it. And he was like, we organize shit, but if it wasn't for the cops, it probably wasn't as good as it was. (Ady)

Ady and other activists I have interviewed repeatedly referred to the media savviness of the media and press working group and their central role for the increasing support and growth of the movement as mainstream media first blacked out and later often mitigated the movement as uncoordinated and ineffective. The lacking and biased reporting might have its root in the free-press zones in which journalists were placed by the police as Gillham, Edwards and Noakes (2013) argue. Although through the spatial practices of taking Zuccotti Park and claiming Brooklyn Bridge, the activists also aimed to carve out discursive spaces for the movement. As part of this aim, occupiers were able to reveal police tactics and brutality that were constitutive for the struggle about space. The immediate and real-time reporting from events—such as the Brooklyn Bridge March—allowed for the recruitment of supporters over vast distances.

Considering the two earlier movements of the Unemployed Workers in the 1930s and of the Tenants in the 1970s, it becomes clear that there are crucial changes concerning spatial practices in relation to media practices. In the 1930s, the main media for organizing the unemployed were printed outlets such as leaflets and shop papers. Brochures and pamphlets were mainly reproduced with the help of low-cost printing machines, so-called mimeographs, and included not only information about the protest activities but also about relief programmes, the structure and contact details of unemployed councils as well as block committees. Besides sharing information as resource, the outlets also gathered experiences of unemployment, poverty and precarity contributing to a collective experience rather than leaving the unemployed to suffer alone. The production of bulletins and shop papers was self-organized by workers. Harold Lasswell and Dorothy Blumenstock remark in their study that 'the shop unit was usually responsible for gathering the material, and a special shop-paper committee was usually formed in the unit' (Lasswell and Blumenstock 1939, 60). The protest practices of the unemployed can be understood as spatial practices in Lefebvre's sense in two ways. First, the mobilization evolved around the workers' daily, very close spatial reference points, namely the neighbourhoods. With the help of mechanically reproduced printed outlets, organizers and activists aimed to transform the individuals sharing the physical infrastructure of their houses into a community sharing experiences of unemployment and precariousness. Second, gathered for marches the protesters were often considered as mobs having the potential to disrupt the everyday stream of practices in the city, for example, traffic, production and consumption. Hence, the spatial practice of the protesters claiming the streets of the city was identified as dangerous and was met by the extensive police force. A march of thirty-five thousand unemployed workers in New York City on the International Day of Unemployment on 6 March 1930 ended with two dead demonstrators and several hundred being injured after the police tried to disperse 'the violent mob' as they were described by the *New York Times* the next day (*New York Times* 1930).

While the tenants' movement in the 1970s followed similar, very local organizing principles as the unemployed workers movement, they operated in a very different media ecology; a media ecology that was far more complex, including not only mainstream newspapers and the radio, but also a growing number of television channels. In that context, central organizations such as the Metropolitan Council on Housing orchestrated larger and more creative events such as the housing crimes trial in 1970. They prepared and staged the event together with numerous organizations emphasizing the spectacle and performance aspects of protest in order to attract media coverage and intercept in the perpetual flow of television programming (Williams 1974). At the same time, this and similar events created a platform to exchange shared experiences among activists, organizers and tenants. In order to extend the sense of shared experiences, media coverage by mainstream media was of utmost importance and as part of the preparations of direct actions, the organizers reached out to newspapers, radio and television channels and invited journalists to participate. Often the events were audio recorded and in the case of the housing crimes trial, a student team was working on a documentary. This event was particularly successful not only in attracting between one and two thousand attendees, but also in generating press coverage in bigger and smaller outlets.[1] The major objective of the housing crimes trial was a negotiation of the right to space and to challenge those having the power over urban housing and public spaces. As part of the attempt, the organizers on the one hand approached and frequented the media and forums that are of concern for the power holders, for example, mainstream news media such as the *New York Times*. On the other hand, community media—Jane Benedict ran a monthly radio show with a local radio channel and the *Tenants' Voice* paper—became a locus for internal identification and solidarity among diverse minority groups all being affected by the housing crisis.

FROM SPACE BIAS TO HYPER-SPACE BIAS

In contrasting OWS to two previous important events in the context of crisis, it becomes apparent that the repertoires of spatial practices, contentious action and media practices are integrated with each other. Activists of all three movements are employing rather taken-for-granted, established media technologies to externally and internally communicate their causes. Taking OWS as an example, I argue that the major media technologies employed were well-established infrastructures such as Facebook and Twitter. OWS activists had no major interest to establish alternative channels. There were attempts for OWS social networking platforms—global square and occupii—which however never really took off (Fuchs 2014). Instead, activists worked predominantly with *banal* media technology for organizational and mobilization purposes. At the same time, they were demystifying taken-for-granted media channels, providing workshops and best-practice advice. The Press and Media working group of OWS was staffed with well-trained, media-savvy personnel that aimed to carve out space within established media.

In terms of the production of space, the movements share that the media employed are characterized by a space bias while remaining ephemeral in terms of their durability. The Canadian economist and media theorist Harold Innis considers both time and space as central configurations of civilizations and suggests that premodern societies were characterized by a time bias, while modern societies were obsessed with space, that is, the expansion over large territories (Innis 2007/1950). In that context, he distinguishes between media technologies that emphasize time and those that emphasize space (Paine 1992):

> Media that emphasize time are those that are durable in character, such as parchment, clay and stone (. . .) Media that emphasize space are apt to be less durable and light in character, such as papyrus and paper. The latter are suited to wide areas in administration and trade. (Innis 2007/1950, 26)

Hence, changes in media technologies have consequences for communities and democracy. According to Innis, media technologies alter 'the structure of interest (the things thought about) by changing the character of symbols (the things thought with), and by changing the nature of community (the arena in which thought developed)' (Carey 1989, 180).

Although the movements' media practices share a spatial bias, there is an extension or acceleration of the bias discernable since the 1930s. While the unemployed workers movement mobilized for direct action based on a neat infrastructure of local Unemployed Councils and Block Committees and a broad citywide coalition organized the Mock Housing Crimes Trial in 1970, the Occupy Wall Street Movement extended this spatial net even further, attracting activists and occupiers from all over the country and connecting to encampments throughout the United States and globally. The global connectedness in real time could be understood as a further extension of the spatial bias that Innis identified for modern societies towards a hyper-space bias. Hyper-space biased communication does not only emphasize connections over space, but also questions the boundaries and constitution of space as such, suggests André Jansson (2007). Social media are crucial for OWS in this context, making it possible to connect over vast distances. At the same time, the very local occupation of a physical room seemed to have been the most effective protest strategy of activists. OWS was characterized by the need to express resistance against the current ideology of hyper-spatial bias and the end of geography fostered by among others social media. This need to occupy a physical space as resistance is reflected in the difficulties of sustaining the movement after the eviction in November 2011. This spatial or hyper-spatial bias is closely linked to the temporal organization of the movement as is argued in the following.

Media technologies such as mimeographs (copy machines) and the television helped both the unemployed workers movement and the tenants' movement to speed up the production, distribution and consumption process of information. However, the activists engaging with diverse media practices still faced a time lag in the circulation of messages from production to consumption. In contrast, social media—successfully employed by OWS—are collapsing production and consumption into one immediate experience. Without any circulation time, activists and supporters potentially engage with messages in real time. Connected to temporal changes through media technologies, spatial practices are potentially altered. While modern media were connecting different places over vast distances and in Innis's terms embraced a space bias, social media contribute to what Jansson has called hyper-space bias in which space loses its character as a reliable variable. The hyper-space biased ideology is closely connected to the ideology of globalization and reflects a changing emphasis moving from limitless progress of modernity to limitless communication of post- or late modernity (Mattelart 1996/2000).

FROM MECHANICAL SPEED TO DIGITAL IMMEDIACY

Besides a shift from space to hyper-space bias, there is a change from mechanical speed to digital immediacy. In the 1930s, spatial and media practices were linked to mechanical speed that was still effortful. Reproducing the printed materials to organize the unemployed was executed with the help of mimeographs. The employment of machines to reproduce brochures, pamphlets and shop papers helped to speed up the process and consequently it was possible to reach out to more people. In the first version of his famous essay on the work of art, Walter Benjamin quotes Paul Valery in order to describe the process of reproduction in the era of mechanical speed:

> Just as water, gas, and electricity are brought into our houses from far off to satisfy our need in response to a minimal effort, so we shall be supplied with visual or auditory images, which will appear and disappear at a simple movement of the hand hardly more than a sign. (Valery 1934/1964, 225)

For Benjamin, the reproducibility encompassed that media images no longer had a unique place in time, which coincided with its increased mobility. Benjamin suggests '(. . .) technical reproduction can place the copy of the original in situations which the original itself cannot attain. Above all, it enables the original to meet the recipient halfway, (. . .)' (Benjamin 1936/2008, 21). This argument suggests a democratization of the image through its reproduction, but also political potential to spread it to the masses for resistance against fascism. Benjamin writes:

> If the natural utilization of production forces is impeded by the property sys-
> tem, the increase in technical means, in speed, in the sources of energy will
> press for an unnatural use. This is found in war, and the destruction caused by
> war furnishes proof that society was not mature enough to make technology its
> organ (. . .). (Benjamin 1936/2008, 42)

Benjamin's arguments resonate with the experience of acceleration of speed with the possibilities of mechanical reproduction in the 1930s. Although Benjamin points out the dangers of immature usage of technology and the increasing alienation of recipients, he remains hopeful of the potential that comes with reproducibility for political mobilization of the masses.

In the 1970s, there is a further acceleration of speed in the (re)production process of media content that intersects with the increased commercialization and globalization of the media technologies employed. Analysing television as the dominant media technology of the 1970s, Raymond Williams (1974) is especially concerned with a change of sequence as programming to sequence as flow. Referring to flow, he aims to capture the integration of previously separate segments, for example, a theatre play or musical piece, through commercial breaks and trailers. Commercial breaks and trailers for future programmes create a constant flow of parallel narratives, capturing the viewer for the whole evening. Writing at the threshold of the twenty-four-hour news cycle, Raymond Williams already captures the experience of a constant stream of new experiences that television offered, while diminishing real beginnings and endings of the presented items.

Current discussions of digital culture emphasize the increasing speed and immediate character of digitally enabled communication especially through social media (Tomlinson 2007; Bolter 2000; Bolter and Grusin 2000). During the industrial era, speed was mainly associated with social progress (Benjamin 1936/2008). With the postindustrial era, the acceleration of speed is increasingly dictated by global capital and culture that is facilitated by means of communication. Tomlinson argues, hence, that we are witnessing a development from effortful speed to effortless, immediate delivery. In extension, Vincent Manzerolle refers to ubiquitous computing as 'tending towards real-time, networked communication and a collapsing of spatial distance, with a tendency of contemporary media to accelerate the circulation of information' (Manzerolle 2014, 211), which leads to the contemporary condition of immediacy. Social media that are largely based on user-generated content are contributing to a collapse of and blurring of boundaries between production and consumption, which contributes to accelerating the circulation towards immediacy and real time (Manovich 2009). Hence, social media are expressions of the condition of immediacy, particularly as they emphasize newness and presentness (Kaun and Stiernstedt 2014).

In their spatial practices, Occupy activists clearly established the encampment and direct actions as protest spaces against the everyday, speedy flow of the neoliberal city. Out of necessity their media practices are, however, relying on communication technologies following a hyper-spatial bias potentially questioning the constitution of space as such. The social media infrastructures employed however are based on the acceleration of message exchanges towards immediacy, while the participatory practices of decision making by Occupy Wall Street require time for deliberation and critique. Consequently their media practices came to stand in a stark contrast to the attempt of challenging the hegemonic order by 'making it slow', namely relying on decision-making processes following the principles of participatory democracy that need time (Polletta 2002). The OWS General Assembly and the spokescouncil became emblematic for the slowness of participatory practices giving all attendees the right to speak, but also block decisions. Break-out-sessions figured as a way to reach consensus in case suggestions were not supported by all or blocked. The character of the GA changed over time with new participants arriving all the time. Consequently, not only organizing the everyday life in the camp, but also and in particular developing a structure for decision making was an effortful and time-consuming process. Mark Bray describes the shifting roles of the GA and spokescouncil as follows:

> The hope was that the GA could return to being an outward-facing tool for recruitment and larger political decisions and discussions while the more tedious issues that bored new people could be moved to the spokescouncil. (Bray 2013, 89)

Reaching decisions through the slow process of participatory practices namely tedious discussions and planning, has been a central feature of OWS, even though the organizing was never completely nonhierarchical and all-inclusive (Bray 2013). Social media that are based on principles of immediacy, presentness and newness contribute potentially to a desynchronization between time of media practices and political time of participatory practices (Rosa 2013, Kaun and Stiernstedt 2014). Hartmut Rosa (2013, 2003) argues that desynchronization between political practices (slow politics) and other societal spheres—especially the economic system (fast capitalism)—is a symptom of general social acceleration of late modernity. Consequently, technological infrastructures such as social media that are so vividly used by activists need to be repoliticized not only in terms of the content exchanged, but also in terms of the principles that steer the platforms.

CONCLUSION

This chapter traces the changes of how protest movements are producing space in relation to their practices involving media technologies. In that context, deterritorialization, the dispossession of urban space and shifts in the location of power are current dominant developments. Consequently citizens—individually and collectively—are increasingly dispossessed in terms of time and space. Almost every waking hour is dedicated either to production (labour) or consumption (Crary 2013). At the same time, common public spaces in a physical sense are disappearing (Nemeth and Hollander 2010), since they are increasingly turned into commercial, corporate spaces dedicated to consumption or production. Media technologies are an important part of these changes as they are constitutive of a particular mode of production in capitalist societies that are based on knowledge and information.

Protest movements such as OWS are actively challenging this dominant logic of spatial and temporal dispossession, while operating in the very regime of capitalist production. Hence, they partly adopt logics of communicative capitalism particularly visible in their media practices (Dean 2008). This leads to unresolvable tensions between the time-consuming practices of participatory democracy and media practices that are immediate and ephemeral. The chapter aimed to identify these tensions that particularly social media produce in the context of protest movements, while contextualizing them historically. In general, two major shifts have been identified. First, I have identified a shift from space bias to a hyper-space bias. The ideological impetus that space is annihilated as a category as such by social media is questioned through the spatial practices of occupying Wall Street as the most radical form of resistance. Hence being in the square 24/7 provides a powerful counter picture to the flow of social media that was often characterized as spaceless. Second, the ideology of annihilation of space is based on new temporalities and acceleration in the production, distribution and consumption of content through social media (Virilio 1986). These changes constitute a second shift since the 1930s from mechanical speed to digital immediacy. Negotiating the relationship between resistance and adaptation, protest movements face challenges beyond the discussion of reform versus revolution in highly mediatized societies. Beyond decisions on media tactics, protest movements need to develop long-term strategies about how to relate to social media that are constitutive of communicative capitalism. In that sense media technologies and infrastructures need to be (re)politicized.

NOTE

1. Articles about the trial appeared, for example, in the *Daily Worker*, the *Village Voice*, the *New York Times*, *New Yorker*, the *Guardian*, *Columbia Spectator*, *Columbia Owl* and the *Unionist*.

REFERENCES

Baker, Al, Colin Moynihan and Sara Maslin Nir. 2011. "More Than 700 Arrested as Protesters Try to Cross Brooklyn Bridge." *New York Times*. October 2.
Benjamin, Walter. 1936/2008. "The Work of Art in the Age of Its Technological Reproducibility: Second Version." In *The Work of Art in the Age of Its Technological Reproducibility and Other Writings of Media*, edited by Michael Jennings, Brigid Doherty and Thomas Levin, 19–55. Cambridge, MA and London: Belknap Press of Harvard University Press.
Bolter, David, and Richard Grusin. 2000. *Remediation: Understanding New Media*. Cambridge, MA: MIT Press.
Bolter, Jay David. 2000. "Remediation and the Desire for Immediacy." *Convergence* 6 (1): 62–71.
Bolton, Matthew, Emily Welty, Meghana Nayak and Christopher Malone. 2013. "We Had a Front Row Seat to a Downtown Revolution." In *Occupying Political Science: The Occupy Wall Street Movement from New York to the World*, edited by Emily Welty, Matthew Bolton, Meghana Nayak and Christopher Malone, 1–24. New York: Palgrave Macmillan.
Bourdieu, Pierre. 1989. "Social Space and Symbolic Power." *Sociological Theory* 7 (1): 14–25.
Bray, Mark. 2013. *Translating Anarchy: The Anarchism of Occupy Wall Street*. Winchester, WA: Zero Books.
Carey, James. 1989. *Communication as Culture: Essays on Media and Society*. Boston: Unwin Hyman.
Castells, Manuel. 1977. *The Urban Question: A Marxist Approach*. Cambridge, MA: MIT Press.
———. 2000. *The Rise of the Network Society, Vol. 1*. Oxford and Malden: Blackwell Publishers.
Crang, Mike, and Nigel Thrift. 2000. "Introduction." In *Thinking Space*, edited by Mike Crang and Nigel Thrift, 1–30. New York: Routledge.
Crary, Jonathan. 2013. *24/7: Late Capitalism and the Ends of Sleep*. London: Verso.
Dean, Jodi. 2008. "Communicative Capitalism: Circulation and the Foreclosure of Politics." In *Digital Media and Democracy*, edited by Megan Boler, 101–21. Cambridge, MA and London: MIT Press.
Elden, Stuart. 2007. "There Is a Politics of Space Because Space Is Political: Henri Lefebvre and the Production of Space." *Radical Philosophy Review* 10 (2): 101–16.
Feigenbaum, Anna, Fabian Frenzel and Patrick McCurdy. 2013. *Protest Camps*. London and New York: Zed Books.
Flinn, Andrew, Mary Stevens and Elizabeth Shepherd. 2009. "Whose Memories, Whose Archives? Independent Community Archives, Autonomy and the Mainstream." *Archival Science* 9:71–86.
Foster, John B., and Robert McChesney. 2012. *The Endless Crisis: How Monopoly-Finance Capital Produces Stagnation and Upheaval from the USA to China*. New York: Monthly Review Press.
Fuchs, Christian. 2010. "Labor in Informational Capitalism and on the Internet." *The Information Society* 26 (3): 179–96. doi: 10.1080/01972241003712215.
———. 2014. *OccupyMedia! The Occupy Movement and Social Media in Crisis Capitalism*. Hants, UK: Zero Books.
Gerbaudo, Paolo. 2012. *Tweets and the Streets: Social Media and Contemporary Activism*. London: Pluto Press.

Gillham, Patrick, Bob Edwards and John Noakes. 2013. "Strategic Incapacitation and the Policing of Occupy Wall Street Protests in New York City, 2011." *Policing and Society: An International Journal of Research and Policy* 23 (1): 81–102.

Gitlin, Todd. 2012. *Occupy Nation*. New York: HarperCollins Publishers.

Graeber, David. 2013. *The Democracy Project: A History, A Crisis, A Movement*. New York: Spiegel and Grau.

Harvey, David. 1990. *The Condition of Postmodernity: An Enquiry into the Origins of Cultural Change*. Oxford: Blackwell.

Innis, Harold. 2007/1950. *Empire and Communications*. Lanham, MD: Rowman & Littlefield.

Jansson, André. 2007. "Texture: A Key Concept for Communication Geography." *European Journal of Cultural Studies* 10 (2): 185–202. doi: 10.1177/1367549407075904.

Kaun, Anne. Forthcoming. *Crisis and Critique: A History of Media Participation in Times of Crisis*. London: Zedbooks.

Kaun, Anne, and Fredrik Stiernstedt. 2014. "Facebook Time: Technological and Institutional Affordances for Media Memories." *New Media & Society* 16 (7): 1154–68.

Lasswell, Harold D., and Dorothy Blumenstock. 1939. *World Revolutionary Propaganda: A Chicago Study*. New York: Knopf.

Lefebvre, Henri. 1991. *The Production of Space*. Maiden and Oxford: Blackwell.

Manovich, Lev. 2009. "The Practice of Everyday (Media) Life: From Mass Consumption to Mass Cultural Production?" *Critical Inquiry* 35 (2): 319–31. doi:10.1086/596645.

Manzerolle, Vincent. 2014. "Technologies of Immediacy/ Economies of Attention: Notes on Commercial Development of Mobile Media and Wireless Connectivity." In *The Audience Commodity in a Digital Age*, edited by Lee McGuigan and Vincent Manzerolle, 207–28. New York: Peter Lang.

Massey, Doreen. 2005. *For Space*. London, Thousand Oaks, CA and New Delhi: Sage.

Mattelart, Armand. 1996/2000. *Networking the World 1794–2000*. Minneapolis: University of Minnesota Press.

Maxwell, Richard, and Toby Miller. 2013. "Cultural Materialism, Media and the Environment." *Key Words: A Journal of Cultural Materialism* 11:86–102.

McLuhan, Marshall. 1964. *Understanding Media: The Extensions of Man*. London: Routledge.

Merrifield, Andy. 2013. *The Politics of Encounter: Urban Theory and Protest Under Planetary Urbanization*. London and Athens: University of Georgia Press.

Mosco, Vincent. 2005. *The Digital Sublime. Myth, Power, and Cyberspace*. Cambridge, MA and London: The MIT Press.

Nemeth, Jeremy, and Justin Hollander. 2010. "Security Zones and New York City's Shrinking Public Space." *International Journal of Urban and Regional Research* 34 (1): 20–34.

New York Times. 1930. "Reds Battle Police in Union Square; Scores Injured, Leaders Are Seized; Two Dead, Many Hurt in Clashes Abroad."

Paine, Robert. 1992. "Time–Space Scenarios and the Innisian Theory: A View from Anthropology." *Time & Society* 1 (1): 51–63.

Polletta, Francesca. 2002. *Freedom Is an Endless Meeting: Democracy in American Social Movements*. Chicago and London: University of Chicago Press.

Rosa, Hartmut. 2003. "Social Acceleration: Ethical and Political Consequences of a Desynchronized High-Speed Society." *Constellations* 10 (1): 3–33.

———. 2013. *Social Acceleration: A New Theory of Modernity*. New York: Columbia University Press.

Sewell, William. 2005. *Logics of History: Social Theory and Social Transformation*. Chicago: University of Chicago Press.

Silverstone, Roger. 2007. *Media and Morality: On the Rise of Mediapolis*. Cambridge: Polity.

Thompson, John. 1995. *Media and Modernity: A Social Theory of the Media*. Cambridge: Polity Press.

Tomlinson, John. 1999. *Culture and Globalization*. Chicago: University of Chicago Press.

———. 2007. *The Culture of Speed: The Coming of Immediacy*. Los Angeles: Sage.

Valery, Paul. 1934/1964. "The Conquest of Ubiquity." In *Aesthetics: The Collected Works of Paul Valery*, 225–28. New York: Pantheon Books.

Virilio, Paul. 1986. *Speed and Politics: An Essay on Dromology*. New York: Semiotext(e).

Weltevrede, Esther, Anne Helmond and Carolin Gerlitz. 2014. "The Politics of Real-Time: A Device Perspective on Social Media Platforms and Search Engines." *Theory, Culture & Society* 31 (6): 125–50. doi:10.1177/0263276414537318.

Williams, Raymond. 1974. *Television: Technology and Cultural Form*. New York: Schocken Books.

III

Surveillance, Censorship and Political Economy

Chapter Six

Social Media Censorship, Privatized Regulation and New Restrictions to Protest and Dissent

Arne Hintz

In November 2014, Robert Hannigan, newly appointed Director of the British Government Communications Headquarters (GCHQ), outlined his view of key challenges for national security. He pointed to social media networks as 'terrorists' command and control networks of choice' and singled out internet companies for failing to address the misuse of their platforms by criminals and terrorists (Hannigan 2014). Shortly after, Prime Minister David Cameron announced he would 'step up pressure on web companies such as Facebook and Twitter to do more to co-operate with the intelligence agencies' as they have a 'social responsibility' to help fight terrorism (*Guardian* 2015a). This focus on social media companies and their platforms is a significant shift from earlier discourses. Whereas social media were celebrated as harbingers of democratic citizen action during the Arab Spring, they are now increasingly under pressure to comply with state interests of restricting and monitoring their use. They are called upon for 'responsible behaviour', state representatives are demanding their proactive contribution to state-based content policies and laws and regulations focus on their role as key nodes in communication networks.

At the same time, these companies are taking an active role in shaping the uses of their platforms and intervening into what can be published and distributed. Google, Facebook, Apple and others are creating rules that limit the range of acceptable content, and resource and infrastructure providers like PayPal and Amazon have excluded clients (such as WikiLeaks) from their services. The Snowden revelations of mass online surveillance have highlighted the key role of social media platforms in large-scale data collection

and their—sometimes reluctant, sometimes complicit—integration in surveillance programmes by state agencies such as the NSA and GCHQ. Policy
developments in further areas such as intellectual property protection have
contributed to an emerging shift in regulatory authority to private intermediaries.

This shift points to new challenges for dissident content and activist media uses. First, as private intermediaries are enlisted in regulatory mechanisms and assigned a greater role in implementing laws and policies, the state
outsources interventions into citizens' communication to these platforms.
Second, as internet companies themselves formulate and set policy that affects freedom of expression, they set new standards for legitimate online
communication and bypass established legal rules.

This chapter addresses these two dynamics as it discusses the role of
private intermediaries in limiting dissent and protest. It focuses on content
control by social media companies but also considers related challenges of
surveillance and copyright restrictions, and it situates these issues in the
wider context of the privatization of communication policy. I start by outlin-
ing the context of current communication policy research which increasingly
addresses the role of nonstate actors, such as their participation in networked
multistakeholder processes, standard-setting by technical developers and policy advocacy by both civil society and the private sector. Then I highlight
key areas of the current debate around internet freedoms and restrictions,
focusing on the three dimensions of censorship, surveillance and intellectual
property. The third section of the chapter emphasizes the role of social media
platforms, which is then broadened towards a wider perspective on commercial intermediaries and the privatization of communications policy in the
context of neoliberal restructuring. Finally, I connect this analysis with practices of resistance and contestation which increasingly take place, similarly,
in the arena of private, nonstate media actors and infrastructures. I argue that
the trend of outsourcing regulatory decisions and privatizing policy, particularly with regard to social media companies, has serious implications for
freedom of expression and forms of protest.

COMMUNICATIONS POLICY
AND NETWORKED GOVERNANCE

Classic understandings of policy may focus on national law and regulation,
complemented by some intergovernmental coordination at international institutions such as the United Nations. However, the spaces and actors of policy
making have expanded and diversified over the past few decades. Developments taking place at other levels than the national, and both normative and
material influences by a variety of nonstate actors, increasingly transform

traditional regulatory procedures. National policy has 'become embedded within more expansive sets of interregional relations and networks of power' (Held and McGrew 2003, 3), and policy authority is now located at 'different and sometimes overlapping levels—from the local to the supra-national and global' (Raboy and Padovani 2010, 16). Policy fora such as the World Summit on the Information Society (WSIS) and the Internet Governance Forum (IGF) have experimented with new forms of multistakeholder processes that include civil society and the business sector. The main internet governance institution, the Internet Corporation for Assigned Names and Numbers (ICANN), has relegated governments to an advisory function. Thus the vertical, centralized and state-based modes of traditional regulation have been complemented by collaborative horizontal arrangements, leading to 'a complex ecology of interdependent structures' with 'a vast array of formal and informal mechanisms working across a multiplicity of sites' (Raboy 2002, 6–7).

Despite a lack of actual authority to adopt laws and regulations, nonstate actors have been able to use this complex environment for normative interventions into policy debate by setting agendas, exerting public pressure, lobbying and public campaigns and by lending or withdrawing legitimacy to policy goals, decisions and processes (Keck and Sikkink 1998). Furthermore, both civil society groups and the business sector have changed the communications environment by developing new technologies and platforms, and with them new standards, protocols and practices that have become de-facto cornerstones of communication technology. As technical standards and protocols typically allow some actions and disallow others, and enable some uses and restrict others, their development constitutes a latent and invisible form of policy making (e.g., Lessig 1999; Braman 2006; DeNardis 2009). Media activists, equally, have often focused on the creation of alternative infrastructure that bypasses regulatory obstacles, rather than advocating for policy change. Interactions with the policy environment, in this case, take place neither through lobbying 'inside' nor protesting 'outside' institutional or governmental processes, but through prefigurative action that creates alternative infrastructure and by adopting a tactical repertoire of circumvention (Hintz and Milan 2013; Milan 2013).

Business actors have, for a long time, been engaged with these different forms of policy interventions. During the early development of international radio standards, for example, they drafted declarations which were then adopted by government representatives, and they shaped the radio as a unidirectional broadcast medium by pursuing certain avenues of technological development and neglecting others (Hamelink 1994). They are heavily engaged with contemporary internet debates, from promoting certain standards and platforms (e.g., operating systems) to involvement with public campaigns (e.g., on intellectual property protection) and to intense lobbying (e.g., on net neutrality).

CENSORSHIP AND OTHER CHALLENGES
TO DIGITAL COMMUNICATION

Complex interactions between state and nonstate actors have also shaped internet policy and the struggles around the freedoms and restrictions of online communication. Many of the key components of the internet have been developed in a decentralized, informal and experimental fashion by technologists rather than governments and as 'bottom-up, grassroots process-es' (Kahn 2004, 18), 'without a great deal of governmental or other over-sight' (Cerf 2004, 14). The end-to-end principle gave a maximum of power and control to the edges of the network, that is, the user, rather than central nodes. 'Governments of the Industrial World, leave us alone!' John Perry Barlow famously proclaimed in his Declaration of the Independence of Cy-berspace: 'You have no sovereignty where we gather' (Barlow 1996). Cyber-space challenged the law's traditional reliance on territorial borders and thus questioned government's ability to control citizens' behaviour (Johnson and Post 1996).

However, gradually such borders were introduced and drawn around the previously borderless cyberspace (Goldsmith and Wu 2006). The 'Great Firewall of China' has demonstrated that control over major backbones and access points can allow governments to draw a virtual fence around a state territory and restrict access to both services and information from outside that territory (e.g., Deibert et al. 2008). The Egyptian government, at the height of the Arab Spring uprising in January 2011, proved that internet access in a country can be reduced or even shut down during protest situa-tions, and other governments have applied this new capability with increas-ing frequency and flexibility (Webster 2011).

Inside a country's borders, filtering and blocking certain content has be-come common practice across the globe (Open Net Initiative 2012). Informa-tion that transcends moral, religious or political limits set by governments has been blocked, most prominently in the Middle East and Asia, but increas-ingly also in Western countries. The UK has occupied a questionable pioneer role as internet service providers, mandated by the government, have estab-lished 'Parental Control Filters' that censor a range of different content types deemed inappropriate for minors.

While child protection and the restriction of, particularly, child pornogra-phy, may be admirable goals, the creation of an extensive censorship archi-tecture for these purposes typically raises demands for wider content restric-tions. As Ron Deibert notes, 'once the tools of censorship are in place, the temptation for authorities to employ them for a wide range of purposes are large' (Deibert 2009, 327). In Thailand, for example, the initial blocking of pornographic material was gradually extended to politically sensitive material. The adoption of a child-pornography filtering law in Germany in 2009 was quickly followed by demands to extend the law to a broader range of content deemed illegitimate (Hintz and Milan 2011). But filtering can also lead to unintended overblocking because of the imperfections or technical configuration of the software. An attempt by an internet service provider in Canada, for example, to block one site caused more than six hundred nonrelated websites to be blocked (Villeneuve 2006), and the child protection filters in the UK have blocked access to, for example, sexual education websites, parental guidance sites, the support site childline.org.uk and the website of the Electronic Frontier Foundation, an important digital rights organization (Robbins 2013).

A more indirect form of content restrictions has emerged with the debate on net neutrality. As a network of cables and wireless connections that move data packages from A to B regardless of their content, the internet has largely been a neutral platform for information exchange, rather than a broadcaster that makes editorial decisions. As such, it has become an important public sphere and a crucial space for free expression and democratic participation (Loeblich and Musiani 2014). However, the increasing practice by ISPs and telecommunications services of blocking and/or throttling (i.e., slowing down) some content, and speeding up the delivery of other content and services, has substantially altered this space. This form of content discrimination through infrastructure control provides particular challenges for noncommercial content and small businesses that may not be able to pay the fee required to be on a 'fast lane', and for oppositional and dissident news sources whose exposure a network provider may want to limit (Balkin 2009).

A second area of intervention and change has been privacy and surveillance. In contrast to earlier celebrations (or concerns, depending on the perspective) of anonymity, electronic communication has vastly increased the capabilities of governments and corporate actors to monitor citizens' interactions, exchanges, locations and movements. In contemporary 'surveillance societies', 'all manner of everyday activities are recorded, checked, traced and monitored' (Lyon 2007, 454). As Sandra Braman notes, the traditional notion of panopticon-style surveillance has been replaced with the 'panspectron', in which information is gathered about everything, all the time (Braman 2006, 315).

The revelations by whistleblower Edward Snowden about mass surveillance by security agencies such as the NSA and the GCHQ have demonstrated this impressively. Programmes such as Prism, Tempora, Muscular, Edgehill, Bullrun and Quantumtheory have provided evidence of mass surveillance of our social media uses; interception and monitoring of most online and phone communication; state-sponsored hacking into telecommunications services; the sabotage of security tools and the compromising of internet infrastructure (*Guardian* 2015b). They have included paying security software firms to weaken the security of their products, and infecting citizens' computers with malware to see their screen or use their webcam. The extent to which this has allowed governments to collect, store and analyse data amounts to—in the words of John Perry Barlow—'monitoring the communication of the human race' (Barlow 2013).

National and international law has expanded governments' ability to monitor citizens' communication. For example, the data retention Directive in the European Union, which was adopted in 2006 and implemented by most European countries in 2009 (but revoked by the European Court of Human Rights in 2014), required telecommunications operators and internet service providers to store their customers' connection data and to make it available to the authorities upon request. This concerns detailed information on who communicates with whom, at what times, for how long, and at which physical location. According to civil rights lawyer T. J. McIntyre, the Directive resulted in the creation of 'a comprehensive digital dossier about every individual' (McIntyre 2008, 327). In the wake of the Snowden revelations, states have replaced the Directive with national law and have expanded the legality of data collection further—for example, in the UK, through the controversial Data Retention and Investigatory Powers Act of 2014.

Blanket surveillance and pervasive monitoring of people's movements, actions and communication undermine critical debate and dissident voices. Just a few days before the first Snowden leaks were published in June 2013, the United Nations Special Rapporteur on Freedom of Expression and Opinion delivered a landmark report on state surveillance and freedom of expression in which he highlighted that the right to privacy is an essential requirement for the realization of the right to freedom of expression (UN General Assembly 2013). This was confirmed by a PEN study in the aftermath of the Snowden leaks, which found that journalists and other writers have self-censored their work as a result of mass surveillance. Fears that engaging with controversial issues may cause them harm have led them to avoid or treat cautiously, among other issues, protest reporting and critical investigations into government policies (PEN 2013). Critical and investigative reporting is particularly challenged by surveillance as it requires confidential communication with sources and, occasionally, the anonymity of authors (Rusbridger 2013).

Finally, the increasingly rigid interpretation (and enforcement) of intellectual property has led to further restrictions. The free availability of protocols and standards has been essential for how we use the net today, and the hacker slogan 'information wants to be free' has been a cornerstone for infrastructure development, the emergence of free and open source software and many aspects of digital culture, such as remixes and mash-ups (Benkler 2006; Lessig 2008). The internet is a 'gigantic, globally distributed, always-on copying machine' (Mueller 2010, 131) and a huge library that allows us to share files, share knowledge and benefit from an abundance of ideas. However, control over these ideas and knowledge through the means of intellectual property has become a key economic resource and source of power and is therefore enforced fiercely. In what has been termed the 'second enclosure' (Boyle 2003), knowledge and information have been commodified and put under the control of the business sector. As scarcity—and thus a market—is created for informational and immaterial goods, we have witnessed 'the making of knowledge and information into property' (May 2009, 364). The state has regulated and supported this process through the draconic punishment of intellectual property violations (Klotz 2004) and multiple attempts to develop international agreements (such as ACTA) (Geist 2010).

SOCIAL MEDIA AND (UN)FREE COMMUNICATION

Social media and other digital platforms have been important means of activist and dissident communication, but also key sites where the tension between free communication and the emerging reality of restrictions is played out. From Indymedia to Facebook, these platforms have been used to spread alternative information and to organize and mobilize. The Indymedia network, created in 1999 and expanded around the globe over the following years, pioneered citizen journalism by bringing alternative news to a global audience and by allowing every internet user to publish their stories via its open publishing system and thus to contribute to a user-generated news platform (Hintz 2014). In its wake followed the rise of blogging as a mass phenomenon and the widespread practice of 'citizen witnessing' (Allan 2013) of key news events, with citizen reports, pictures and audiovisual footage complementing and transforming traditional journalist reporting.

From the 'sms protests' in Spain and the Philippines in the early 2000s to the alleged 'Twitter'- and 'Facebook-Revolutions' in Iran in 2009 and Egypt in 2011 (and many other places before and after), social media have been widely credited as an important force in supporting social and political change. As 'liberation technology', as Diamond (2010) notes, social media and other information and communications technology (ICT) applications enable 'citizens to report news, expose wrong-doing, express opinions, mobilize protest, monitor elections, scrutinize government, deepen participation, and expand the horizons of freedom' (Diamond 2010, 70). While overenthusiastic and technologically deterministic notions of social media 'revolutions' have increasingly been criticized (Morozov 2011; Christensen 2011), many observers maintain that digital platforms have been 'effective catalysts' (Khamis and Vaughn 2011, 1) of change and amplifiers of social movement activism, not least as they have enabled the creation of forums for free speech and for shared social and political criticism, and generated a social space for developing critical discourses where an open public sphere did not exist (see Haunss's chapter in this volume). Beyond the instrumental uses of social media for protest and activism, these observations point to the broader democratic and participatory potential of digital platforms which have been used for debate and creative peer production, and which have been key components of participatory cultures (Benkler 2006; Jenkins 2008).

However, social media have also been a prime target in the increasing attempts by states to control online communication. 'Like all technologies that threaten to subvert prevailing authority', as Greenwald (2015) notes, social media are increasingly subject to 'police measures of control, repression and punishment' (Greenwald 2015). Criminal cases for online speech have risen significantly. In Britain alone, at least six thousand people a year were investigated between 2012 and 2015 for comments made online, in some cases leading to severe sentences (Bloodworth 2015). These investigations concern a variety of offensive comments and hate speech, but definitions of what is deemed offensive and therefore leads to persecution depend on socio-political contexts. Criticism on social media of Western military interventions in the Middle East, for example, has been interpreted as 'promotion of terrorism' and carried heavy sentences (Greenwald 2015). Social media commentators on the London riots in August 2011 have been sentenced for incitement of violence (*Guardian* 2011). As the boundaries between democratic forms of contentious communication and illegal hate speech are shifting, social media are a site that is under increasingly close observation by the police and are used by the state to enforce speech regulation.

This targeted form of monitoring and limiting online dissent is complemented by state disruptions of digital infrastructure, including the blocking of social media platforms. Twitter, YouTube and other social media have been blocked in countries such as China, Iran, Pakistan, Thailand and Turkey, and similar blocks have been discussed by Western governments (Deibert et al. 2008; Howard et al. 2011). Typical rationales given for such action are threats to national security and the preservation of cultural or religious morals. In practice, most blocks have occurred as a reaction to protests, uprisings and criticism of governments, and have thus served to protect political authority and mitigate dissidence. In many cases, 'the targets (victims) are active domestic civic society movements' (Howard et al. 2011, 220).

Social media platforms are thus an object of observation and control, but they have also become a subject of intervention. In addition to state-sanctioned and law-based content restrictions, internet companies, social networking platforms and app stores have created their own practices for what they deem acceptable content. A strict interpretation of rules to prevent 'indecency', for example, caused Facebook to censor pictures of breastfeeding mothers, as well as cartoons depicting naked people (such as a naked Adam and Eve in the garden of Eden) (Norton 2014). Apple deleted an app from its app store that marked US drone strikes on a geographic map. The app was not illegal but certainly politically sensitive (Bonnington and Ackerman 2012). Activists and political dissidents have experienced increasingly restrictive content policies, as Facebook, for example, has discontinued activist pages in the run-up to protest events. Despite the platform's reputation of supporting protests and uprisings in the Middle East and elsewhere, it has taken down pages dedicated to anticapitalist and antiracist causes 'as part of a growing effort by Facebook to crack down on the presence of political groups on its network' (Dencik 2014).

Interventions by human censors are complemented by algorithmic interventions. Most social media companies are adapting content feeds automatically according to their users' preferences and are therefore manipulating what users see in their news feeds. Facebook has actively experimented with affecting user behaviour regarding a core feature of the democratic system— voting. By providing selective information about voting behaviour by a user's friends, it has created statistically significant changes in voting patterns (Sifry 2014). Changes to Google's ranking of search results can have similar effects as the relevant algorithm has profound implications for the visibility of online information. Incorporating the 'truthfulness' of an article in the search ranking, as was discussed in early 2015, may mean that mainstream narratives and official reports are highlighted whereas activist and dissident information which typically questions established 'truths' are moved down to the less visible search results (Watson 2015). While these practices may not qualify as censorship by internet companies, they have considerable impact on the availability of activist and political information on the web.

At the intersection between external interventions into, and internal interventions by, internet companies, measures provided by those companies to monitor user behaviour are sometimes used strategically. For example, the Facebook Report Abuse button which allows users to flag content that is deemed inappropriate has been applied as a tool for stifling dissent. Critical online publications, journalists and activist Facebook groups have faced mass reports of alleged abuse and their accounts were taken down by Facebook as a consequence (Brandom 2014).

The various forms of content restrictions on social media often go hand in hand with the surveillance of content and user activities. The 'big data' generated through social media platforms is at the heart of current surveillance trends, as highlighted by the Snowden leaks (Lyon 2014). The 'data mine' (Andrejevic 2012, 71) of social media allows for the detailed monitoring and analysis of internet users, including their locations, activities, preferences, friends and networks, and political orientations. Applications (such as widgets and share buttons) that are included on an increasing number of websites allow the tracing of users across the web, both by social media companies and their commercial partners. As social media render human connections measurable, information about people is not just inferred from their own activities and preferences but also from those of their friends and acquaintances (Trottier and Lyon 2012). Unsurprisingly, Google, Facebook and others have been both at the centre of surveillance programmes such as Prism and in the spotlight of debate since the start of the revelations. Even before Snowden, Google specified in its Transparency Report some of the more official ways in which governments use social media to collect information about its users. Between July and December 2013, for example, Google received requests for the data of over eighteen thousand users in the United States, and over three thousand users in the UK (which is, in the case of the United States, requests for one hundred different users each day) (Google Transparency Report 2014).

Protesters and dissidents have often been the target of social media-based surveillance, particularly in situations of major uprisings. The 'social media revolutions' in the Middle East and elsewhere demonstrated how the use of platforms such as Facebook, Twitter and YouTube not only helped mobilize the public and spread information but also served as a means for the state to monitor protesters. As Hofheinz (2011, 1420) notes about the 'Green Revolution' in Iran in 2009: 'While people in New York cafés were forwarding tweets that gave them the thrilled feeling of partaking in a revolution, Iranian conservatives tightened their grip on power using YouTube videos and other internet evidence to identify and arrest opposition activists.' In Iran, Tunisia, Syria and elsewhere, authorities used social media to scrape user data, and in some occasions to infect the computers of opposition supporters with malware; for example, spying software to capture webcam activity (Villeneuve 2012).

The incorporation of social media into information control and surveillance is not accidental. Corporate services like Facebook and Google are based on a business model of collecting and analysing user data. As Leistert and Rohle (2011) note, their users are customers, not citizens. The provision of a public sphere of democratic communicative interactions and activist mobilizations aligns with this strategy as it offers the company increased access to user data and improves insights into the preferences, networks and activities of people. However, its rationale does not stem from a concern for civil rights and democratic participation; rather, user expectations for freedom of expression and privacy are only accepted as long as they concur with the broader goal of marketization. Thus, for example, Facebook has established requirements for the use of 'real names' rather than pseudonyms and experiments with automatic facial recognition, even though this violates users' right to anonymity (Leistert and Rohle 2011).

All interactions on corporate platforms take place in the context of commerce and marketing. Similar to 'the replacement of the downtown city centre by the shopping mall' (Andrejevic 2012, 82), the privatized infrastructure of commercial social media offers a confined and controlled space for semipublic interactions, under the conditions of the commercial imperative. Political activism, in this context, becomes a side note that is tolerated as long as it does not threaten the broader commercial goal.

The prefix 'commercial' social media remains important as noncommercial alternatives and earlier forms such as Indymedia do not monitor, store and exploit user data, and therefore operate in a different context. However, the monopolization of social media services and the dominant role of companies such as Google and Facebook mean that most social media interactions are subject to both the commercial logics of, and restrictive interventions by, these actors. Increasingly, the 'internet' equals services provided by a small oligopoly of social media companies (Patelis 2013; Fuchs 2014). The often close and friendly interactions between these companies and the state—for example, between Google and the US government (Assange 2014)—suggest cooperative and mutually supportive relations between the major commercial and state forces in internet business and governance.

LOCATIONS OF CONTROL:
THE PRIVATIZATION OF INTERNET POLICY

As we can see from both the trends in internet policy and the interventions and logics of social media companies, private intermediaries play an increasing role in enforcing regulations, setting new rules and providing significant resources for surveillance and information control. They allow us to observe a shift in the location of policy making and regulation.

This is particularly apparent in the area of censorship and content limitations. As app stores and social media have created their own rules and practices for accepting and rejecting content on their platforms, internet companies are making decisions with severe political and human rights implications. They have become a 'social media police force' (Dencik 2014) that is bound by its own terms of service, commercial logics and political leanings, rather than civil rights and the rule of law. Together with other intermediaries such as ISPs and search engines, they act as 'proxy censors' (Kreimer 2006, 13).

These actors also encompass providers of other relevant infrastructure, including server space, domain registration and funding. In December 2010, Amazon, PayPal and others demonstrated their crucial gatekeeping role when they closed the services they had previously provided for WikiLeaks, depriving the leaks platform of its domain name and of access to necessary funds in the middle of a major release (the Cablegate leaks). This 'denial of service' (Benkler 2011) demonstrated the significant power of so-called 'cloud' services in allowing and disallowing access to information and in controlling the gates that enable internet users to participate in increasingly cloud-based communication exchanges. Furthermore, the actions by Amazon, PayPal and others highlighted the vulnerability of these services to political interventions, as they coincided with pressure from members of the US political elite, both inside and outside government (Benkler 2011).

While the theme of censorship points to direct interventions by the private sector into communication practices and information exchange, surveillance highlights how business practices are used for state goals. Both the Snowden leaks and corporate transparency reports have demonstrated the extent to which private intermediaries, and social media in particular, are now at the centre of state efforts to monitor citizens and internet user behaviour. While some of the programmes revealed by Snowden (such as 'Muscular') have been used to intercept data traffic between the servers of social media companies without the latter's knowledge, the more prominent programmes (such as 'Prism' and 'Tempora') have relied on the knowledge and cooperation of internet companies and telecommunications providers. They demonstrate the position of private intermediaries between object and subject of intervention. Furthermore, as the collection and storage of data is outsourced to social media companies, telecommunications services and ISPs, so is the development of specific mechanisms for targeted intrusion, monitoring and analysis of user data. Companies such as Finfisher and Blue Coat provide sophisticated tools for surveillance and filtering to governments around the world, including both Western democracies and authoritarian states (Citizen Lab 2013; Marquis-Boire et al. 2013).

The third area of online restrictions that was introduced earlier—the fight against file sharing and remixing—offers particularly useful insights into the outsourcing of policy as it focuses largely on interactions between private companies. Intellectual property owners or their representatives, such as the Recording Industry Association of America (RIAA), typically commission law firms to request the ISP or content provider to take down particular content or a link. Such private-sector-based processes have led to requests to remove, on average, twenty to twenty-five million URLs from Google searches each month, by summer 2014 (Google Transparency Report 2014). Agreements between the copyright holder industry and ISPs have included, for example, the US Copyright Alert System in which copyright holders identify shared copyrighted material and ISPs exert punishment by warning the respective customer or, as a last resort, cancelling their internet connection. Such mechanisms bypass governmental and judicial oversight and put both the definition of, and the punishment for, copyright infringement in the hands of content owners and ISPs (Flaim 2012).

According to Mueller (2010, 149), 'the regulatory trend that constantly emerges from the [intellectual property] tension is a shift of the responsibility for monitoring and policing internet conduct onto strategically positioned private sector intermediaries.' By 'delegating responsibility to the private sector' (Mueller 2010, 149), the state enlists businesses and other nonstate actors in implementing communications policy and, furthermore, transfers quasi-policy functions. Internet companies have been the recipient and executor of take-down requests (such as Google searches, see above), but they have also participated in creating nonstate rules and practices. YouTube, for example, makes agreements with copyright holders on a country-by-country basis on whether copyrighted material uploaded by users is either taken down or monetarized. Rather than waiting for a court order, its ContentID system detects copyrighted material and acts upon it immediately, based on the respective agreement with the copyright holder (see also Elmer's chapter in this volume).

Social media companies are thus at the core of an increasing privatization of media policy in which authority and decision-making power are transferred to private environments, often underpinned by commercial and market logics. This development can be situated within the broader context of neoliberal politics in which the legitimacy of the public sector has been questioned and authority has been moved away from the public realm. Operating outside of democratic control, market-driven politics has challenged—and often weakened—democratic processes and legitimacy (Crouch 2004; Couldry 2010). Privatized forms of policy making and implementation may thus be seen as a component of what Freedman calls 'neo-liberal media policy' (Freedman 2008, 47).

While the trend towards internet censorship, content restrictions and pervasive surveillance relies heavily on the role of private intermediaries, the contestations of this dynamic are not entirely focused on state-related solutions either. Campaigns for digital rights and protests against restrictive policies have been complemented by the development of technological alternatives and encryption tools, and changes in individual communication practices. Emerging autonomous and civil-society-based media infrastructure has included internet services such as Riseup.net, alternative forms of social networking such as Lorea.org and the use of anonymization and encryption tools such as TOR and PGP. Rather than advocating for policy change, many internet activists see their task in creating 'self-managed infrastructures that work regardless of "their" regulation, laws or any other form of governance' (Indymedia activist, quoted in Hintz and Milan 2009, 31). Their strategies focus on prefigurative action, rather than attempts to influence policy processes they regard as dominated by existing powers (Hintz and Milan 2013).

In their efforts, they thus mirror privatized forms of policy authority and implementation as they trust in their own ability to develop solutions to perceived problems, rather than in the abilities of public institutions.

Where policy advocacy does take place, it is sometimes combined with prefigurative action towards a strategy of do-it-yourself policy making (or 'policy hacking') by developing new model laws and regulatory frameworks, rather than waiting for the state to do that. These forms of civil-society-led policy development have extended from the local level (e.g., the making of a new transparency law in the city of Hamburg) to the national (e.g., the Icelandic Modern Media Initiative which created proposals for new media laws in Iceland) to the international (e.g., the development of a model law on net neutrality in Europe) (Hintz 2015). Here, the 'outsourcing' of policy making has involved civil society actors who have taken legislative development into their own hands.

CONCLUSION

Social media are at the centre of a trend towards restrictions to online communication by both state and private actors. The deterritorialized spheres of the internet have partly been reterritorialized by states; the practice of filtering and blocking content is expanding; information and ideas are being commodified and digital surveillance has become pervasive. Social media companies and other commercial intermediaries are subjected to these trends as they are enlisted by the state to police the net and required by governments to monitor their users and store data exchanges. Yet they also play an active role in developing and enforcing new rules for allowing as well as restricting information, they define and punish objectionable user behaviour and they provide and withdraw, accordingly, vital spaces and resources for communication. In that sense, they may operate 'responsibly' (as Robert Hannigan demanded) but this responsibility refers to commercial logics and interactions with the state, rather than the protection of civil rights and a democratic public sphere. For activists and dissident information, the incorporation of social media into restrictive policies and practices provides a serious challenge and a significant shift as platforms used for protest and public debate are transformed into controlled spaces. What was regarded as 'liberation technology' is increasingly enclosed.

These processes, as we have seen, are part of a broader trend—the privatization of internet policy. Responsibility and authority for policy making and implementation are thus shifting to the private sector in the shape of ISPs, telecommunications services, social media platforms and other providers of online services. At the same time, resistance to censorship and surveillance may equally be transitioning from a state focus to prefigurative action by civil society groups. Established forms of advocacy and campaigning are complemented with the development of alternative platforms, tools for circumvention, and model laws and regulations. Demands for privacy, free expression, an open internet and unrestricted exchange of knowledge are thus not just raised through protest and lobbying but through the self-organized creation of technological as well as policy alternatives that embody and implement these values. Contestations over censorship and surveillance take place increasingly in the arena of private, nonstate media actors and infrastructures.

REFERENCES

Allan, S. (2013) *Citizen Witnessing: Revisioning Journalism in Times of Crisis.* Cambridge: Polity.

Andrejevic, M. (2012) "Exploitation in the Data Mine." In C. Fuchs, K. Boersma, A. Albrechtslund and M. Sandoval, eds., *Internet and Surveillance: The Challenges of Web 2.0 and Social Media*, 71–88. Abingdon: Routledge.

Assange, J. (2014) *When Google Met WikiLeaks.* New York: OR Books.

Balkin, J. M. (2009) "The Future of Free Expression in a Digital Age." *Pepperdine Law Review* 36 (2): 427–44.

Barlow, J. P. (1996) "A Declaration of the Independence of Cyberspace." http://homes.eff.org/~barlow/Declaration-Final.html.

——— (2013) Interview by Sky News with John Perry Barlow and Julian Assange, 10 June 2013. https://www.youtube.com/watch?v=_DO8mdrPYWw.

Benkler, Y. (2006) *The Wealth of Networks: How Social Production Transforms Markets and Freedom.* New Haven, CT and London: Yale University Press.

——— (2011) "A Free Irresponsible Press: WikiLeaks and the Battle over the Soul of the Networked Fourth Estate." Working draft. http://www.benkler.org/Benkler_Wikileaks_current.pdf.

Bloodworth, James (2015) "Katie Hopkins' Views Are Now Considered Matters for Law Enforcement, and It Is Utterly Terrifying." *Independent*, 1 January 2015. http://www.independent.co.uk/voices/comment/katie-hopkins-views-are-now-considered-matters-for-law-enforcement-and-it-is-utterly-terrifying-9953339.html.

Bonnington, C. and Ackerman, S. (2012) "Apple Rejects App that Tracks U.S. Drone Strikes." *Wired*, 30 August 2012. http://www.wired.com/2012/08/drone-app/.

Boyle, J. (2003) "The Second Enclosure Movement and the Construction of the Public Domain." *Law and Contemporary Problems* 66 (1-2): 33–74.

Braman, S. (2006) *Change of State: Information, Policy, and Power.* Cambridge, MA: MIT Press.

Brandom, Russell (2014) "Facebook's Report Abuse Button Has Become a Tool of Global Oppression." *The Verge*, 2 September 2014. http://www.theverge.com/2014/9/2/6083647/facebook-s-report-abuse-button-has-become-a-tool-of-global-oppression.

Cerf, V. G. (2004) "First, Do No Harm." In D. MacLean, ed., *Internet Governance: A Grand Collaboration*, 13–15. New York: United Nations ICT Task Force.

Christensen, C. (2011) "Twitter Revolutions? Addressing Social Media and Dissent." *The Communication Review* 14 (3): 155–57.

Citizen Lab, The (2013) *Planet Blue Coat: Mapping Global Censorship and Surveillance Tools.* https://citizenlab.org/wp-content/uploads/2013/01/Planet-Blue-Coat.pdf.

Couldry, N. (2010) *Why Voice Matters: Culture and Politics after Neoliberalism.* London: Sage.

Crouch, C. (2004) *Post-Democracy.* Cambridge: Polity.

Deibert, R. (2009) "The Geopolitics of Internet Control: Censorship, Sovereignty, and Cyberspace." In A. Chadwick and P. Howard, eds., *The Routledge Handbook of Internet Politics*, 323–36. London: Routledge.

Deibert, R. J., Palfrey, J. G., Rohozinski, R., and Zittrain, J. (2008) *Access Denied: The Practice and Policy of Global Internet Filtering*. Cambridge, MA: MIT Press.

DeNardis, L. (2009) *Protocol Politics: The Globalization of Internet Governance*. Cambridge, MA: MIT Press.

Dencik, L. (2014) "Why Facebook Censorship Matters." *JOMEC Blog*, 13 January 2014. http://www.jomec.co.uk/blog/why-facebook-censorship-matters/.

Diamond, L. (2010). "Liberation Technology." *Journal of Democracy* 21 (3): 69–83.

Flaim, S. M. (2012) "Op-ed: Imminent 'Six Strikes' Copyright Alert System Needs Antitrust Scrutiny." *ars technica*, April 2012. http://arstechnica.com/tech-policy/news/2012/03/op-ed-imminent-six-strikes-copyright-alert-system-needs-antitrust-scrutiny.ars.

Freedman, D. (2008) *The Politics of Media Policy*. Cambridge: Polity.

Fuchs, C. (2014) *Social Media: A Critical Introduction*. London: Sage.

Geist, Michael (2010) "The Trouble with the Anti-Counterfeiting Trade Agreement (ACTA)." *SAIS Review* 30 (2).

Goldsmith, J., and Wu, T. (2006) *Who Controls the Internet? Illusions of a Borderless World*. Oxford: Oxford University Press.

Google Transparency Report (2014). http://www.google.co.uk/transparencyreport/.

Greenwald, Glenn (2015) "With Power of Social Media Growing, Police Now Monitoring and Criminalizing Online Speech." *The Intercept*, 6 January 2015. https://firstlook.org/theintercept/2015/01/06/police-increasingly-monitoring-criminalizing-online-speech/.

Guardian, The (2011) "Facebook Riot Calls Earn Men Four-Year Jail Terms Amid Sentencing Outcry." 16 August 2011. http://www.guardian.co.uk/uk/2011/aug/16/facebook-riot-calls-men-jailed.

——— (2015a) "Facebook and Twitter Have Social Responsibility to Help Fight Terrorism, Says Cameron." 16 January 2015. http://www.theguardian.com/world/2015/jan/16/cameron-interrupt-terrorists-cybersecurity-cyberattack-threat.

——— (2015b) "The NSA Files." http://www.theguardian.com/us-news/the-nsa-files.

Hamelink, C. (1994) *The Politics of World Communication: A Human Rights Perspective*. London: Sage.

Hannigan, Robert (2014) "The Web Is a Terrorist's Command-and-Control Network of Choice." *Financial Times*, 3 November 2014. http://www.ft.com/cms/s/2/c89b6c58-6342-11e4-8a63-00144feabdc0.html#axzz3TywRsOQ2.

Held, D., and McGrew, A. C. (2003) "The Great Globalization Debate." In David Held and Anthony G. McGrew, eds., *The Global Transformations Reader*, 1–50. Cambridge: Polity Press.

Hintz, A. (2014) "Independent Media Center." In Harvey, K. ed., *Encyclopedia of Social Media and Politics*, 653–54. Thousand Oaks, CA: Sage.

——— (2015, forthcoming) "Policy Hacking: Citizen-Based Policymaking and Media Reform." In D. Freedman and R. McChesney, eds., *Strategies for Media Reform: International Perspectives*. New York: Fordham University Press.

Hintz, A., and Milan, S. (2009) "At the Margins of Internet Governance: Grassroots Tech Groups and Communication Policy." *International Journal of Media & Cultural Politics* 5 (1): 23–38.

——— (2011) "User Rights for the Internet Age: Communications Policy According to Netizens." In R. Mansell and M. Raboy, eds., *The Handbook of Global Media and Communication Policy*, 230–41. Oxford: Wiley-Blackwell.

——— (2013) "Networked Collective Action and the Institutionalised Policy Debate: Bringing Cyberactivism to the Policy Arena?" *Policy & Internet* 5 (1): 7–26.

Hofheinz, A. (2011) "Nextopia? Beyond Revolution 2.0." *International Journal of Communication* 5 (2011). http://ijoc.org/ojs/index.php/ijoc/article/view/1186.

Howard, P. N., Agarwal, S. D. and Hussain M. M. (2011) "When Do States Disconnect Their Digital Networks? Regime Responses to the Political Use of Social Media." *The Communication Review* 14 (3): 216–32.

Jenkins, H. (2008) *Convergence Culture: Where Old and New Media Collide*. New York: New York University Press.

Johnson, D. R., and Post, D. (1996) "Law and Borders: The Rise of Law in Cyberspace." *Stanford Law Review* 48 (5): 1367–402.

Kahn, R. E. (2004) "Working Code and Rough Consensus: The Internet as Social Evolution." In D. MacLean, ed., *Internet Governance: A Grand Collaboration*, 16–21. New York: United Nations ICT Task Force.

Khamis, S., and Vaughn, K. (2011) "Cyberactivism in the Egyptian Revolution: How Civic Engagement and Citizen Journalism Tilted the Balance." *Arab Media & Society* (13).

Keck, M. E., and Sikkink, K. (1998) *Activists Beyond Borders. Advocacy Networks in International Politics*. Ithaca, NY: Cornell University Press.

Klotz, R. J. (2004) *The Politics of Internet Communication.* Lanham, MD: Rowman & Littlefield.

Kreimer, S.F. (2006) "Censorship by Proxy: The First Amendment, Internet Intermediaries, and the Problem of the Weakest Link." *University of Pennsylvania Law Review* 155 (11).

Leistert, O. and Rohle, T. (2011) Identifizieren, Verbinden, Verkaufen. Einleitendes zur Maschine Facebook, ihren Konsequenzen und den Beiträgen in diesem Band." In O. Leistert and T. Rohle, eds., *Generation Facebook: Über das Leben im Social Net*, 7–30. Bielefeld: transcript.

Lessig, L. (1999) *Code and other Laws of Cyberspace.* New York: Basic Books.
——— (2008) *Remix: Making Art and Commerce Thrive in the Hybrid Economy.* London: Bloomsbury.

Loeblich, M., and Musiani, F. (2014) "Net Neutrality and Communication Research: The Implications of Internet Infrastructure for the Public Sphere." In E. L. Cohen, ed., *Communication Yearbook 38*, 536–65. London: Routledge.

Lyon, D. (2007) "Surveillance, Power, and Everyday Life." In R. Mansell, C. Anthi Avgerou, D. Quah and R. Silverstone, eds., *The Oxford Handbook of Information and Communication Technologies*, 449-472. Oxford/New York: Oxford University Press.
——— (2014) "Surveillance, Snowden, and Big Data: Capacities, Consequences, Critique." *Big Data & Society* (July–December 2014): 1–13.

Marquis-Boire, M., et al. (2013) *For Their Eyes Only: The Commercialisation of Digital Spying,* Toronto: The Citizen Lab. https://citizenlab.org/storage/finfisher/final/fortheireyesonly.pdf.

May, C. (2009) 'Globalizing the Logic of Openness: Open Source Software and the Global Governance of Intellectual Property." In A. Chadwick and P. Howard, eds., *The Routledge Handbook of Internet Politics*, 364–75. London: Routledge.

McIntyre, T. J. (2008) "Data Retention in Ireland: Privacy, Policy and Proportionality." *Computer Law & Security Report* 24 (4): 326–34.

Milan, S. (2013) *Social Movements and their Technologies: Wiring Social Change.* Basingstoke: Palgrave MacMillan.

Morozov, E. (2011) *The Net Delusion: The Dark Side of Internet Freedom.* New York: Public Affairs.

Mueller, M. (2010) *Networks and States: The Global Politics of Internet Governance.* Cambridge: MIT Press.

Norton, B. (2014) "Fascist Facebook? The Social Network Giant's Double Standards." *Counterpunch*, 10–12 January 2014.http://www.counterpunch.org/2014/01/10/fascist-facebook/.

Open Net Initiative (2012) "Global Internet Filtering in 2012 at a Glance." Blog post, 3 April 2012.http://opennet.net/blog/2012/04/global-internet-filtering-2012-glance.

Patelis, K. (2013) "Political Economy and Monopoly Abstractions: What Social Media Demand." In G. Lovink and M. Rasch, eds., *Unlike Us Reader: Social Media Monopolies and Their Alternatives*, 117–26. Amsterdam: Institute of Network Cultures.

PEN (2013) *Chilling Effects: NSA Surveillance Drives U.S. Writers to Self-Censor.* New York: PEN American Center. http://www.pen.org/sites/default/files/Chilling%20Effects_PEN%20American.pdf.

Raboy, M. (2002) *Global Media Policy in the New Millennium.* Luton: University of Luton Press.

Raboy, M., and Padovani, C. (2010) "Mapping Global Media Policy: Concepts, Frameworks, Methods." Available at http://www.globalmediapolicy.net.

Robbins, M. (2013) "Cameron's Internet Filter Goes Far Beyond Porn—And That Was Always the Plan." *New Statesman,* 23 December 2013. http://www.newstatesman.com/politics/2013/12/camerons-internet-filter-goes-far-beyond-porn-and-was-always-plan.

Rusbridger, A. (2013) "David Miranda, Schedule 7, and the Danger That All Reporters Now Face." *The Guardian,* 19 August 2013. http://www.theguardian.com/commentisfree/2013/aug/19/david-miranda-schedule7-danger-reporters.

Sifry, Micah (2014) "Facebook Wants You to Vote on Tuesday. Here's How It Messed with Your Feed in 2012." *Mother Jones,* 31 October 2014. http://www.motherjones.com/politics/2014/10/can-voting-facebook-button-improve-voter-turnout.

Trottier, D., and Lyon, D. (2012) "Key Features of Social Media Surveillance." In C. Fuchs, K. Boersma, A. Albrechtslund and M. Sandoval, eds., *Internet and Surveillance: The Challenges of Web 2.0 and Social Media,* 89–105. Abingdon: Routledge.

UN General Assembly (2013) Report of the Special Rapporteur on the Promotion and Protection of the Right to Freedom of Expression. Frank La Rue, 17 April 2013. http://www.ohchr.org/Documents/HRBodies/HRCouncil/RegularSession/Session23/A.HRC.23.40_EN.pdf.

Villeneuve, N. (2006) "The Filtering Matrix: Integrated Mechanisms of Information Control and the Demarcation of Borders in Cyberspace." *First Monday* 11 (1–2). http://firstmonday.org/htbin/cgiwrap/bin/ojs/index.php/fm/article/view/1307/1227.

———— (2012) "Fake Skype Encryption Software Cloaks DarkComet Trojan." *Trend Micro Malware Blog,* 20 April 2012. http://blog.trendmicro.com/fake-skype-encryption-software-cloaks-darkcomet-trojan/.

Watson, Steve (2015) "Google Moving to Shut Down Alternative Media by Ranking Sites on 'Facts' Rather than Popularity." *Global Research,* 2 March 2015. http://www.globalresearch.ca/google-moving-to-shut-down-alternative-media-by-ranking-sites-on-facts-rather-than-popularity/5434328.

Webster, S. C. (2011) "Vodaphone Confirms Role in Egypt's Cellular, Internet Blackout." *The Raw Story,* 28 January 2011.http://www.rawstory.com/rs/2011/01/28/vodafone-confirms-role-egypts-cellular-internet-blackout/.

Chapter Seven

Social Media Protest in Context

*Surveillance, Information Management
and Neoliberal Governance in Canada*

Joanna Redden

This chapter argues that understanding current and future uses of social media platforms for protest and campaigning requires placing these uses within
their wider communication ecology. Specifically, I focus on the Canadian
context to raise concerns about how political repression, conventional surveillance practices, the ubiquity and increasing uses of big data driven surveillance practices and the political management of information are being
used in ways to discourage dissent and protest participation. Emerging
government uses of surveillance and information management are central to
understanding contemporary protest communication ecologies (Altheide
1995), and evolving governmental processes to manage and control dissent.
Furthermore, I argue that greater understanding of the emerging political
practices to monitor and control people and information can help us better
understand and respond to the harsher, intensified mode of neoliberal
governance which has emerged since the financial crisis of 2007–2008 (Mirowski 2013; Peck 2010; Hall, Massey, and Ruskin 2013).

In the wake of the financial crisis it has become increasingly obvious, and
accepted by many, that neoliberal capitalism does not work for most people:
it is prone to crises (Harvey 2010), and is leading to increasing poverty and
inequality (Navarro 2007; Ruckert and Labonté 2014; Jacobs and Myers
2014). Support for capitalism in Canada, and globally, has declined since the
crisis (Environics Institute 2012; Pew Research Center 2012). In the wake of
these findings, and the increasing opposition to neoliberalism, we are learning more about what I contend are related practices; the increasing state

127

efforts to control and manage people and information. The Snowden leaks have drawn considerable attention to how governments are using new technologies to monitor their own populations (Greenwald 2014). In addition, there are increasing accounts of government and corporate monitoring of activists offline and online as well as their mobile communications to destabilize, silence and prevent protest (Juris 2005; Lübbers 2012; Leistert 2013; Uldham 2014; ACLU 2013). The use of social media monitoring by the state as an attempt to watch and manage protestors is part of a much longer, and important, history of political repression. In combination with the attempts to manage people, there are also increasing state efforts to control and limit the type of information that is available to those who might challenge the status quo.

In this chapter I detail and bring together these related practices, in the Canadian context, to argue that contemporary surveillance and information management are essential to understanding: (1) how protest activities are changing, and will change, as groups and individuals develop strategies to escape surveillance, and conduct and share research and information, and (2) the emerging, and harsher, forms of neoliberal governance that we must contend with. The chapter is organized in four sections. First, I outline the theoretical framework informing this discussion. I draw upon discussions of neoliberal governance and rationality as outlined by Foucault (2008), Brown (2015, 2005), Couldry (2010), and Renzi and Elmer (2013) to contextualize contemporary political practices. Second, my research approach and sources are detailed. Third, an historical overview of state efforts to monitor and contain activists is provided as the groundwork for section 4, which raises questions about the contemporary surveillance of activists. Section 4 reads these surveillance practices as part of a lengthier and troubling history of the political repression of dissent in Canada. An emerging problem relating to political repression in Canada is the managing, and in some cases the elimination, of sources of information which activists use to challenge neoliberal programmes and policies.

NEOLIBERAL GOVERNANCE AND RATIONALITY

This work begins from the position that neoliberalism is a political, economic and social project (Peck 2010; Mirowski and Plehwe 2009). But, as argued by Foucault, the neoliberal project is about more than changing policies and regulations. It is also a project which aims to change the way we think; so that neoliberalism becomes a method of thought, 'a grid of economic and sociological analysis' (Foucault 2008, 218). The goal is for the rationalities of the market, for market-based thinking, to be extended to all facets of life (Couldry 2010; Brown 2015, 2005). Here history is important, as from the outset, neoliberals recognized that the extension of market values to all spheres of life and the transformation of people into *homo oeconomicus* (self-entrepreneurs) is not natural and must be constructed and organized by law and political institutions, and requires political interventions and force (Brown 2005, 41). Significantly, in Foucault's account, neoliberalism is a deliberate approach to political practice and must be viewed as more than a series of governmental techniques. As argued by Lemke (2002, 58), 'Foucault's discussion of neoliberal governmentality shows that the so-called retreat of the state is in fact a prolongation of government: neoliberalism is not the end but a transformation of politics that restructures the power relations in society.' Power is about guidance and 'structuring the possible field of actions of others' (Lemke 2002, 53). In the neoliberal view, the role of the state is to ensure market criteria are applied in as many areas of social, economic and cultural life as possible (Klassen 2009).

In practice, neoliberalism is exercised differently in various contexts as it is shaped and influenced by adaptations on the ground and is forced to respond to its own contradictions, 'botched efforts' and the considerable opposition generated as it is introduced (Peck 2010). However, Mirowski argues that there are a number of central tenets that neoliberals generally support. The six that are important in relation to this discussion are: (1) the need for political effort and organization to ensure the conditions for neoliberal governance; (2) the 'reformation of society by subordinating it to the market,' (3) that neoliberal market society must be promoted and treated as if it is the natural state of mankind; (4) that the shape and functions of the state must be redefined in ways that promote marketization and diminish collective action through, for example, audit devices, privatization and reregulation to inhibit change; (5) the promotion of an economic theory of democracy and citizen as consumer and (6) that neoliberal policies lead to an expansion of prisons and criminalization (Mirowski 2013, 53–66).

A great deal of strategizing and effort was required to move this set of ideas from the margins of political and economic life in the early twentieth century to its current position as dominant political paradigm. Neoliberal ascendance required battling and undermining the postwar consensus about the need for organized capitalism, particularly given the widespread view that markets were prone to crises following the market crash of 1929 and the widespread experiences of poverty which followed. The efforts of corporate leaders, public relations professionals, economists and politicians to advance neoliberalism have been carefully detailed elsewhere (Miller and Dinan 2008; Harvey 2007). In the end, it took these efforts and the crises of the 1970s for neoliberalism to take root (Couldry 2010, 4).

I provide this overview as necessary background because from here on in I argue that neoliberal governance still requires a great deal of political intervention. Neoliberal governance is productive in the efforts made to produce particular kinds of behaviours and practices; for example, to encourage people to become entrepreneurs of themselves and to promote the expansion of markets into new areas of social life. But, neoliberal governance is restrictive in the ways effort is made to limit, manage and control dissent. Of course political attempts to control and manage dissent are not new. Opposition to the inequality, exploitive practices and oppression caused by pursuits of profit and expansion at all costs are 'as old as capitalism itself' (Boltanski and Chiapello 2005, 36), as are the political attempts to manage this opposition. The aim of this chapter is not to argue that the monitoring and management of dissent are new, but rather to trace the trajectory of the surveillance and management of dissent in order to draw attention to the significance of contemporary surveillance practices. I provide a brief history of the use of surveillance practices to control and manage dissent in North America, with a focus on Canada. I argue that surveillance practices are increasingly technologies of neoliberal capitalist governance. An identification of political efforts to manage and silence dissent raise significant questions about the state of contemporary democracy in Canada. Contrary to the normative democratic ideal of the state as neutral and in service to the public, the account detailed below presents an active state heavily invested in managing and preventing opposition (Whitaker, Kealey and Parnaby 2012). Couldry, citing Ranciere, draws attention to contemporary political practices of 'hollowing out,' of the 'compulsion to get rid of people and politics,' and concludes that neoliberal democracy is an oxymoron (Couldry 2010, 25).

Method

In this chapter I explore a variety of material in order to detail contemporary practices of governance that I argue are essential to understanding the present and future activist uses of social media. I draw upon historical accounts and government documents to provide an overview of the extent of government surveillance and infiltration of activist organizations throughout the last century. This history has been chronicled by Canadian historians, but can also be gleaned from the now published Royal Canadian Mounted Police Security Bulletins spanning 1919–1945 (Kealey and Whitaker 1993); further a government inquiry into RCMP conduct provides additional material (McDonald 1981). Insight into contemporary protest policing is gained through intelligence reports as detailed by Monaghan and Walby (2012a, 2012b), who received these reports through access to information requests. Also drawn upon are published reports and letters by the Office of the Privacy Commissioner of Canada (OPC), and Government of Canada protest reports released to the House of Commons in 2014. In addition, I use news accounts of documents leaked by Edward Snowden (now available directly through the Snowden archive: https://cjfe.org/snowden), as well as documents produced by nonprofit advocates and organizations, and surveys. In combination, these documents are used to place contemporary practices of political repression in historical context. These documents, when combined, also provide us with a fuller image of what the emerging, and intensified, form of neoliberal governance looks like. Furthermore, these documents provide an indication of the democratic rights being threatened and the effort being extended to silence and prevent protest.

MANAGING DISSENT: THE IMPORTANCE OF HISTORY

Attempts to monitor and control dissent are not new, and contemporary surveillance practices are part of a long history of state efforts to manage opposition. What is new is the sheer size, scope and ubiquity of contemporary data surveillance as a result of technological developments. Of concern is how data surveillance may be used to reinforce the neoliberal system in the face of widespread opposition. There have been ongoing attempts, across a variety of disciplines, to document state and private efforts to prevent, control and constrain protest. These practices are commonly referred to as political repression (Earl 2011), and the present efforts to research and uncover state and corporate monitoring of social media for the purposes of political repression must be viewed as part of this longer political project. Much of the work detailing political repression and its effects has focused on the United States and Europe. A history of these practices is beyond the scope of this chapter, but a very brief history of some American practices is provided given its proximity to Canada. In the United States, some of the most widely known examples of state efforts to monitor, manage and prevent protest include FBI and police domestic surveillance practices targeting the trade union movement beginning in the early twentieth century. In the 1950s, 1960s and 1970s, efforts focused on those identified as communists and/or 'subversive', such as civil rights group members, including Dr. Martin Luther King, Jr., anti-Vietnam War protestors and feminist activists and organizations (Murray and Wunsch 2002; Cunningham 2004; Irons 2006; Rosen 2000; McKnight 1998). It is important to underline that many of the groups and individuals under surveillance and labelled as 'subversive' were advocating social and political changes that most of us now agree were right, justified and necessary, such as the end of gender and racist segregation and discrimination. The now infamous tactics of the FBI through its Counterintelligence Program (COINTELPRO) included infiltration, spying, blackmail and threats to various group members (Johnson 2004; US Congress 1976).

In Canada, government domestic spying on individuals can be traced back to Confederation (Whitaker et al. 2012). The origins of Canada's secret service has been dated as early as the 1860s, as the government of the time targeted Irish republicans and South Asian radicals who promoted independence from British rule for surveillance (Kealey and Parnaby 2003). Surveillance and monitoring continued into the twentieth century as secret agents were hired to monitor those opposed to the status quo: for example, organizers of coal strikes in 1915, those vocally opposed to conscription in 1916, and those participating in antiwar and prolabour activities in this early period (Kealey 1992). Kealey notes that Canada's response to the 'Red Scare' was to ban various socialist, ethnic and labour publications and organizations (1992). Early reports and memos suggest the use of agent provocateurs as early as 1918, and the employment of secret agents to watch perceived Bolshevik and socialist sympathizers. The goal was to prevent 'the efforts of misguided persons to subvert and undermine the settled Government of Canada' (Kealy 1992). These agents were to 'become fully acquainted with all labour and other organizations in their respective districts' (as quoted in Kealey 1992). Reminiscent of contemporary surveillance, these secret agents were also to survey radical pamphlets and publications, to record questionable public speeches and to watch street meetings (Kealy 1992).

An average of 427 Canadians per year had files created on them between 1919 and 1929 (Kealey 1992). The list of those surveyed includes women, clergy, doctors, military, elected officials, and union members. Police attempts to 'sabotage and suppress' left-wing dissent are documented in police reports of the period. Tactics included raids, harassment, the interception of mail, arrests and providing misleading information to the public (Kealey 1992; Whitaker, Kealey and Parnaby 2012; Lonardo 1995). RCMP Intelligence Section reports spanning the first half of the twentieth century demonstrate the extent of government-sponsored surveillance of those challenging political and economic power. As detailed by Earle (2001), the activities deemed 'subversive' were activities condemning capitalism, trade union activity such as strikes and demonstrations by the unemployed. Earle argues that these activities were labelled 'subversive' because they might disrupt business through losses to production and profit, or challenge those holding political power (Earle 2001, 141).

In this way, as argued by Hewitt and Sethna (2012), subversion is used in the twentieth century as a classification to justify state monitoring of domestic groups and individuals. Grace and Leys (1989, 62) note that the framing of opposition as subversive is used to delegitimize protestors (who are acting lawfully) and legitimize the state actors who are acting against them. A significant element of the identification of domestic threats is labelling them as subversive individuals and denying the 'relevance of social and economic factors as the cause of unrest' (Donner 1992, 76). In Canada, the list of groups labelled as subversive is long. For example, women's liberation groups in the 1960s were labelled as subversive. The RCMP Security Service spied on women's liberation groups and viewed these groups as a threat because it was thought they were connected to other groups on the left like the Trotskyists (Hewitt and Sethna 2012).

By 1977, as detailed by Whitaker, Kealey and Parnaby (2012), the RCMP had a name index with 1.3 million entries and eight hundred thousand files on individuals. According to the 1971 census, the population of Canada at that time was 21,568,000. This means that information was being kept on more than one out of every twenty-seven Canadians (Whitaker, Kealey and Parnaby 2012, 546). They argue that while state surveillance has targeted other groups such as the Ku Klux Klan and terrorist organizations, a history of secret service policing in Canada shows that political policing for more than a century in Canada has demonstrated an 'ideological bias against the left'.

> There is a kind of secret history of conservatism to be deciphered from the records of the security service. What we learn from this secret history is that the established order and the elites that defend it have not contented them-selves with arguing their case in Parliament and in the court of public opinion, but have resorted to secret police spies, undercover agents, agents provoca-teurs, and occasional dirty tricks. We also learn that an interest in legitimately worrisome peoples and organizations often provides the political cover neces-sary for advancing other objectives, which cannot be attained as quickly, or at all, by democratic means. (Whitaker, Kealey and Parnaby 2012, 11).

As also noted by Whitaker, Kealey and Parnaby (2012, 12), 'one genera-tion's subversion is another generation's conventional wisdom', and their history of surveillance in Canada is an apt response to those who argue that surveillance is not a concern because they are not doing anything wrong. History demonstrates that a citizen may become a target of surveillance the minute he or she begins challenging dominant economic, social or political norms and values. Furthermore, this history also challenges the normative ideal of the democratic state as neutral and influenced by 'the court of public opinion' (Whitaker, Kealey and Parnaby 2012, 11). What this history demon-strates are the lengths to which the authorities will go to silence, manage and prevent protest. It is in this context that we must consider how new techno-logical capabilities and the opportunities provided for ubiquitous surveillance are influencing the communication ecologies of contemporary protest.

MANAGING DISSENT: CONTEMPORARY ACCOUNTS

We know about the history of political repression in Canada largely through the meticulous collection of data via access to information requests. Similar-ly, we are learning more about the political repression of contemporary protest activities through the same access to information request processes.

Monaghan and Walby's (2012a) collection of threat assessment reports from 2005 to 2010 shows troubling trends in the production of threat categories after 9/11 which target those engaged in democratic protest for surveillance and management. They note the expansion of threat categories to include one entitled 'Multi-Issue Extremism'. Groups in this category are described as activist groups, indigenous groups, environmentalists and others who are publicly critical of government policy. They raise concerns about how government agencies have blurred threat categories and expanded the purview of security intelligence agencies so that terrorism, extremism and activism are now categorized and captured into 'an aggregate threat matrix.' The reports link terrorist entities with other 'ideologically motivated' groups. Furthermore, in the new framework for antiterror policing 'subversive and simply suspicious conduct is lumped under the categories of terrorism and extremism' (Monaghan and Walby 2012a, 146). Given what we know about how activists have been monitored and controlled in the past, we need to be concerned about how these new threat categories may enable interference with those engaged in political dissent.

Of concern is how the blurring of threats in security and policing discourse and practices may be used to justify domestic spying on social movements and to also criminalize protest (Monaghan and Walby 2012a, 142; Renzi and Elmer 2013). Similar to the findings of Whitaker, Kealey and Parnaby (2012), these more recent reports demonstrate the relationship between the Canadian security establishment and corporate interests as authorities blur the protection of corporate property with national security. Monaghan and Walby note that the focus of the new security intelligence hub is 'the global justice movement as a force confronting global capitalism.' These more recent security reports demonstrate that it is the perceived threat to capital from these new social movements, described as a 'combination of eco, indigenous and anarchist movements,' which is the major concern of Canada's security establishment (Monaghan and Walby 2012a, 146). In 2014, in response to opposition requests, the Government of Canada tabled reports in Parliament which show that about eight hundred public demonstrations and events were monitored by government agents and law enforcement agencies between 2006 and 2014. These reports demonstrate the continued monitoring and surveillance of protest activities. They were collected by the Government Operations Centre, which is responsible for responding to emergencies. While some of these reports focused on international protests, most of them focused on events in Canada, 'especially First Nations protests and environmental activism' (Boutilier 2014). We also learned in 2014, through a leaked email, that the federal government is trying to monitor all 'known demonstrations' in Canada (Pugliese 2014). The email was sent by the Government Operations Centre to all federal departments in June 2014. We do not know what kind of information is being collected and what reports of these events look like. Government representatives argue that this monitoring is to ensure public safety. But, as previously detailed, history demonstrates that surveillance of protest has been used to aid in managing, manipulating and limiting future protest activities. At the very minimum, this history demonstrates a need for greater transparency and accountability of government and police surveillance practices concerning protestors.

The contemporary surveillance of social movements and advocacy practices must be viewed within the wider context of protest policing and aggressive attempts to neutralize and preempt resistance (Renzi and Elmer 2013; Elmer and Opel 2008). The aim of this preemption it has been argued is to 'disable and displace rigorous political and democratic debate' (Elmer and Opel 2008, 74–75). Canada's adoption of the Miami model of preemptive policing, designed to control and contain protest, was most evident during the policing of the G20 protests in Toronto in 2010 (see also Elmer in this volume). The policing and security of the G20 Summit was 'the largest security operation in Canadian history' (Milberry and Clement 2014, 128). There was an initial budget of $1 billion to fund things like the installation of new video-surveillance cameras, security fencing and twenty thousand police, military and private security personnel (Milberry and Clement 2014, 128; Chase 2010). In addition, the police turned to facial recognition techniques and internet monitoring. Access to information requests reveals that police set up an internet-monitoring unit to monitor 'all open source internet links related to the G8/G20 summits' (Milberry and Clement 2014, 136), and also that authorities 'developed maps of activists' social networks and drew inferences about their behaviour based on whom they followed and were followed by on Twitter, the events they said they would attend, and other personal information disclosed on social media' (Bennett et al. 2014). The federal government monitored internet chatter and criticism, Twitter accounts, YouTube and photo sites, and produced reports measuring public sentiment about aspects of the G20 (Milberry and Clement 2014, 136). Undercover police officers infiltrated a number of groups leading to the preemptive arrest of seventeen people. Charges were later dropped against eleven of these people, with the remaining six pleading guilty to minor charges. As Bennett et al. (2014) note, it is significant that these activists were excluded from participating in democratic protests that were mostly peaceful. More recent examples of social media monitoring of protestors include the Department of Aboriginal Affairs and Northern Development's weekly situational awareness reports of Idle No More activities in 2012 and 2013. Idle No More is a movement to raise awareness of First Nations issues, build allies and protect the environment. The reports contain information about indigenous activists' demonstrations and events obtained from a range of sources including social media (Davis 2013).

Government uses of new technologies to monitor Canadians, including social media monitoring more generally, has been in the news in recent years. While social media monitoring is being used to monitor public opinion and responses to various government practices and initiatives, it is also being used to monitor specific people and groups. However, we don't know the extent to which social media monitoring is being used to watch protestors in Canada. There are examples suggesting such practices. In 2012–2013, the OPC responded to a complaint by First Nations activist Cindy Blackstock that two federal departments had contravened the Privacy Act by collecting her personal information. The OPC found that departments had been monitoring social media sites, including Blackstock's personal Facebook page. The OPC concluded that 'the public availability of personal information on the internet' does not 'render personal information non-personal' (OPC 2013).

In 2014, the OPC issued a special report to government in response to concerns about increasing government surveillance of social media. In February of 2014, then Privacy Commissioner Chantal Bernier wrote a letter to Treasury Board President, Tony Clement, noting that 'we are seeing evidence that personal information is being collected by government institutions from social media sites without regard for accuracy, currency, and accountability.' The OPC called for the Treasury Board to develop specific guidelines for the 'collection, use and dissemination' of the information gathered through social media sites and other online sources. The OPC revealed that government agencies had asked nine telecom and social media companies for user data 1.2 million times in 2011 (Evans 2014). Given the history of monitoring political dissent in Canada, the monitoring of activists' social media in relation to the G20 protests in 2010, the effort being put into monitoring protests across the country, the widespread and increasing surveillance practices of spy agencies as well as the move within police departments across the country toward predictive policing, it is fair to assume that activists' social media sites are being monitored. There is need for more empirical research in this area.

A series of documents released by Snowden demonstrate the capabilities of government authorities and the Communications Security Establishment of Canada (CSEC) to monitor communications and that Canadians are being monitored. These documents raise significant questions and concerns about the extent of media surveillance, the nature and purpose of this surveillance and how it might be used to preempt and manage dissent. For instance, CSEC used a Canadian airport's Wi-Fi service to track the wireless devices of thousands of airline passengers for days after they left the terminal. It appears this was a trial run of a new software-tracking programme developed by CSEC and the NSA (Weston, Greenwald and Gallagher 2014). Other documents released by Snowden demonstrate the extent to which CSEC shares information with the NSA in the United States and other Five Eyes agencies (Greenwald 2014), and also that CSEC tracks millions of downloads around the world daily (Hildebrandt, Pereira and Seglins 2015). At the time of writing, March 2015, the Government of Canada is attempting to increase the surveillance, detention and intervention powers of intelligence agencies and the police. Bill C-51, the Anti-Terrorism Act, has passed second reading and, despite national protest, appears set to pass third reading and be made into law given the governing Conservative Party's majority position within Canada's House of Commons. Bill C-51 is at present opposed by the Canadian Privacy Commissioner, former prime ministers, former CSIS officials, politicians from all parties, national news organizations and a long list of civil society and social justice organizations. The Bill is widely criticized as too broad and vague in language. In the Bill threats can be any 'interference' with the Government's ability in relation to diplomatic relations, critical infrastructure and economic stability. Those opposing the Bill worry it will be used to increase the surveillance and criminalization of activists, particularly those involved in political, First Nations and environmental activism.

Canada's privacy commissioner, who was blocked from participating in the government committee hearings on the bill, warns that the bill provides 'excessive' and 'unprecedented' powers to federal agencies to monitor and profile all Canadians. 'Bill C-51 opens the door to collecting, analysing and potentially keeping forever the personal information of all Canadians in order to find the virtual needle in the haystack. To my mind, that goes too far' (Therrien 2015b).

The Act would enable government to collect and analyse massive amounts of information through the use of data analytics as an attempt to spot trends, predict behaviours and make connections. Therrien argues this raises serious privacy concerns given how much sensitive information the Canadian government has about Canadians, and the extent to which the Act would enable federal agencies to share information about Canadians if deemed relevant (Therrien 2015a).

We know that Canadian activists, advocates and those who publicly oppose some political positions and policies are already feeling targeted. Those involved in generating information challenging neoliberal policies and rhetoric have lost valuable resources as key information bodies have been cut. Canadian activists and advocates who use social media to access and share information, organize and strategize are operating within this political climate. These cuts have mobilized some scientists, civil servants and activists in Canada to create a movement called the 'Death of Evidence'. Since 2006, some of the agencies and institutions which have been cut include: the Courts Challenges Program, the Canadian Council on International Co-operation, the Status of Women Canada, the National Council of Welfare, Statistics

Canada's Long Form Census and a wide range of environmental agencies including the Canadian Foundation of Climate and Atmospheric Science. Also, scientists, academics and bureaucrats are being systematically silenced. In a recent survey by the Public Service Alliance of Canada, 90 percent of scientists said they cannot speak freely (PIPSC 2013). Some of the charities who have publicly opposed government practices have been recently targeted by the Canada Revenue Agency (CRA) for a political activities audit, leading journalists and others to ask publicly if there is a connection (Beeby 2014; Broadbent Institute 2014). Critics argue that it is the 'data sources that enable us to hold on to a sense of belonging to an entity called society that are being eliminated' (Walton-Roberts et al. 2014), and furthermore, that we are witnessing a deliberate move from evidence-based policy making. The significance of this cannot be overstated. One of the most often cited advantages of social media for activists is that it makes it easy for people to access and share information. In this way the internet, and more recently social media sites, level the playing field by enabling activists to become informed and also increase public awareness about issues. The internet and social media sites also enable activists to share information quickly, and make it easier to strategize and organize based on the latest information. Eliminating the ideas, arguments and evidence activists use to justify action and inform others about the gravity of various situations 'hollows out' the potential for social media spaces to be used for protest-related activities. In most cases, activists simply do not have the kind of resources needed to produce the kind of evidence needed to justify changing current practices and policies, for example, environmental impact assessments, or income and inequality statistics.

CONCLUSION

More research is needed into how emerging practices of surveillance, control and management are limiting critique by 'hollowing out' democratic spaces, including social media spaces, of people and content. Those using social media platforms for protest and campaigning are operating within a larger communication ecology that is overdetermined by specific neoliberal political interventions. As argued by Foucault, if we want to understand contemporary power relations and the specific rationalities underlying these power dynamics, we should study resistance to it. This approach:

> [C]onsists of taking the forms of resistance against different forms of power as a starting point. To use another metaphor, it consists of using this resistance as a chemical catalyst so as to bring to light power relations, locate their position, and find out their point of application and the methods used. Rather than analysing power from the point of view of its internal rationality, it consists of

analysing power relations through the antagonism of strategies. (Foucault 1982, 780)

I think Foucault is right about this, and in the Canadian context we can learn a lot about the emerging practices of neoliberal governance by detailing the efforts by the Government of Canada to monitor and manage people and information in order to preempt and control dissent. Studying these interactions, these points of surveillance and contact brings to light the changing nature of power relations. What this analysis indicates is that power is being used to limit the kind of information available to the public, to limit the ability for people to organize and publicly express their views through protest, to hollow out public spaces so that alternative ways of thinking that counter neoliberal rationality are simply not present, to expand the power of authorities to monitor the public, to increase the ability for authorities to secretly watch what Canadians are saying to each other and to limit processes of accountability and oversight.

The simple point being raised is that if we want to understand how activists are using social media to protest we need to recognize that activists are aware of surveillance practices and acting based on their knowledge of government monitoring and interventions. A further argument put forward in this chapter is that the monitoring and managing of dissent, and the efforts to increase the abilities of authorities to monitor and manage people and information suggests a political elite that views information and dissent as a threat. I argue that surveillance practices are key in the neoliberal transformation of politics, in the political interventions and force required to maintain neoliberal extensions in the face of widespread contestation. Although there is a long history of surveillance and management of dissent in Canada, the failings of neoliberalism have expanded and entrenched the need for ever-expanding social control, a need that is facilitated by new technological capabilities and expanded powers of surveillance. Neoliberalism requires ignorance (Davies and McGoey 2012). Ignorance is required to undermine the ability of central planners who might wish to direct resources in ways that run counter to market goals, and to undermine those trying to challenge neoliberal policies and rhetoric. In this light, it becomes clear that controlling information, access to information and therefore the quality and nature of debate and political engagement is central to neoliberal governance, and surveillance practices are the means through which much of this control has historically been achieved. Given this, we need to pay attention to the surveillance abuses we already know about, to do more empirical research into emerging practices of surveillance and be very cautious and skeptical of attempts to increase the surveillance powers of authorities.

REFERENCES

Altheide, David L. 1995. *An Ecology of Information*. New York: Walter de Gruyter, Inc.

American Civil Liberties Union. 2013. "Spy Files: Spying on First Amendment Activity State-by-State." https://www.aclu.org/maps/spying-first-amendment-activity-state-state (accessed 20 February 2015).

Beeby, Dean. 2014. "Pen Canada Hit with Political-Activities Audit by Canada Revenue Agency." *Globe and Mail*, 21 July. http://www.theglobeandmail.com/news/politics/pen-canada-hit-with-political-activities-audit-by-canada-revenue-agency/article19699773/ (accessed 15 March 2015).

Bennett, Colin J., Haggerty, Kevin D., Lyon, David and Steeves, Valerie. 2014. *Transparent Lives: Surveillance in Canada*. Edmonton: Athabasca University Press.

Boltanski, Luc, and Chiapello, Eve. 2005. *The New Spirit of Capitalism*. New York: Verso.

Boutilier, Alex. 2014. "Ottawa Admits to Tracking Hundreds of Protests." *Toronto Star*, 18 September. http://www.thestar.com/news/canada/2014/09/18/ottawa_admits_to_tracking_hundreds_of_protests.html (accessed 10 February 2015).

Broadbent Institute. 2014. "Stephen Harper's CRA: Selective Audits, 'Political' Activity, and Right-Leaning Charities." https://www.broadbentinstitute.ca/en/issue/stephen-harpers-cra-selective-audits-political-activity-and-right-leaning-charities (accessed 4 March 2015).

Brown, Wendy. 2005. "Neoliberalism and the End of Liberal Democracy." *Edgework: Critical Essays on Knowledge and Politics*. Princeton, NJ: Princeton University Press.

———. 2015. *Undoing the Demos: Neoliberalism's Stealth Revolution*. Cambridge, MA: Zone Books.

Chase, Steven. 2010. "G8/G20 Security Bill to Approach $1 Billion." *Globe and Mail*, 25 May. http://www.theglobeandmail.com/news/world/g8g20-security-bill-to-approach-1-billion/article1211436/ (accessed 1 March 2015).

Couldry, Nick. 2010. *Why Voice Matters: Culture and Politics after Neoliberalism*. London: Sage.

Cunningham, David. 2004. *There's Something Happening Here: The New Left, The Klan, and FBI Counterintelligence*. Los Angeles: University of California Press.

Davies, William, and McGoey, Linsey. 2012. "Rationalities of Ignorance: On Financial Crisis and the Ambivalence of Neo-Liberal Epistemology." *Economy and Society* 41 (1): 64–83.

Davis, Stephen Spencer. 2013. "Canada's Spy Agency Kept Close Watch on Rapidly Growing First Nations Protest Movement: Documents." *National Post*, 11 August. http://news.nationalpost.com/2013/08/11/canadas-spy-agency-kept-close-watch-on-rapidly-growing-first-nations-protest-movement-documents/ (accessed 3 March 2015).

Donner, Frank. 1992. *Protectors of Privilege: Red Squads and Police Repression in Urban America*. Berkeley: University of California Press.

Earl, Jennifer. 2011. "Political Repression: Iron Fists, Velvet Gloves, and Diffuse Control." *Annual Review of Sociology* 37:261–84.

Earle, Michael. 2001. "The Mounties and the Red Menace." *Acadiensis* 30 (2): 141–48. http://journals.hil.unb.ca/index.php/Acadiensis/article/view/10756/11503 (accessed 9 February 2015).

Elmer, Greg, and Opel, Andy. 2008. *Preempting Dissent: The Politics of an Inevitable Future*. Winnipeg: Arbeiter Ring Publishing.

Environics Institute. 2012. Focus Canada 2012. http://www.environicsinstitute.org/institute-projects/current-projects/focus-canada (accessed 2 September 2013).

Evans, Pete. 2014. "Chantal Bernier Says Ottawa Snooping on Social Media." CBC.ca, 8 May. http://www.cbc.ca/news/business/chantal-bernier-says-ottawa-snooping-on-social media-1.2635998 (accessed 3 March 2015).

Foucault, Michel. 2008. *The Birth of Biopolitics: Lectures at the College de France 1978–1979*. New York: Palgrave Macmillan.

———. 1982. "The Subject and Power." *Critical Inquiry* 8 (4): 777–95.

Government of Canada. 2014. Order of the House of Commons. Protest Reports Collected by Government Operations Centre. Mr. Brison. 5 June 2014. http://www.scribd.com/doc/

240110830/Protest-Reports-collected-by-Government-Operations-Centre (accessed 10 January 2015).

Grace, Elizabeth, and Leys, Colin. 1989. "The Concept of Subversion and Its Implications." *Dissent and the State*, 62–85. C. E. S. Franks, ed. Oxford: Oxford University Press.

Greenwald, Glen. 2014. *No Place to Hide: Edward Snowden, the NSA, and the U.S. Surveillance State*. New York: Metropolitan.

Hall, Stuart, Massey, Doreen and Ruskin, Michael. 2013. *After Neoliberalism: The Kilburn Manifesto*. Soundings. http://www.lwbooks.co.uk/journals/soundings/manifesto.html (accessed 10 June 2014).

Harvey, D. 2007. "Neoliberalism as Creative Destruction." *The Annals of the American Academy of Political and Social Science* 610 (1): 21–44.

Harvey, David. 2010. *The Enigma of Capital and the Crises of Capitalism*. Oxford: Oxford University Press.

Hewitt, Steve, and Sethna, Christabelle. 2012. "Sex Spying: The RCMP Framing of English-Canadian Women's Liberation Groups during the Cold War." *Debating Dissent: Canada and the Sixties*, 135. Lara Campbell, Dominique Clement and Gregory S. Kealey, eds. Toronto: University of Toronto Press.

Hildebrandt, Amber, Pereira, Michael and Seglins, Dave. 2015. "CSE Tracks Millions of Downloads Daily: Snowden Documents." CBC.ca, 27 January. http://www.cbc.ca/news/canada/cse-tracks-millions-of-downloads-daily-snowden-documents-1.2930120 (accessed 10 March 2015).

Irons, Jenny. 2006. "Who Rules the Social Control of Protest? Variability in the State-Countermovement Relationship." *Mobilization* 11 (2): 165–80.

Jacobs, David, and Myers, Lindsey. 2014. "Union Strength, Neoliberalism, and Inequality: Contingent Political Analyses of U.S. Income Differences Since 1950." *American Sociological Review*, 9 June. 1–23. http://asr.sagepub.com/content/ (accessed 1 September 2014).

Johnson, Loch K. 2004. "Congressional Supervision of America's Secret Agencies: The Experience and Legacy of the Church Committee." *Public Administration Review* 64 (1): 3–14.

Juris, Jeffrey. 2005. "The New Digital Media and Activist Networking Within Anti-Corporate Globalization Movements." *Annals of the American Academy of Political and Social Science* 597:189–208.

Kealey, Gregory S. 1993. "The Early Years of State Surveillance of Labour and the Left in Canada: The Institutional Framework of the Royal Canadian Mounted Police Security and Intelligence Apparatus, 1918–26." *Intelligence and National Security* 8 (3): 129–48.

———. 1992. "The Surveillance State: The Origins of Domestic Intelligence and Counter-Subversion in Canada, 1914–21." *Intelligence and National Security* 7 (3): 179–210.

Kealey, Gregory S., and Parnaby, Andrew. 2003. "The Origins of Political Policing in Canada: Class, Law, and the Burden of Empire." *Osgoode Hall Law Journal* 41 (2–3): 211–40.

Kealey, Gregory S., and Whitaker, Reginald. 1993. *RCMP Security Bulletins: The Depression Years*. Canadian Committee on Labour.

Klassen, Jerome. 2009. "Canada and the New Imperialism: The Economics of a Secondary Power." *Studies in Political Economy* 83:163–90.

Larsen, Mike, and Walby, Kevin. 2012. *Brokering Access: Power, Politics, and Freedom of Information Process in Canada*. Vancouver: UBC Press.

Leistert, Oliver. 2013. *From Protest to Surveillance—The Political Rationality of Mobile Media: Modalities of Neoliberalism*. Frankfurt: Peter Lang.

Lemke, Thomas. 2002. "Foucault, Governmentality, and Critique." *Rethinking Marxism* 14 (3): 1–17.

Lonardo, Michael. 1995. "Under a Watchful Eye: A Case Study of Police Surveillance during the 1930s." *Labour / Le Travail* 35:11–41.

Lübbers, Eveline. 2012. *Secret Manoeuvres in the Dark: Corporate and Police Spying on Activists*. London: Pluto Press.

McDonald Commission. 1981. Commission of Inquiry Concerning Certain Activities of the RCMP. Second Report, Volume 1, *Freedom and Security under the Law*. Ottawa: Minister of Supply and Services, 518.

McKnight, Graham. 1998. *The Last Crusade: Martin Luther King, Jr., the FBI, and the Poor People's Campaign.* Boulder, CO: Westview Press.

McQuaig, Linda. 2010. "Making It Easier to Ignore the Poor." *Rabble.ca.* http://rabble.ca/columnists/2010/07/harpers-attack-census-bad-news-poor (accessed 20 August 2011).

Milberry, Kate, and Clement, Andrew. 2014. "Policing as Spectacle and the Politics of Surveillance at the Toronto G20." *The State on Trial: Policing Protest*, 127–47. Vancouver, BC: UBC Press.

Miller, David, and Dinan, William. 2008. *A Century of Spin.* London: Pluto Press.

Mirowski, Phillip. 2013. *Never Let a Serious Crisis Go to Waste: How Neoliberalism Survived the Financial Crisis.* London: Verso.

Mirowski, Phillip, and Plehwe, Dieter. 2009. *The Road from Mont Pelerin: The Making of the Neoliberal Thought Collective.* Cambridge, MA: Harvard University Press.

Monaghan, Jeffrey, and Walby, Kevin. 2012a. "Making Up 'Terror Identities': Security, Intelligence, Canada's Integrated Threat Assessment Centre and Social Movement Suppression." *Policing and Society: An International Journal of Research and Policy* 22 (2): 133–51.

———. 2012b. "'They Attacked the City': Security Intelligence, the Sociology of Protest Policing and the Anarchist Threat at the 2010 Toronto G20 Summit." *Current Sociology* 60 (5): 653–71.

Murray, Nancy, and Wunsch, Sarah. 2002. "Civil Liberties in Times of Crisis: Lessons from History." *Massachusetts Law Review* 87 (2). http://www.massbar.org/publications/massachusetts-law-review/2002/v87-n2/civil-liberties-in-times-of/ (accessed 1 February 2015).

Navarro, Vicente, ed. 2007. *Neoliberalism, Globalization, and Inequalities: Consequences for Health and Quality of Life.* Amityville, NY: Baywood Publishing.

Office of the Privacy Commissioner of Canada. 2013. Findings Under the Privacy Act 2012-2013. Ottawa: Government of Canada. https://www.priv.gc.ca/cf-dc/pa/2012-13/pa_201213_01_e.asp (accessed 10 February 2015).

———. 2014. Checks and Controls: Reinforcing Privacy Protection and Oversight for the Canadian Intelligence Community in an Era of Cyber-Surveillance. Special Report to Parliament. Ottawa: Minister of Public Works and Government Services Canada. 28 January. https://www.priv.gc.ca/information/sr-rs/201314/sr_cic_e.asp (accessed 3 March 2015).

Peck, Jamie. 2010. *Constructions of Neoliberal Reason.* Oxford: Oxford University Press.

Pew Research Center. 2012. "Global Attitudes Project." http://www.pewglobal.org/files/2012/07/Pew-Global-Attitudes-Project-Economic-Conditions-Report-FINAL-July-12-2012.pdf (accessed 3 September 2013).

Professional Institute of the Public Service of Canada. 2013. "The Big Chill, Silencing Public Interest Science: A Survey." Ottawa, Canada. http://www.pipsc.ca/portal/page/portal/website/issues/science/bigchill (accessed 15 October 2013).

Pugliese, David. 2014. "Government Orders Federal Departments to Keep Tabs on All Demonstrations Across Country." *Ottawa Citizen*, 4 June. http://ottawacitizen.com/news/politics/government-orders-federal-departments-to-keep-tabs-on-all-demonstrations-across-country (accessed 3 March 2015).

Renzi, Alessandra, and Elmer, Greg. 2013. "The Biopolitics of Sacrifice: Securing Infrastructure at the G20 Summit." *Theory, Culture & Society* 30 (5): 45–69.

Rosen, Ruth. 2000. *The World Split Open: How the Modern Women's Movement Changed America.* New York: Penguin.

Ruckert A., and Labonté R. 2014. "The Global Financial Crisis and Health Equity: Early Experiences from Canada." *Globalization and Health* 10 (2).

Therrien, Daniel. 2015a. "Bill C-51, the Anti-Terrorism Act, 2015." Submission to the Standing Committee on Public Safety and National Security of the House of Commons. 5 March. https://www.priv.gc.ca/parl/2015/parl_sub_150305_e.asp (accessed 14 March 2015).

———. 2015b. "Without Big Changes, Bill C-51 Means Big Data." *Globe and Mail*, 6 March. http://www.theglobeandmail.com/globe-debate/without-big-changes-bill-c-51-means-big-data/article23320329/ (accessed 14 March 2015).

Uldham, Julie. 2014. "Corporate Management of Visibility and the Fantasy of the Post-Political: Social Media and Surveillance." *New Media & Society* 1–19.

US Congress. 1976. Select Committee to Study Governmental Operations with Respect to Intelligence Activities (Church Committee). *Final Report.* 95th Cong., 1st sess., May, S. Rept. 94-755.

Walton-Roberts, Margaret, Beaujot, Roderic, Hiebert, Daniel, McDaniel, Susan, Rose, Damaris and Wright, Richard. 2014. "Why Do We Still Need a Census? Views from the Age of 'Truthiness' and the 'Death of Evidence.'" *The Canadian Geographer* 58 (1): 34–47.

Weston, Greg, Greenwald, Glenn and Gallagher, Ryan. 2014. "CSEC Used Airport Wi-Fi to Track Canadian Travellers: Edward Snowden Documents." CBC.ca, 30 June. http://www.cbc.ca/news/politics/csec-used-airport-wi-fi-to-track-canadian-travellers-edward-snowden-documents-1.2517881 (accessed 3 March 2015).

Whitaker, Reg, Kealey, Gregory S. and Parnaby, Andrew. 2012. *Secret Service: Political Policing in Canada from the Fenians to Fortress America.* Toronto: University of Toronto Press.

Chapter Eight

Preempting Dissent

*From Participatory Policing
to Collaborative Filmmaking*[1]

Greg Elmer

There has always been a relatively clear distinction between participating in and observing or witnessing a political protest. Those on the streets, marching to a rally or other destination often waved at observers on the sidewalks, imploring those on the sidelines to join them. Observers or bystanders did not chant or hold signs—they mostly just watched and witnessed the protest event unfold with their eyes. With the introduction of handheld media devices or smartphones with video and photo capabilities, however, this divide has seemingly collapsed, or has at least blurred. Protestors now also observe, routinely holding their arms up in the air, not with raised fist, but with the hope of a better point of view for their media devices. Witnesses and bystanders too have turned to capturing protests on their smartphones. Protest events have never been so mediated—or to be more precise, captured.

Much has been made of the popular impact of images captured by protestor-witnesses, as an increasingly integral component of social movements and other expressions of dissent (Archibald 2011; Cammaerts 2012; Mattoni and Teune 2014). Lacking, however, is a discussion of the distinction between the large-scale capture of mediated images of protests and the common sharing—and wide circulation—of such files without strict licencing and copyright restrictions.

While the practice of sharing of photos in general has been growing of late,[2] the overwhelming majority of protest photos remain unshared, and unseen—mired on the memory cards of individual smartphones around the world. Even recent progressive efforts at collectivizing video infrastructure at Occupy camps resulted in much protest footage being squirreled away, never to be shared with other protestors or media activists. Joan Donovan, in her discussion with Tiziana Terranova (2013) reflecting on the end of the Occupy LA media committee, tellingly noted that:

> [T]he loss of the camp revealed a lot about the motivations of many in the media committee. Subsequently, we found out that some who were using the media committee's resources, such as power and access to Wi-Fi, never intended on sharing the video footage they captured during the days of the camp; they were either embedded mainstream media who were filming for a private company, others were paid by unions to push a certain agenda, or they were independent documentary filmmakers who seemed to disappear with the camp. (Terranova and Donovan 2013, 301)

For the independent documentary filmmaker, media activist and historians, such images and sounds represent an untapped resource—and one that documents the distinct vantage point of the protestor and/as witness.[3] Indeed, files on the handheld device represent a site of opportunity for storytellers and media activists—they are yet to be copyrighted by the mainstream social media platforms once uploaded and shared on such corporate properties. Once uploaded to Facebook, for example, the protestor/witness grants the platform 'a non-exclusive, transferable, sub-licensable, royalty-free, worldwide license to use any IP content that you post on or in connection with Facebook'.[4]

There are of course valid reasons for not wanting to share images of protests irrespective of questions of ownership and intellectual property. The fear on the part of many protestors is that citizens and protestors might be compelled to provide their media files to police and other security agencies, turning their mediated witnessing into yet another node in an ever expanding surveillance apparatus. It is this contemporary figure, the protestor as witness for the prosecution and defence, (to borrow a cliché) the protestor with smartphone raised in the air, that compelled and informed the making of the creative commons documentary *Preempting Dissent*, of which I am a codirector.[5] In this chapter, I review the attempts of the film's production team to engage with the archive of the protestor/witness, in the process of making a collaborative, creative commons feature documentary film. The chapter seeks to illuminate and analyse the obstacles that the producers faced in creating a collaborative and creative commons documentary focused on the history of protest policing, again as an effort at soliciting the participation of the protestor/witness—an effort at making the handheld media device an integral component of media activism and counter surveillance strategies.

Theoretically, the impetus behind making a collaborative documentary film came about through a previously published book by the codirectors (Elmer and Opel 2008) that sought to rethink dominant modes of political surveillance. Of course activists remain, and will continue to be for the foreseeable future, under visual surveillance from various police, law enforcement and security agencies. The active monitoring and intelligence gathering of protest communities, organizers and movements is well documented, and seemingly unrelenting (see also Redden in this volume).[6] Surveillance is, however, not exclusively visual—surveillance should not be conceived narrowly as the act of watching; rather, surveillance is inherently linked to other acts of policing (through arrests, violence or forms of intimidation). There is, in other words, a 'participatory' element of surveillance, where watching and intelligence gathering gives way, or is displaced by police actions designed to preempt protest and dissent. In this respect, countersurveillance strategies by activists and media makers cannot be restricted to visual tactics alone, meaning that sous-veillance (Mann, Nolan and Wellman 2003)—a bottom-up, democratic form of 'watching the watchers'—is but one response to expansive forms of surveillance. Attempts by police to preempt dissent, in the form of protests, marches and the like, are again not restricted to intelligence gathering. Moving forward, this chapter subsequently works with a preemptive definition of surveillance, one that integrates (or better still *folds*) visual practices into the act of policing, be it arrests, violent strikes of a baton or the all-too-carefree deployment of so-called less-than-legal weaponry. Samuel Weber's (2005) *Targets of Opportunity* captures this dynamic most succinctly. He writes:

> [I]t is a question not just of targets but targets of *opportunity*, which is to say where time and space are decisive factors in the establishment of the target. Even without this explicit reference to temporal localization, it is difficult to conceive how a "target" could be construed simply as self-contained or self-present. What is involved here is the difference between something simply "seen" and something being "sighted"—that is, discovered, localized, identified in order to be hit or struck. (Weber 2005, 7–8)

Such a preemptive definition of surveillance thus calls into question a much broader array of tactics and technologies deployed to detain, suspend, ban and intimidate potential protests and protestors. As a consequence any counter (preemptive) surveillance strategies that engage media must similarly invoke a discussion of media infrastructures that enable, circulate and govern images and sounds from protests, marches and rallies.

BAD APPLES: UPLOADING DISCRETE INCIDENTS

In the first instance, our film was inspired by a particularly egregious aspect of participatory surveillance, the use of undercover police in the province of Quebec during a protest against a proposed North American security protocol

(April 2007) to provoke violence among a group of peaceful protestors. A video of the agent provocateurs was posted online,[7] and later led to a mea culpa by the provincial police force in Quebec.[8] At the 2001 FTAA protest, the police were not acting as agents of surveillance, though to be sure reports were filed on the activities of protestors and protest groups; rather, they were proactively participating in the protest, indeed suggesting violent and criminal actions. In this respect, participation does not adequately capture the meaning of agent provocateurs, given the attempt to govern and lead a set of behaviours. The intervention of the YouTube-posted video thus raised an important question for us: given the amount of media images stored on personal media devices around the world, some inevitably capturing other questionable and illegal police tactics during political protests, could we assemble some of these images into a compelling story, into somewhat of a conventional documentary film? There is a steady stream of short handheld witness videos depicting police violence at protests and elsewhere, yet surprisingly few feature-length films that bring these images together into a forceful argument.

While the producers of the film were intrigued by the active role that police played in the Quebec protests, we wanted to better reflect on the limits of police and security surveillance, again as a way to understand police action, in particular preemptive police action. In many respects, participatory and preemptive surveillance are both an outgrowth and logical extension of the failures of surveillance systems, failures of intelligence gathering processes, mechanisms and technologies. Clearly, in the post-9/11 environment, the failure of knowing what is coming next, or indeed the failure of being able to conduct telling surveillance campaigns, called forth an impulse on the part of police agencies to act, even in absence of so-called 'intelligence' or in the absence of criminal acts. As media producers and filmmakers, we asked ourselves not only how we could elicit participation, but also visually and aurally represent preemptive acts—which is in some respects a paradox. Popular representations of surveillance often depict a deeply visual process—it can be easily communicated on film, through the use of cameras, CCTV technology, an individual gaze or better still, glance (see Shields 2004). But how could we as media producers capture the logic of preemption, the decision on the part of police agencies to forgo the process of intelligence gathering and head straight for police action—arrest, violence or less brutally through efforts to divert or otherwise thwart participation at political events? Ultimately we settled on two strategies, the first being a focus on history and policy, that is, political documents and protocols that expressly adopted the language of preemption—George Bush's preemptive national security document (2002), being the prototypical example. The second example, of police actions, would form the main basis for our calls for participation from protestor/witnesses and for the most part provides a focus for this chapter.

While consent to participate in the making of a document film or any other media product is an essential ethical component to media production, we felt compelled to solicit participation from those individuals and groups who had already explicitly identified their media content as seeking not only distribution publicly, but also available for many other uses through a creative commons licence. Initially our goal was not only to produce a collaborative documentary, but to also provide a larger resource and infrastructure—in the form of an open source archive of media clips of protests, arrests and the like—that future media makers could draw upon. What we found very quickly, however, was that there was a very limited amount of creative commons content on the internet and elsewhere. Thus in many respects the film was in its infancy, at least more of an experiment in media collaboration than in scripting, directing or producing—or any other conventional terms used to connote documentary filmmaking. The production team was not convinced that we would be able to locate or solicit enough creative commons media files to adequately tell a story—and of course a compelling story, about the emergence and spread of preemptive policing technologies, protocols and practices. This was not merely an effort at convincing media activists and protestors/witnesses to give up their content for inclusion in our film, it went one step further—it sought to convince those individuals to adopt a licencing protocol (creative commons) which at its heart sought to make freely available media for download, remix and reuse. The goal in so doing was, again, to grow a larger media infrastructure for media activists. We could simply have engaged each owner of media content and negotiated the inclusion of files into our film, but such a process would have ended there. At the start of the project we were encouraged by the creative commons efforts at rethinking the ownership and circulation of media files in perpetuity. In other words, once a media file was tagged with a 'share-a-like' creative commons licence it could not be revoked, as such a media resource would be created indefinitely for other media activists to use as they see fit down the road. The media file would therefore not only enter the public domain, it would actively denote share-ability, and unfettered use by media producers (subject to some attributions and other restrictions).[9]

Lastly, in terms of the contours and requirements we set for ourselves at the beginning of the process, we agreed that upon laying out the terms of participation in the film (simply an agreement to the linking of the media files), we would in no way alter the media files once they had been shared with the producers. In other words, if the protestor/witness sent us a standard-definition video file (which occurred with some regularity), we would not return to ask for a high-definition file. We would, in other words, represent—if we deemed it important to include in the final version of the film—

the shared media document 'as is'. In this respect, the film was designed to represent not only a story and political concept (preemption), but also certain aesthetics of media sharing. There was no colour correction or postproduction modifications to files that were shared with us. And with the historical focus of the film, its various sections, going back to the 1960s through to the present decade, provide a compelling account of video-capture technologies available to various media activists, institutions and of course more recently, everyday citizens. *Preempting Dissent* thus conceived might be viewed as a practice in—or form of—media archeology (cf. Parikka 2012).

THE COLLABORATIVE MEDIA MAKING PLATFORM: OPEN SOURCE CINEMA

With such lofty (read unrealistic!) ambitions—to seek out participation, cultivate a creative commons community, tell a complex story and create a long-lasting, creative commons archive or media material—the project team required a dynamic and flexible media collaboration platform. The project called for a series of requirements. How and through what medium would we reach our collaborators? How could they deliver their content to us? Where and how could we store, and later make available, such media content? And in a more general sense, how could we promote this project to interested parties and later audiences, including media activists?

Director Brett Gaylor's 2008 film *Rip: A Remix Manifesto*[10] provided some initial inspiration and a possible way forward. Focused on questions of copyright, music, ownership and remix culture, Gaylor sought to promote and produce the film as itself an example of remix culture and creative commons media. To facilitate some contributions—albeit relatively small—to the film, the director collaborated with some other media producers and distributors in Canada to produce the Open Source Cinema project. The main focus of the project was the construction of a web platform where media producers could in effect house their creative commons films. The platform would serve as a site for solicitation of participation (through social media add-ons), file uploading, downloading and an online editor that could be used to splice together or remix samples of work. The reality was of course much more complicated, and was in effect the very first fatality and dose of reality for our ambitious goals. Opensourcecinema.org served as a stand-alone platform with multiple functions, it did not aggregate or otherwise coordinate functions from distributed sites, it was all hosted in one place, the result being that if one function failed, often the whole platform failed. Cue, for instance, the process of logging in and creating user accounts. A colossal failure. And ultimately so much so that users were turned away. It was just far too difficult to create an account even before one could get to the main functions of the site—which given the heavy amounts of bandwidth required, were inevitably compromised to the point of critical dysfunction. This was, however, just the start. Or perhaps, the start of the end.

Apart from its functional limits and general user-unfriendliness, to put it mildly, the platform also suffered from, for lack of a better term, poor management and resourcing, saying nothing about its poor security which resulted in endless streams of phishing and spamming comments. Once its founder left for a new job, the site lost its main supporter and eventually went dark. Proposals from our team to revive it, ironically as a creative commons platform, were for unexplained reasons rejected. We were left with no site from which to launch our calls for participation or to host our archive of creative commons media files.

MEDIA ACTIVISM: SOLICITATION AND PARTICIPATION

Having decided that it would be too unwieldy, expensive and time-consuming to effectively reproduce and code an open source cinema-like platform, the team concluded that a social media campaign would be the best option moving forward, specifically as we sought to solicit media files and other participation from media activists and producers. Facebook and Twitter accounts of course form the backbone of most such accounts—yet a robust network of friends and followers is a challenge, and it too would be time-consuming, requiring constant updates to encourage those working on similar activist media projects to follow our progress and retweet and cross promote to their own networks and communities. Such platforms thus served as largely promotional devices, driving some traffic to a web page that contained more specific and long-winded descriptions of the project and calls for participation.[11]

A more targeted strategy for soliciting participation in our film, however, was facilitated by and through the YouTube platform, which at the time did not have many video-hosting and social media competitors (Vimeo was relatively underdeveloped at the time). While social media bursts (largely on Twitter and Facebook) provided a series of leads that were followed up, YouTube offered a searchable database that could match our more specific needs and interests. Again, given our intentions to produce a creative commons-only feature documentary film, YouTube posed some technical and practical obstacles or limitations. When uploading content to the platform users are not prompted to choose a licence; the site works with a default set 'standard YouTube licence',[12] meaning that if users don't actively search for other licences for their work, the standard licence will apply as a default. Such a default technicity thus severely limits the pool of creative commons content on YouTube, while conversely highlighting the degree to which a small minority take the effort to licence their media files through the creative commons system.[13] That said, in an effort at engaging media activists and recognizing YouTube's licencing lay system, the production team actively sought specific YouTube-hosted videos from users through email solicitations on the platform. Two examples of such efforts prove illustrative. First, we approached an individual who had posted a series of compelling videos from protests at a political convention in New York City, exactly the kind of event that the Miami model of policing was designed for. Since the videos were tagged with YouTube's 'standard Licence' we asked if the individual would be willing to share the videos with us using a creative commons licence. The specifics of the exchange were repeated a number of times with a series of other users on YouTube. At first the user requested payment for the footage. When we noted that this was a scholarly project that used a noncommercial creative commons licence we were again rebuffed, the reason given that our hosting of the content would potentially reduce the traffic (page views) to the user's own account. As YouTube developed more user-centred functions, designs and practices, the site would encourage its users to produce and brand their own 'channels', of which the more successful ones would be highlighted on the home page of the site (Senft 2013).

Our YouTube solicitations in short served to highlight the pitfalls of the 'me-centric' or first-person architecture and conventions of social networking and social media (Elmer 2015), especially for those media producers and activists intent on freely circulating compelling media content. The paradox of social media platform and interfaces lies herein: while social media promises connections to networks, friends and acquaintances and affords small-group discussions and networking, such opportunities are all presented through a first-person—or personalized—interface. While such platforms offer little variation from account to account, still no two user accounts are substantively the same. That is to say, that we all 'view' the socially mediated world through our own filtered lenses (or better still algorithms), our own profiles, browsing histories, aggregation of 'likes' and so on. And moreover, content is now filtered, and customized, and options highlighted and recommended, in response to a user's own profile. In this respect, social media is an intensely insular, 'me-centric' and distorted view of the world—always outward from the 'I'.

That said, there is no lack of literature arguing that the internet has in fact heightened our ability to connect with others in meaningful ways (cf. Wellman and Rainie 2014). Yet, our experience showed, conversely, that social media platforms, one of the preferred spaces of sharing media files and organizing protests, is an intensely individuated and personalized space, or interface. While social media platforms clearly facilitate connectivity, they do so through personalized, first-person frames and screens, and correspondingly customized content where fleeting attention spans and tickers can only be matched by efforts by users to increasingly self-brand online spaces to attract attention. Such a networked environment calls for a particular form of sharing—efforts at sharing ideas, and thoughts that serve to drive or direct attention and time to exclusively hosted—that is, unshared—media images, sounds, experiences and testimonies. Hence, one could imagine in such an economy of attention that the most shocking—or simply, attention-getting— images and sounds would in effect be 'hoarded', or closely guarded by individual users so as to increase traffic and potentially increase a user's on and offline reputation.

Not all discussions and negotiations with media activists, however, ended in self-branded, personalized web channels and blogs. Our production team located a YouTube-hosted video of the very first known use of a 'long-range acoustic device' (LRAD) at the 2009 G20 protests in Pittsburgh. Better known as a 'sound cannon', the footage of the military weapon was like many others tagged with YouTube's standard licence. The owner of the footage had been approached by news networks to use the footage and was unsure how our use of the footage would affect any such plans. Briefly put, the conversation emerged into an engaging discussion over the commercial possibilities of videos under a creative commons licence. We suggested a noncommercial licence for our use, and the owner would be free to sell other rights to whomever he chose. The video producer agreed and we included the footage in the final version of the film—it is arguably one of the most compelling moments in the film, a robotic voice emitted from the LRAD warns protestors that that they must leave the area immediately. The images and sounds are unmistakably militaristic, and in keeping with the Miami model or protest policing developed in the wake of 9/11,[14] deployed with such sonic force as to literally chase citizens out of the public space.

The production team was, however, not so lucky in negotiations with Britain's *Guardian* newspaper. But again, while frustrating in the end, the conversation was an important one for our research goals, and ultimately for our understanding of the limits of the creative commons production model that we had embarked upon. During the making of our film, the British parliament, newspapers and activists were engaged in a heated debate over the policing of student protests. Of particular concern was the police tactic of kettling, or boxing in protestors from all sides. In this heated environment, a tragic story emerged, the death of Ian Tomlinson as he made his way home through a protest in central London. A video of the event, posted to YouTube from the *Guardian* newspaper, shows Tomlinson with hands in his pockets violently pushed from behind by a police officer.[15] Unable to cushion his fall, Tomlinson's head strikes the pavement hard. While Tomlinson is able to steady himself and leave the area, he collapses and dies moments later. Our production team contacted the *Guardian* to explain the goals and intent of our creative commons documentary film project. We asked to include the Tomlinson video. The discussion, and back and forth, continued for months, with the conversation leading up the chain of command at the *Guardian*. In the end the *Guardian* declined and later explained that while as an innovator and supporter of digital content platforms, they chose to maintain control over the circulation of the video. In short, they were concerned that if we put a share-a-like creative commons licence [16] on the clip that anyone on the web could remix or reedit the video in any way they chose. The *Guardian* ultimately felt as though they had a duty to the family of Tomlinson, a duty to maintain some integrity to the video and to not enable its reuse that might unintentionally or not offend the family. The *Guardian*'s decision was hard to argue with, particularly since a video we included in the film of a student being violently Tasered for no defendable reason had been previously remixed by a number of YouTube users to the tune of MC Hammer's 'Can't Touch This'. [17]

Not all social media platforms, however, required such extensive discussions, negotiations and ethical considerations. The photo-hosting and sharing website Flickr proved to be an immensely valuable resource for our creative commons media project. The site's programmers though, unlike YouTube, placed a much greater emphasis on different media licences, placing creative commons licences on an even playing field with other more proprietary models. The ability to search for creative commons licences is also far more advanced and user-friendly than on many other social media platforms. And while there is comparatively far less video content on Flickr, digital photos from protests around the world are very much in abundance on the site, a number of which were included in the final version of the film *Preempting Dissent*.

While some historical footage has over the years entered the public domain, our interest in including media that was purposefully circulated and shared with a creative commons licence also took us over (and over) to archive.org—originally a project that sought to archive the entire web. Over the years, archive.org has emerged into a multimedia site, of which again creative commons searchable content proved invaluable to our goals, and ultimately to our ability as filmmakers to tell a richer historical story about the emergence of policing protocols. Our team also sought out a number of music-focused archives that specialized in creative commons content to assemble a musical score for the film.

THE EVENT—THE TORONTO G20

As much as one sets out to solicit, seek out networks, partners, participants and allies, the protest event can in a matter of hours bring it all together. And of course working on protest policing, the G20 summit in Toronto, Canada, in the summer of 2010 provided a ready-made time and space from which to engage media activists and populate our film-in-the-making with compelling images of preemptive policing efforts. We would not be disappointed, unfortunately. The G20 event would witness the largest mass arrest in Canadian history, with some nine hundred overwhelmingly peaceful protestors detained—many without formal charges. The summit, staged in the centre of the city's financial district, was with very few variations a classic example of the Miami model policing policy. The security budget for the summit (along with the G8 event held a few days earlier just north of the city) approached nearly $1 billion Canadian dollars. The government rejected appeals from city officials to hold the event at an amusement park at the edge of the downtown core—a site that provided obvious benefits for security planning. Instead, the federal government in conjunction with various levels of government, the security community and many police forces from the area, descended upon the centre of the city, shutting down most daily events and disrupting countless citizens and businesses. The core of the financial district that housed the summit's central meeting sites was ringed with a 3.5-kilometer temporary security fence costing $5.5 million (CDN) alone. A flood of pictures and video of the fence was sent our way, and eventually served as a key visual trope in the film. The city was not only under a form of marshal law; it was literally encircled by a security fence.

The Doc

As the production team sifted through the shared media files, it became apparent that representing the story of preemption that is the history of the policing protocol would be a challenge. To provide some analysis and history, the team interviewed a series of scholars, lawyers and activists to serve as narrators for the various sections of the film. The footage we received from protestors, activists and citizen journalists conversely often caught police in various interactions with protestors; they served, in other words, as examples of the effects of a preemptive mind-set and set of policies. And of course the issue of preemption, while being front and centre in our call for participation, was rarely the specific focus of much of the footage we received. The scale of the event in Toronto was evident, however. In addition to the security fence, many photos and videos simply capture the starkly militarized landscape—the endless lines of police, the military equipment and clothing and the intimidating yells and instructions of individual officers.

Overall, we found ourselves struggling in the last days of the production to acquire more footage, reflecting upon perhaps the too strict limits we placed on ourselves by committing to a creative commons-only framework. Yet, as we searched long and hard through the sites and archives noted above, the larger debate that emerged in producing and editing this collaborative film became an aesthetic one. We were always concerned and sensitive to making a film overburdened with images of police brutality, or 'riot porn'. Much low-budget, activist filmmaking tends to use lower-resolution video equipment and overplay violence in an effort at shocking their audiences at worst, or merely focusing on one specific police-protestor dynamic. Conversely, recent films of global protest such as Jehane Noujaim's *The Square*[18] could be accused of focusing too heavily on the image, with high HD aesthetics and beautifully lit scenes. Given the scarcity of images, and the focus of our film, we drew upon a vast range of images, perhaps to a fault. Indeed, at one of the first rough-cut screenings of our film, an audience member—self-identified as a radical researcher—bemoaned our use of low-resolution footage. 'Could you not get better resolution?' he asked.

In moving through the history of protest policing policies from the 1960s civil rights era in the United States, through to Vietnam-era protests, Reagan's war on poverty and use of policing to 'clean the streets' under New York Mayor Giuliani, to the groundbreaking protests at the WTO summit in Seattle in 1999, our film drew upon a range of video documents, colours and resolutions. Indeed, the film in many respects, represents a history of video technology and capture throughout the decades, from professional use of cameras in the 1960s, 1970s and 1980s, through to the introduction of consumer video technology—handicams and other low-cost video cameras—that ushered in a new wave of poor-quality video (in retrospect through our contemporary HD lens). Regardless of our efforts to tell a story, through interviews, stock footage or solicited footage, the film cannot escape its place as a media document and the subsequent expectations that various audiences have for the big or small screen.

The reactions and feedback of contributors to our film, the protest-witnesses, have unfortunately been rather muted, perhaps in part because many have yet to see the film or the G20 protests have started to fade from their radars. This did not stop us, however, from engaging in a rather heated discussion at times among our production group about the lengths to which we needed to provide attribution and credit to our contributors—again an important component of the creative commons framework. The question surrounded due diligence. After we did succeed in having an individual share images stored on his or her smartphone, coaxing the individual into moving from witness to participant of another kind—as a media activist after the fact, perhaps—how could we be absolutely sure that the media files were indeed owned by the person who shared it with us? This matter was even more complicated on the web, where we poured through creative-commons-attached materials and archives. In so doing, it was more than obvious that some individuals had no right to tag a television news broadcast from NBC, for instance, with a creative commons license. With such obvious examples, the question became, should we therefore assume that there are many other less-obvious examples of tagging of content that fell outside of creative commons guidelines? And how would we ever determine such examples? Unfortunately, there are no clear guidelines for such a process, only best practices and best intentions.[19] In the end, we made an honest effort to verify the ownership of each media file and provided proper attribution in the film's final credits.

CONCLUSION

To be sure, in retrospect the project was an overly ambitious one. Our team was too small and lacked the training, experience and resources to complete all aspects of the project (the open source media archive remains incomplete, for example). Yet calls for media innovation, engagement of various production communications and transmedia products are now very much the norm, especially for those media producers seeking to distribute their films and acquire funding. Our use of the creative commons framework was one effort to rethink the dominant mode of media documentation, and to a lesser degree norms within media activist communities as well. In so doing, our project succeeded in at least asking some structural questions about the limits on the sharing economy, technological reasons why default settings and software preferences on handheld devices and accompanying web and social media platforms dissuade or otherwise ex-distance the tagging and sharing of creative commons media files. At the time of writing this chapter, no major photography apps or platforms set their sharing protocols as default creative commons licences—a move that would surely create a steady flow of protest images from the devices of many protestors and witnesses. That said, our experience also tells us that often creative commons projects are designed to have participants merely contribute to the direction of media producers; that is, they are not meaningful participants, only contributors to someone else's vision—a model more in keeping with the notion of crowdfunding. Likewise, the promise of creative commons and open source software to 'free' code, and enable anyone to improve and build upon media, was lost on the producers and owners of the open source cinema platform—the means of production were still very much in the hands of the funders in that instance.

Thus as an effort at addressing the preemptive forces of surveillance and protest policy, the documentary film-experiment did prove useful on a number of counts. The assembling and editing of all these discrete images and sounds—some known to the public, others not—did succeed in telling a cohesive story about the history of protest policing, showing examples of its impact on protest movements and individuals and casting an important light on the sources of funding for such policies and protocols. The film clearly documented police efforts at preplanning arrests at various so-called security events around the world, most notably during the 2010 G20 summit in Toronto, Canada. With few other examples, the film succeeded in positing a new documentary genre, the creative commons documentary, that while failing to ultimately link this in a systematic way to centralized archives of creative commons content, did serve as a conduit for logging such resources, and making share-able—through creative commons licenced resources—media files. Such an effort serves as perhaps the most compelling component of this larger project, that is the effort at establishing infrastructures for media activists, social movements and protest communities, an infrastructure that challenges the first-person, selfie-obsessed interface and images, that narrow and internalize our fields of vision, imaginaries and potential sites of political engagement and struggles for social justice.

NOTES

1. The author would like to recognize the key collaborators on the documentary film *Preempting Dissent*: Andy Opel, Steven James May, Alessandra Renzi and Boaz Beeri. A full list of credits for the film, including all those whose media files were used in the final documentary, can be found at http://preemptingdissent.com/credits/. The author would also like to thank the editors Lina Dencik and Oliver Leistert for their immensely helpful comments and revisions to this piece. Original funding for this project was provided by the Social Science and Humanities Research Council of Canada.

2. http://www.pewinternet.org/2013/10/28/photo-and-video-sharing-grow-online/ (accessed 18 December 2014).

3. For lack of space here, I will forgo a discussion of the protest selfie, a digital artifact that moves from an embodied gaze (often raised, shaking hand)—not unlike the extended corporeal view points of the HD sports camera GoPro (Cartwright 2014)—to a posed foregrounding of the self against an unseen backdrop. Ben Valentine (2013) offers an optimistic view of the protest selfie, making the case that 'This is me [self image], and I am for this [protest background]'. The claim is perhaps a bit too quickly made, and intention—as an endorsement—problematically inferred. An outstretched hand/camera clearly seeks what the eye perhaps cannot; it searches for the ability to witness an event, images and sounds. Valentine, however, removes the intent of the embodied camera, claiming that the protest selfie is a convergence of the individual and the crowd/protest. While some might use the protest selfie to ally with a social movement or goal of a protest, the camera's self-reflexive trajectory is more intent on providing visual evidence of one's presence at an event. Building on Esposito (2012), the selfie could therefore be seen as merely an effort to extend the first person view, though not outward as witness, but inward from an absent other (the photographer).

4. https://www.facebook.com/legal/terms (accessed 2 March 2015).

5. The film (2014) was codirected by Andy Opel and coproduced by Alessandra Renzi, Steven James May and Boaz Beeri. www.preemptingdissent.com.

6. In Canada, surveillance of native peoples and environmentalists has grown as critics of Alberta's tar sands and opponents of oil pipelines have gained worldwide attention. Cf. http://www.amnesty.ca/blog/canada-surveillance-of-indigenous-protests-and-rule-of-law.

7. https://www.youtube.com/watch?v=St1-WTc1kow

8. http://www.cbc.ca/news/canada/quebec-police-admit-they-went-undercover-at-montebello-protest-1.656171

9. https://creativecommons.org/licenses/

10. https://www.nfb.ca/film/rip_a_remix_manifesto/

11. CALL FOR PARTICIPANTS PREEMPTING DISSENT: OPEN SOURCING SECRECY An Open Source Documentary Film Project Call for Videos, Testimonials, Photographs, and other Audio Visual Materials. This project examines new forms of social control including

the proliferation of Tasers and the rise of 'no-fly' and watch-lists. We are seeking contributions to this project in the form of video, still images and testimonials. This content will be made available for others to mix and remix into their own documentaries. HOW TO CONTRIBUTE: We are seeking video content from those of you who have experienced and/or captured on video new forms of surveillance and social control. Have you been Tasered by police, security guards or other citizens? Did you witness someone being Tasered and record it on video? Has your name been placed on a 'no-fly' list—or similar exclusionary watch-list? If so, we invite you to submit your video footage, personal video testimonials, audio testimonials, photographs, news footage, cell phone videos, mash-ups and any other audio-visual medium which will convey your story.

12. While YouTube's default 'standard YouTube Licence' accompanies a user's posted content, there is no hyperlink on the licence, nor is the term itself explicitly defined anywhere on the site. A rather lengthy and complex description of the platform's terms of service, however, can be found at https://www.youtube.com/static?template=terms.

13. While there are no stats on the number of videos hosted by YouTube, the company reported in 2012 that over four million videos used some form of creative commons licencing. While an impressive number at first glance, one has to put this in the context of YouTube's extensive userbase, totalling over one billion users. http://youtube-global.blogspot.ca/2012/07/heres-your-invite-to-reuse-and-remix-4.html.

14. The Miami model is commonly defined as a set of police and law enforcement strategies developed by US state and federal agencies in the aftermath of 9/11. The overarching logic behind the Miami model is preemption—efforts at limiting the possibility of public protest before an event has even occurred. Such an effort thus relies heavily on tactics designed to redirect or detain protestors from reaching the intended protest site. For further reading, see Elmer and Opel (2008) and Vitale (2007).

15. https://www.youtube.com/watch?v=HECMVdl-9SQ (accessed 16 December 2014).

16. http://creativecommons.org/licenses/by-sa/2.5/ca/

17. https://www.youtube.com/watch?v=Xzkd_m4ivmc (accessed 16 December 2014).

18. http://www.imdb.com/title/tt2486682/

19. https://wiki.creativecommons.org/Best_practices_for_attribution; see also http://www.cmsimpact.org/fair-use/best-practices/documentary/fair-use-frequently-asked-questions#commons.

REFERENCES

Archibald, David. (2011). "Photography, the Police and Protest: Images of the G20, London 2009," in S. Cottle and L. Lester, eds., *Transnational Protests and the Media*, 129–43. New York: Peter Lang.

Cammaerts, Bart. (2012). "Protest Logics and the Mediation Opportunity Structure." *European Journal of Communication* 27 (2): 117–34.

Cartwright, Lisa. (2014). "My Hero: A Media Archaeology of Body-Mounted Camera Technologies of the Self." Public lecture, University of Toronto, 30 January.

Elmer, Greg. (2015). "Scraping the First Person," in G. Langlois, J. Redden and G. Elmer, eds., *Compromised Data: From Social Media to Big Data*. London: Bloomsbury.

Elmer, Greg, and Andy Opel. (2008). *Preempting Dissent: The Politics of an Inevitable Future*. Winnipeg: Arbeiter Ring Press.

Esposito, Roberto. (2012) *Third Person: Politics of Life and Philosophy of the Impersonal*. London: Polity.

Mann, Steve, Jason Nolan and Barry Wellman. (2003). "Sousveillance: Inventing and Using Wearable Computing Devices for Data Collection in Surveillance Environments." *Surveillance and Society* 1 (3): 331–55.

Mattoni, Alice, and Simon Teune. (2014). "Visions of Protest: A Media-Historic Perspective on Images in Social Movements." *Sociology Compass* 8 (6): 876–87. doi:10.1111/soc4.12173.

Parikka, Jussi. (2012). *What Is Media Archeology?* Cambridge: Polity.

Renzi, Alessandra, and G. Elmer. (2012). *Infrastructure Critical: Sacrifice at Toronto's G20 Summit*. Winnipeg: ARP.

Senft, Theresa. (2013). "Microcelebrity and the Branded Self," in J. Hartley, J. Burgess and A. Bruns, eds., *A Companion to New Media Dynamics*, 346–54. Malden: Blackwell.

Shields, Rob. (2004). "Visualicity: On Urban Visibility and Invisibility." *Visual Culture in Britain* 15 (1): 23–36.

Terranova, Tiziana, and Joan Donovan. (2013). "Occupy Social Networks: The Paradoxes of Using Corporate Social Media in Networked Movements," in G. Lovink and M. Rasch, eds., *Unlike Us Reader: Social Media Monopolies and Their Alternatives*, 296–311. Amsterdam: INC.

Valentine, Ben. (2013). "A Survey of the Protest Selfie." *The Civic Beat Reader*, http://reader.thecivicbeat.com/2013/11/the-protest-selfie/ (accessed 20 March 2015).

Vitale, Alex. (2007). "The Command and Control and Miami Models at the 2004 Republican National Convention: New Forms of Policing Protests." *Mobilization: An International Quarterly* 12 (4): 403–15.

Weber, Samuel. (2005). *Targets of Opportunity: On the Militarization of Thinking*. New York: Fordham University Press.

Wellman, Barry, and Lee Rainie. (2014). *Networked: The New Social Operating System*. Cambridge, MA: MIT press.

IV

Dissent and Fragmentation
from Within

Chapter Nine

The Struggle Within

Discord, Conflict and Paranoia in Social Media Protest[1]

Emiliano Treré

In this chapter, I begin by introducing three sketches that outline the problems of control, surveillance and the everyday frustrations and anxieties that are linked to practices of social media protest. The first sketch concerns an attempt of delegitimization of the #YoSoy132 movement by the government carried out on the YouTube video platform (as we will see in details, Cossío, the creator and manager of the yosoy132.mx website, was in reality an infiltrated agent of the Mexican Secret Service who used his inside knowledge of the movement to try to discredit it). The second sketch tells the story of a technical infrastructure that is not working properly and prevents us from fulfilling our activist 'job'. The last example relates the negative emotions that we feel when we perceive that authorities are using our digital traces on social media platforms to control us and possibly indict us.

It's the 18th of June and student activist Saúl Alvídrez cannot believe what he is seeing and hearing . . . He's playing a YouTube video that contains a mix of audio files, recorded without his consent, where he speaks about the #YoSoy132 movement and its connections with politicians of the Mexican Left. . . . Shocked, Saúl suddenly recognizes who uploaded the video, Manuel Cossío, supposedly a friend and an activist of the movement, owner and manager of the yosoy132.mx website.

It's the 23rd of June of 2012, the rain is falling heavily in Mexico City, and Rodrigo, an activist of the #YoSoy132 movement, is sitting in his room, desperately trying to access the internet to send one important message to his Facebook comrades: the planned meeting of the day after has been cancelled and rescheduled in another location, far away from the previous one. The internet connection is not working properly, because every five minutes the electric current crashes, making it impossible to access the social media platform. After one hour of struggling, everything goes completely dark: the room, the street, the whole neighborhood . . . Rodrigo reaches at his mobile phone: 'No signal'. 'This always happens when you have something important to do,' Rodrigo thinks, puffing at the windows while the rain keeps falling in the dark.

4th of December 2012—During a meeting at the Autonomous University of Mexico City to decide what actions have to be taken following the brutal police repression of the 1st of December, Laura is nervous . . . She has just disassembled her mobile phone and removed her chip, but even after that she does not feel safe, she is thinking about all her posts and pictures on Facebook during the last mobilization that may compromise her, may lead authorities to question her. 'If only I had been more cautious,' she thinks, nervously tapping her fingers on the desk . . . 'I have to delete all those compromising pictures as soon as this meeting ends'.

During my extensive fieldwork in Mexico with the #YoSoy132 movement in 2012 and 2013, I have encountered these sorts of complications many times, and my vision of digital activism has also been deeply affected. I have come to realize that communication practices around digital media, and social media in particular—given their paramount role in contemporary activism—are constantly plagued by daily conflicts and clashes, discomfort and struggles, fights and discord. The vision that emerges from my research is different from the celebratory literature developed around the movement that has praised the role of social media in the development of a 'fifth state' (Islas and Arribas 2012), and conceived them as alternative media to the so-called Mexican *telecracy* (Andión Gamboa 2013). Everyday frictions and struggles, together with issues of exploitation, dataveillance, control and intents of delegitimization have contributed to a much more controversial image of social media activism in the Mexican context.

In this chapter, I offer an in-depth exploration of the many issues that plagued the digital resistance of the #YoSoy132 movement. In so doing, I first aim to deconstruct the celebratory narratives around the potential of social media that have dominated the literature on this movement. Furthermore, my aim is to contribute to the critical literature on digital activism by showing that the political economy lens—the most influential approach in the field—can benefit from the integration of a focus on negotiations among activists that underline everyday conflicts and frictions. In other words, while investigating how capitalism is shaping and constraining social media (resistance) is a fundamental task that is being accomplished by a wide variety of scholars, one has not to overlook the daily disputes around the use of social media for social change, struggles that are inherent to the recognition that technologies are not mere instruments that activists use to fight against neoliberal power, but complex ecologies of mediations that are constantly crossed by clashes and conflicts and inhabited by suspicion and paranoia.

MANUFACTURING (DIGITAL) CONSENT: TELECRACY AND DIRTY DIGITAL WARS IN THE 2012 MEXICAN ELECTIONS

The 2012 electoral process in Mexico represented, without a doubt, a historical moment: after twelve years of PAN (National Action Party), the PRI (Institutional Revolutionary Party) that had governed the country for seventy years was credited by polls as the favorite party, with a young, smiling, attractive candidate, omnipresent in the media: Enrique Peña Nieto (EPN) who was leading the coalition 'Commitment for Mexico'. For six years, Mexican media giant Televisa carefully constructed the candidacy of EPN, while at the same time building a counterstrategy to delegitimize his opponent of the Left, Manuel López Obrador (AMLO) (Tuckman 2012; Villamil 2010). If there was any doubt, these elections made clear the enormous power of the so-called Mexican *mediocracy* or *telecracy*, where the power of the media duopoly Televisa-TvAzteca has been described as a 'wild power' (Trejo 2004) that is able, thanks to its incredible diffusion, massive spread and penetration (they dominate 99 percent of the market; see Huerta & Gómez 2013) and its unmatched economic and cultural relevance, to shape the political decisions in the Mexican Republic. Because they could always count on a powerful media apparatus, politics through digital media has never been a priority within the strategies of Mexican politicians. As Espino Sánchez has demonstrated (2012), Mexican politics still relies mainly on television as the main channel for media campaigning and politicians generally have a really low engagement with the possibilities offered by Web 2.0 social platforms.

Superficially, the 2012 elections seemed to represent a change, with politicians embracing social media such as Facebook, Twitter and YouTube to spread their electoral messages and gain followers. However, as it emerges from more in-depth studies of the social media strategies of Mexican politicians during the electoral campaign, the intensification in the use of digital tools did not correspond to an increase in the level of democratic participation and dialogue between candidates and voters, but to a massive deployment of 'dirty digital strategies' that reached their peak on Twitter (Ricaurte Quijano 2013). These strategies included the creation of false universes of followers, such as the use of Twitter's hashtags to boost a candidate and slander his or her opponents, the use of *bots*[2] to automatically generate tweets, the hiring of *trolls* (people who tweet in favour of a candidate and against his or her opponent), and *ghost followers* (empty accounts with the aim of boosting the candidate's followers). In sum, as the Mexican researcher points out, negative strategies of traditional political campaigns were recreated online and the candidates discarded the possibility of using participatory media to innovate their strategies of political communication (Ricaurte Quijano 2013, 90). Thus, she concludes that: 'These strategies do not incorporate democratic visions in the way of doing politics that allow for the inclusion and the participation of the voters' (Ricaurte Quijano 2013, 102).

MEDIA AS GENESIS: THE BIRTH
OF A NETWORKED MOVEMENT

As we have seen, Mexican politicians were not using social media to foster dialogue and interaction with their constituency, but to artificially impose *trending topics* and manufacturing their online relevance. At the same time, EPN's path to the presidency seemed unstoppable, with the Mexican telecracy boosting his image in continuous spots that portrayed him as the only possible option for the future of the country (Villamil 2012). But on Friday, May 11, 2012, something disrupted his image as the only available option for Mexico. The candidate arrived at the *Universidad Iberoamericana* of Mexico City to give a conference. The Iberoamericana is a private, religious university and the PRI expected the event to run in a smooth, business-as-usual way. However, during the candidate's presentation, several students began to question him regarding the police repression and the killings of Atenco[3] that occurred in 2006 when EPN was governor of the state of Mexico; when EPN justified Atenco's violent repression, the tension rose and he had to leave the university surrounded by a security cordon. Immediately after the event, some PRI politicians qualified students as thugs, violent, fascist and intolerant, going so far as to deny their affiliation with the university. Meanwhile, Mexican television networks and the newspaper chain *Organización Editorial Mexicana* presented versions of the event where EPN was portrayed as a hero against a boycott organized by the Left. The defamatory declarations together with the biased media coverage led 131 university students of the Universidad Iberoamericana to publish a video on YouTube[4] in which they displayed their teaching credentials and read their names to the camera to criticize the politicians who had accused them of being violent thugs manoeuvred by the Left and not affiliated with the university: this powerful act of reclamation of identity marked the beginning of the movement. The power of these eleven minutes lies in their ability to build an event where individual responsibility is assumed and students talk from a 'place of identity' (Reguillo 2012), contrasting the official media discourse, reclaiming their agency and using social media platforms to trigger collective identification processes. The phrase '131 Students from Ibero' quickly became one of the trending topics on Twitter in Mexico and worldwide.[5] Other students began to join the protest, stating, 'I'm one more of you,' 'I'm 132,' thus leading to the creation of the Twitter hashtag #YoSoy132, which went on to identify the whole movement. While the dirty digital tricks of official politics were dominating the virtual landscape, suddenly these students' voices proved that another way of using social media was possible.

MEDIA AS ADDRESSEE AND TOOLS OF THE #YOSOY132 STRUGGLE

Communication has been at the very centre of the #YoSoy132 resistance: in the Mexican movement, media have been 'genesis, tool and addressee of its struggle' (Aroch-Fugellie 2013, 7). We already saw the importance of (social) media in its genesis, now we will tackle the other two dimensions. From the very beginning, the central concern of #YoSoy132 has been the democratization of the Mexican media. As stated in their manifesto, the movement 'wants the democratization of the mass media, in order to guarantee transparent, plural and impartial information to foster critical consciousness and thought'.[6] This emphasis on media democratization is perfectly understandable in the Mexican context that is characterized—as we previously saw—by an influential telecracy, defined as the imposition of the interests of the advertising dealers of the TV monopolies over the interests of the whole Mexican society and the public interest (Esteinou and Alva de la Selva 2011). It is important to recognize, as Aroch-Fugellie has done, that #YoSoy132 'targets the social imaginary orchestrated by the mass media rather than targeting the institutional face of politics, which it views as a mere façade' (Aroch-Fugellie 2013, 7). Thus, Mexican activists address the television networks as *de facto* powers, and in so doing, they show 'how discarding the mass media as "merely" a mediator is to disavow its function as a structural site of capitalist interest' (Aroch-Fugellie 2013, 7). Through a myriad of artistic performances, demonstrations and urban interventions, #YoSoy132 protested against what they saw as the clear imposition of Enrique Peña Nieto by the Mexican telecracy. The movement produced countless documents and reports on how to reform and democratize the Mexican media, and was able to project several radical videos on the walls of the Televisa's headquarters in Mexico City. Moreover, students of the movement organized the first debate among the candidates in Mexican history that was broadcast on social media and on radio stations (only EPN did not participate because he claimed that impartiality was not guaranteed) and the first to be organized by civil society and not by the Federal Electoral Institute (IFE). The symbolic echo of these protests, initiatives and actions that strongly condemn the power of the media to manipulate the everyday reality and influence the political sphere, still resonates within the consciousness of thousands of Mexican people.

Media have also been significant tools for resistance: the Mexican movement has unleashed the full potential of social media such as Twitter, Facebook and YouTube in order to spread critical messages, organize and coordinate mobilizations, cultivate collective identities, build counterhegemonic spaces, forge transnational connections and increase civic engagement and participation (Gómez and Treré 2014). In recent years, a vibrant digital sphere has emerged in Mexico, where young urban middle classes, especially university students, are increasingly using social media to acquire and spread critical contents. In 2011, Internet World Stats estimated that the internet penetration in Mexico was 36.9 percent.[7] According to AMIPCI, in the same year, 90 percent of Mexican internet users used social media (Facebook being the most used online platform).[8]

Research on the #YoSoy132 movement has flourished in the last three years. Available literature has been mainly descriptive and focused on the first days of its eruption (Candón Mena 2013; Galindo Cáceres and González-Acosta 2013; Rovira Sancho 2012; Sosa Plata 2012) and on the relevance of artistic expressions within the movement (Aroch-Fugellie 2013; Red 2013). Others have stressed the importance of social media in the development of a 'citizenship 2.0', a 'Mexican Spring', a 'fifth state' (Islas and Arribas 2012), or as 'unregulated virtual networks' that function as 'alternative media' to the Mexican telecracy and 'participate in the reconfiguration of the global political and economical order' (Andión Gamboa 2013, 48). It is rather surprising that while the controversies and the anomalies of Mexican conventional media have been denounced, finely dissected and widely criticized by almost anyone who has written on the movement, social media platforms have not been problematized, and their power to change the rules of the game have been by and large taken for granted. The literature has tended to polarize the debate: on one side, the *bad* Mexican telecracy with its high level of concentration and with its immense symbolic and political power. On the other side, the *good* social media: new, free, unregulated, alternative, emancipatory and bringers of revolution. In sum, with the exceptions of a few journalistic reports[9] and various tech activists' analyses,[10] literature has viewed social media platforms as mere tools in the hands of rebellious students.

SOFT DETERMINISM, COMMUNICATIVE CAPITALISM AND SOCIAL MEDIA PROTEST

The metaphor of digital media as mere tools for performing contentious activities is not something that concerns only the Mexican context: as one of the most used metaphors for describing the effects of communication technologies (Nardi and O'Day 1999), the simplistic tool metaphor has long since 'infected' the study of digital activism and social movements (Treré and Barranquero 2013). If we look at standard approaches to communication from social movement theories, we find a rather instrumental view of media (Carroll and Hackett 2006; Downing 2008; Huesca 2001). In fact, social movement theories tend to view media as tools that movements use to pursue predefined goals and to conceive them as 'technological message channels rather than as the complex sociotechnical institutions they actually are' (Downing 2008, 41). In their analysis of flash-mobs as challenges to the 'orthodoxy' of the sociology of social movements, Lasén and Albéniz (2011, 14) has pointed out that in many analyses the role that is attributed to technological mediations used in mobilization is still instrumental: 'these mediations are considered mere resources to reach pre-established political goals', the authors conclude. Most of the time, what we encounter in contemporary evaluations of movements and digital communication technologies is not *hard technological determinism* according to which social media are the only causes of global revolutions, but a *soft technological determinism* (Hands 2011; Stalder 2006) that fails to address social media's complexity in the reconfiguration of political participation. The sociologist Manuel Castells, one of the most influential authors on the relations between social movements and communication technologies, is one example of this soft determinism. In his last works, he has further developed his theory of power in the network society, complementing it with the concept of mass self-communication (Castells 2009) and applying his theoretical reflections to the contemporary cycle of contention that originated in 2011 (from Iceland to the Arab Spring, from the *Spanish Indignados* to the Occupy movement) (Castells 2012). According to the scholar, while highly concentrated global multimedia corporations and business politics are trying to 'conquer' online communicative spaces, the development of interactive, horizontal networks of communication has prompted the emergence of a new form of communication: mass self-communication. In this new form of communication, the production of the message is self-generated, the definition of the potential receiver(s) is self-directed, and the retrieval of specific messages or content from the web and digital networks is self-selected. Mass self-communication is providing unprecedented communicative possibilities to insurgent politics and social movements, as Castells shows in his 2012 book that applies this conceptualization to a variety of new uprisings: he argues that digital communications have created a 'space of autonomy' for the exchange of information and the sharing of feelings of collective outrage and hope.

While Castells's theorizations and reflections are undoubtedly relevant and illuminating, and push us to seriously reflect on the role of digital media in contemporary mobilizations, one is left with the impression that the complexity of social media platforms for resistance is somehow left uncharted; in particular, there are two main concerns with Castells's analysis. First of all, his tendency to polarize the description of the communicative scenario with on one side highly concentrated global corporations, and on the other side social movements using mass self-communication to fight back runs the risk of neglecting the ambivalences and contradictions inherent in contemporary 'technocapitalism' (Kellner 1989), or 'communicative capitalism' (Dean 2005). Far from being autonomous spaces from capital, social media represent *corporate enclosures* where citizens' access is not free because the people are sold as 'a prosumer commodity to third parties in order to generate profit' (Fuchs 2009, 96). Thus, 'the actual power of corporations in web 2.0 is much larger than the actual political counter-power that is exercised by the produsers' (Fuchs 2009, 96). Issues of privacy, surveillance, commodification and digital labor characterize Web 2.0 environments and especially social media platforms. Furthermore, digital technologies are far from exempt from the pressures, the influence and the control of the political sphere (Curran et al. 2012; Morozov 2011). Therefore, when Andión Gamboa (2013, 48), in his analysis of social media's relevance within #YoSoy132, asserts that 'mass self-communication brings as a necessary consequence the democratization of the mass media' he is adhering to the digital optimism of Castells's vision where the conflict and the contradictions of capital are somehow not inherent to 'the digital'.

Second, Castells's analysis falls short of recognizing that 'the relationship between social movements and new technologies is a matter of constant negotiation and is defined by a complex dialectics between transformation and continuity, between the technical and the social, and between old and new political repertoires of political action and media activism' (Barassi 2013). In other words, social media's adoptions, uses, appropriations and integrations into movements' 'repertoire of communication' (Mattoni 2013) are multifaceted activities that are not exempt from everyday conflicts, contrasts and tensions. Thus, far from the 'smooth functioning' of counterpower that Castells provides, we should also recognize that the ways through which digital technologies, political imagination and activists' practices mutually shape each other are frequently problematic, contradictory and ambiguous (Barassi and Treré 2012; Cammaerts, Mattoni and McCurdy 2013; Ganesh and Stohl 2010).

In the next sections, breaking with the simplistic assumption that social media exclusively represented alternative emancipatory technologies with which young Mexicans fought Mexican telecracy, I show that these digital technologies represented permanent ecologies traversed by conflict, dissonance and frictions. Web 2.0 technologies were used by the Mexican government to monitor and discredit the students' protest and were cause of incessant controversy within daily activists' practices. This chapter is based on a two-year-long multimodal ethnography that relies on the triangulation of different methodologies: fifty individual interviews with activists of #YoSoy132; four group interviews with protesters of Mexico City, Guadalajara and Querétaro; several short periods of participant observation (during 2012 and 2013) and a qualitative content analysis of digital media and online platforms.

THE 'APOCRYPHAL PAGE': YOSOY132.MX AS A DIGITAL TRAP

> This guy showed up, his name was Manuel Cossío. He said that in the moment he saw that the movement was something important, he bought the domain *yosoy132.mx* (. . .). He told us he wanted to change the country, and that he offered his skills, that he was an expert in social networking platforms. And the web page looked really nice indeed. Yes, we were a bit worried about the whole 'you have to register yourself and give your data' thing . . . But, as we were into lots of other things, we didn't really pay much attention. It was a fatal mistake.

These words extracted from my interview with Iván, the Twitter administrator of the *#Soy132mx* account, recalls the meeting with Manuel Cossío, who offered to #YoSoy132 activists his digital skills and the web portal *YoSoy132.mx*. Cossío was able to enter in the movement almost immediately, contacting prominent activist Saúl Alvídrez ten days after that famous black Friday when #YoSoy132 originated. While Alvídrez and other activists had already bought the *YoSoy132.com* and *YoSoy132.com.mx* domains, it was the *YoSoy132.mx* registered by Cossío that was finally adopted, also thanks to the ability of Cossío to sell 'its valuable, ready-to-go product' (interview with Laura) during various of the first assemblies of the movement. Announced at the end of May 2012 on the official movement's Twitter account and by various prominent activists as the official page of #YoSoy132, this professional-looking website, fully integrated with possibilities of access and interactions from other platforms such as Google and Facebook, was largely used for debate, organization, information spreading and to collect participants' data.

After a month of intense use of the website, something happened. On Monday, 18 of June, two YouTube videos appeared on the home page of the #YoSoy132 portal and in the YouTube account 'Yo Soy'.[11] In the first video, we can see in the background the fixed image of the face of one active protester of the movement, Saúl Alvídrez from the *Tecnológico de Monterrey University*, while at the same time we hear his voice and see yellow subtitles that report the words of the activist. The audio appears as a collage of several of Alvídrez's informal talks—obviously recorded without his consent—where the #YoSoy132 student speaks about the movement and the relations with Andrés Manuel Lopez Obrador, and other intellectuals identified with the Mexican Left, especially a collective named 'México, ahora o nunca' ('Mexico, now or never') supposedly integrated by director Epigmenio Ibarra, investigative journalist Jenaro Villamil and other critical Mexican voices such as Virgilio Caballero, Anabel Hernandez and Alfredo Jalife.

In the second video called 'La verdad nos hará libres' ('Truth will set us free', one of the principal mottos adopted by the movement, a biblical quote that represents the motto of the *Iberoamericana University*), Manuel Cossío speaks to the camera, reading a text where he shows his profound disappointment for discovering that many leaders of the #YoSoy132 movement were coopted by Mexican Left-wing politicians affiliated with the PRD party such as Marcelo Ebrard, López Obrador and Alejandro Encinas. Both of these online attempts of delegitimization were the creation of Manuel Cossío Ramos, owner and manager of the YoSoy132.mx website.

According to an inquiry carried out by the online investigative journalism website *Contralínea* in June 2013 (anticipated by articles on the critical blog *SinEmbargo* and by the magazine *Proceso*, and further analysed on the *Revolución 3.0* blog[12]), Cossío was an agent of the Mexican Secret Service, the Center of National Watch and Security (CISEN), whose mission was to infiltrate the movement, steal data through the use of the Web platform and destabilize the inner power balances within #YoSoy132 before the elections. Activists of the movement, flooded with activities and with increasing organizational matters to solve in the immediate days after the eruption of #YoSoy132, trusted Cossío and fell into his *digital trap*. The two videos caused controversy and conflict: Alvídrez was expelled from the movement and the Mexican telecracy used the event in order to insinuate that the videos represented proof that the Mexican movement had been manipulated from the beginning by the PRD party and by intellectuals of the Left. #YoSoy132 activists eventually realized that the platform was intended as a way to monitor, control and profile them and decided to migrate to another platform: *yosoy132media.mx*. This migration and the dangers related to the use of the other 'apocryphal web page' were announced on Facebook and spread through multiple Twitter accounts in order to inform citizens about the real intentions of Cossío and the nature of the fake portal; other users and critical blogs from the Mexican blogosphere such as *AnimalPolitico* also retweeted the information.

It is estimated that the website was able to steal the information of more than seventy thousand people with yet unexplored consequences for the Mexican resistance.[13] This example clearly shows how political control can use the technological frame where resistance is carried out in order to steal data, monitor protest activities, control the information flowing through the platform and then exploit the same medium to publish online videos in order to compromise and destabilize the reputation of the movement.

THE STRUGGLE WITHIN: PASSWORDS WAR, THE FANTASY OF ABUNDANCE AND SOCIAL MEDIA PARANOIA

The use and appropriations of social media platforms generated constant internal conflicts within student collectives that had to be addressed and solved during the development of the protest. In particular, within different student collectives there were continuous conflicts over the *ownerships of passwords* to access digital platforms. In the case of the student collectives of the city of Querétaro, for instance, there 'was a war over the passwords and the search for platforms' administrators' (interview with Claudia). The initial Facebook *fan page* of the student collective[14] was abandoned in August 2012 for another *personal* Facebook page.[15] Meanwhile, another Facebook page, linked to the activity of the *Agorá Querétaro* collective, is now (May 2015) the most-used platform.[16] Tracking down the evolution of all these different platforms and the reasons behind their adoption and subsequent desertion proved to be problematic. Some activists contend that the first fan page did not generate the 'necessary process of belonging' and had to be dropped; for other protesters, the main issue was instead that nobody remembered who the creator of the first page was (he or she was hiding behind a pseudonym) and thus they could not contact the creator in any way in order to update the page and change its main objectives. The spontaneity and effervescence of the movement's first days of protest, together with the need to spread information and organize actions straightaway, urged people to create myriads of social media platforms whose 'officiality' and 'representativity' had not been discussed and approved by any assembly. That means that often these platforms were created and managed by people who did not play an active role within the movement, who were unknown to most of the other activists and who disappeared after the first intense days of protest. When some of these digital environments were able to consolidate as *de facto* important media of the movement, various issues emerged: Who has access to and what are the passwords to the Facebook or Twitter accounts? Who is able to decide which information is given priority and who has access to more protected areas of the platform? Following the emotional wave of the protest, activists simply joined and used the first available and spreadable platforms, even if later, when the needs for a more organized and coordinated infrastructure arose, they had to migrate, change, adapt, reject and abandon some of the previous digital media.

This also explains other frequent conflicts generated around the belonging of activists to some platforms and the authority to expel people from Facebook closed groups and mailing lists, an aspect that is also associated—as many other aspects are—to a question of time management within grassroots political organizations (Fenton and Barassi 2011). In sum, social movements' work depends on political conjunctures, and often activists have little time to reflect on their communication tactics (see also chapters by Barassi and Kaun in this volume). Controlling the people who are part of a closed group requires time (time to check who is in and time to decide why he or she should not) and this task cannot be easily performed on a daily basis, especially when activists are flooded with countless protest activities. This situation of *digital chaos* usually aggravates, because new groups are incessantly created in order to overcome this problem (if I do not possess the authority to throw you out of a group, I will create another which you are not part of), and platforms reach a point of saturation where they become uncontrollable and unmanageable. All these issues are connected to internal processes of decision making and organization: as in the case of many contemporary movements (Juris 2008), #YoSoy132 activists want these processes to be as participatory and inclusive as possible. But, as many decisions are contingent and often need to be taken rapidly to be effective, they prevent the possibility of summoning other participants and reach a mutual understanding in an assembly. This 'tyranny of assemblearism' (interview with Ambar) prevented many decisions around communication technologies to be effective and created issues of media management, platforms' saturation and dispersion, together with everlasting discussions on 'who should be allowed to be on that platform and who should be allowed to act in order to expel someone from a Facebook group' (interview with Mariana). Here, it is important to recall the reflections of political theorist Jodi Dean on the *fantasy of abundance* that characterizes communicative capitalism. Dean critiques both digital optimists and digital pessimists for sharing the assumption that the abundance of messages and the enhancement of communications accelerate democratic processes. In the case examined here, the abundance of social media platforms is not an indication of democratic potential, but a reflection of inner organizational chaos, since the easiness of creating social media accounts and of spreading protest-related contents is seen as an obstacle for more effective communication. In Dean's words (and in Agamben's terms) 'communicativity hinders communication' (Dean 2005, 58).

Various authors have documented the techno-surveillance practices of the Mexican state that include sophisticated forms of *dataveillance*,[17] several spy softwares, and a long tradition of laws that limit freedom of expression and dissidence (Ricaurte Quijano, Nájera Valdez and Robles Maloof 2014). In the final part of this section, I would like to draw the attention to the activists' reaction to the perception of being spied on and controlled online by the government. While more tech-savvy protesters used social network analysis in order to unmask the use of bots during the electoral campaign, most of the activists developed a general sense of paranoia around social media such as Facebook and their mobile phones. Students referred to this undefined emotional reaction to the sense of being spied on and controlled by institutions as *social media paranoia.* This paranoia was always present within the digital activities of most of the #YoSoy132 activists, but it affected their practices in different ways, according to the evolution of the political situation and the level of violence and repression that the Mexican police were wielding. At the beginning of the movement, some concerned students exhibited a 'light social media paranoia' (interview with Berenice) in relation to Facebook and Twitter, but, after various discussions in the assemblies, these concerns were discarded because of the pressing need to communicate and organize through digital platforms before the elections. On 1 December 2012 (known as #1DMX[18]), day of the official settlement of Enrique Peña Nieto, during the peaceful protest of #YoSoy132 and other civil society's organizations, Mexican police carried out several arbitrary detentions and human rights violations. This event shocked many activists of the movement and had serious consequences on their social media practices of resistance. Many of them quit their Facebook, Twitter and YouTube accounts, while others began feverish work of deleting 'compromising' digital material including pictures and videos during mobilizations and protests and posts that somehow referred to them as active participants in the struggles.

CONCLUSIONS: POWER AND DISSONANCE IN SOCIAL MEDIA PROTEST

In this chapter, by breaking with dominant celebratory visions that conceived social media platforms as revolutionary tools in the hands of the Mexican youth, I have offered an examination of the digital practices of the #YoSoy132 movement that reveal how these communication technologies were used by the government to monitor, control and discredit dissidence. Furthermore, Web 2.0 environments were crossed by incessant controversy, permanent dispute and everyday conflicts that mirrored the organizational issue of the movement: the abundance of participatory media hindered democratic processes instead of easing them. Besides, activists developed a sense of paranoia in relation to social media that deeply affected their digital practices. The image of social media resistance that this chapter has offered is certainly dissimilar from the 'smooth functioning' of counterpower through mass self-communication that we find in Castells's accounts: social media resistance is constrained and controlled by political forces and has to 'compete' in a digital environment where traditional politics unleashes all its repertoire of dirty digital tricks. In addition, internal organizational conflicts reverberate at the technological level, showing that communication technologies are not mere tools that have to be 'taken for granted', but complex spaces of conflict and negotiation that have to be carefully discovered.

The conceptualization of Castells's mass self-communication is indebted to his definition of power, which, based on Weber, consists in 'the relational capacity that enables a social actor to influence asymmetrically the decisions of other social actor(s) in ways that favour the empowered actor's will, interests, and values' (Castells 2009, 10). If we see power also in the terms of Foucault as relational, immanent and ubiquitous (Foucault 1988), we can appreciate that 'relations of power, and indeed relations of oppression, are not only "outside" of us, but are generated by and through the subjects on which limitations are imposed' (Uzelman 2011, 33). In other words, as our perilous adventure amid Mexican social media resistance has showed, conflicts, discords and dissonances unfold not only in the fight *against* the external agents that embody communicative capitalism (the government, the telecracy), but also continuously operate *within* activists' everyday practices. Otherwise, we may be led to believe that once the shackles of capitalism are removed, the full potential of digital technologies will be finally 'revealed' in a somehow unproblematic and frictionless way.

In his critique to the idea of technology as means, Latour (2002, 255) writes: 'the paradox of technology is that it is always praised for its functional utility, or always held in contempt for its irritating neutrality, although it has never ceased to introduce a history of enfoldings, detours, drifts, openings and translations that abolish the idea of function as much as that of neutrality'. If we look at social media as complex ecologies crossed by frictions and frustrations, traversed by clashes and conflicts, inhabited by fantasies and paranoia, we will appreciate that being critical in their exploration means understanding their imbrications into the processes of *communicative capitalism*, as much as recognizing how *the struggle within* operates, shapes and limits the practices of social media protest. In other words, a careful appraisal of the real contributions that social media bring to activism and resistance should strive to consider all the nuances and the new manifestations of (communication) power, in particular those participatory and decentralized practices that constitute the essence of many contemporary movements. Instead of perpetuating what Galloway calls the 'reticular fallacy' (2014), the belief that rhizomatic structures are per se corrosive of power and sovereignty, we should unearth innovative ways of unravelling their functioning in order to find out under which circumstances they still represent sources of struggle, discomfort and suspicion.

NOTES

1. My research for this article was funded by the 2013 FOFIUAQ Grant of the Autonomous University of Querétaro (Mexico) [grant number FCP201410].

2. Bots (short for *software robots*) designate 'computer algorithm that automatically produces content and interacts with humans on social media, trying to emulate and possibly alter their behavior' (Ferrara et al. 2014: xx). Some of them are benign, but many of them are instead malicious entities designed to be harmful, with the purpose of manipulating social media discourse; for instance, by artificially inflating the support of a candidate during the elections,

as in the case discussed in this chapter. Other reported cases regarding the use of bots during elections include the smearing campaign against one US Senate candidate for Delaware (Ratkievicz et al. 2011) and the campaigns for the governor of the State of Mexico (Ricaurte Quijano 2011).

3. The uprisings of San Salvador Atenco of 2006 began on Wednesday, 3 May, when the police prevented a group of flower vendors from selling at the Texcoco local market in the State of México, about thirty kilometres from Mexico City. Police reacted violently against the population and the vendors appealed to the residents of the small community of San Salvador Atenco, about twenty-five kilometres northeast of Mexico City, famous for their strenuous resistance to the construction of an airport on their land four years before. The Atenco residents blocked the highway to Texcoco near their town and, in response, hundreds of state police were sent by the governor of the State of Mexico, Enrique Peña Nieto, to remove the blockade. According to a five-month investigation of the National Human Rights Commission (CNDH), during the confrontations 207 people were victims of cruel, inhuman or degrading treatment, 145 were arbitrarily arrested, twenty-six women were sexually assaulted and five foreigners were beaten and expelled from the country. For additional information on the Atenco case, see http://www.amnesty.ie/our-work/mexico-first-anniversary-san-salvador-atenco-%E2%80%93-untouchable-impunity.

4. http://www.youtube.com/watch?v=P7XbocXsFkI (accessed 18 November 2014).

5. http://capitalsocialmexico.com/2012/05/15/mas-sobre-la-viralizacion-del-tt-sobre-la-ibero-que-dio-la-vuelta-al-mundo/ (accessed 20 November 2014).

6. http://www.youtube.com/watch?v=igxPudJF6nU (my translation from the original Spanish. Accessed 20 November 2014).

7. http://www.internetworldstats.com/stats.htm (accessed 19 September 2014).

8. http://www.amipci.org.mx/?P=esthabitos (accessed 18 October 2014).

9. For instance, the online magazine CONTRALÍNEA that denounced the Cossío case that I analyse in the next sections (http://info/archivo-revista/index.php/2013/09/08/yosoy-infiltrado/—accessed 22 October 2014), and the critical blog *SinEmbargo* (http://www.sinembargo.mx).

10. For instance, the YoSoyRed blog that is now Loquesigue.net, where the Mexican dirty digital wars were often denounced, see http://loquesigue.net/2014/06/tecnofascismo-el-ejercito-de-bots-que-defienden-a-pena-nieto-y-censuran-a-criticos-y-periodistas/ (accessed 26 October 2014).

11. https://www.youtube.com/watch?v=nj2HipB5a1c&list=UUg-S9Qre98WT9kDEb4hixKw and https://www.youtube.com/watch?v=UmuFHcyHSaA (accessed 22 November 2014).

12. For the article in *SinEmbargo*, see http://www.sinembargo.mx/18-06-2012/267821; in the magazine *PROCESO*, see http://www.proceso.com.mx/?p=343793 and in the blog *Revolución 3.0* see http://revoluciontrespuntocero.com/cissen-infiltrado-en-yosoy132-segunda-parte/ (all links accessed 28 November 2014).

13. According to the online magazine CONTRALÍNEA, Cossío was able to gather and steal data of more than seventy thousand students.

14. https://www.facebook.com/QroYoSoy132 (accessed 28 November 2014).

15. https://www.facebook.com/yosoy.queretaro.75 (accessed 28 November 2014).

16. https://www.facebook.com/pages/%C3%81gora-132-Quer%C3%A9taro/574577782578880 (accessed 28 November 2014).

17. Intended as 'the systematic monitoring of people's actions or communications through the application of information technology' (Clarke 1988).

18. The *1Dmx.org* platform was created on 2 December 2012 in order to document human rights violations and police abuse registered during Enrique Peña Nieto's swearing in as president on 1 December. A few days before 1 December 2013, the US Embassy in Mexico ordered the censorship of the website 1Dmx.org, and on 2 December, *GoDaddy.com*, a US-based company that provides internet domains, took down the site. For space reasons, it was not possible to examine this case of online censorship that again confirms the many pitfalls of digital resistance in the Mexican scenario.

REFERENCES

Andión Gamboa, Mauricio. 2013. "Las redes sociales virtuales como medios alternativos al poder de la Telecracia en México." *Versión* 31:42–55. Accessed 12 December 2014.

Aroch-Fugellie, Paulina. 2013. "Leverage: Artistic Interventions of the Mexican Student Movement." *Journal of Latin American Cultural Studies* 22 (4): 353–73. Accessed 12 December 2014. doi: 10.1080/13569325.2013.843056.

Barassi, Veronica. 2013. "Review—Networks of Outrage and Hope." *E-Internacional Relations*. 27 February.

Barassi, Veronica, and Emiliano Treré. 2012. "Does Web 3.0 Follow Web 2.0? Deconstructing Theoretical Assumptions through Practice." *New Media and Society* 14 (8): 1269–85. Accessed 12 December 2014. doi: 10.1177/1461444812445878.

Cammaerts, Bart, Alice Mattoni and Patrick McCurdy, eds. 2013. *Mediation and Protest Movements*. London: Intellect.

Candón Mena, José. 2013. "Movimientos por la democratización de la comunicación: Los casos del 15-M y #YoSoy132." *Razón y Palabra* 82:1–21. Accessed 12 December 2014.

Carroll, William K., and Robert A. Hackett. 2006. "Democratic Media Activism through the Lens of Social Movement Theory." *Media, Culture & Society* 28:83–104. Accessed 12 December 2014. doi: 10.1177/0163443706059289.

Castells, Manuel. 2009. *Communication Power*. Oxford: Oxford University Press.

———. 2012. *Networks of Outrage and Hope. Social Movements in the Internet Age*. Cambridge: Polity Press.

Clarke, Roger. 1988. "Information Technology and Dataveillance." *Communications of the ACM* 31 (5): 498–512.

Curran, James, Natalie Fenton and Des Freedman. 2012. *Misunderstanding the Internet*. London: Routledge.

Dean, Jodi. 2005. "Communicative Capitalism: Circulation and the Foreclosure of Politics." *Cultural Politics* 1 (1): 51–74. Accessed 12 December 2014.

Downing, John. 2008. "Social Movement Theories and Alternative Media: An Evaluation and Critique." *Communication, Culture & Critique* 1:40–50. Accessed 12 December 12 2014. doi:10.1111/j.1753-9137.2007.00005.x.

Espino Sánchez, Germán. 2012. *¿Cyberrevolución en la política? Mitos y verdades sobre la ciberpolítica 2.0 en México*. México, DF: Distribuciones Fontamara.

Esteinou Madrid, Javier, and Alma Rosa Alva de la Selva. 2011. *Los medios electrónicos de difusión y la sociedad de la información*. México, DF: Secretaría de Relaciones Exteriores.

Fenton, Natalie, and Veronica Barassi. 2011. "Alternative Media and Social Networking Sites: The Politics of Individuation and Political Participation." *Communication Review* 14 (3): 179–96. Accessed 12 December 2014. doi:10.1080/10714421.2011.597245.

Ferrara, Emilio, Onur Varol, Clayton Davis, Filippo Menzer and Alessandro Flammini. 2014. The Rise of Social Bots. *arXiv preprint arXiv:1407.5225*.

Foucault, Michel. 1988. "The Ethic of Care for the Self as a Practice of Freedom." In *The Final Foucault*, edited by James Bernauer and David Rasmussen, 1–21. Cambridge, MA: MIT Press.

Fuchs, Christian. 2009. "Some Reflections on Manuel Castells' Book *Communication Power*." *tripleC* 7 (1): 94–108. Accessed 12 December 2014.

Galindo Cáceres, Jesús, and José Ignacio González-Acosta. 2013. *#YoSoy132. La primera erupción visible*. México, DF: Global Talent University Press.

Galloway, Alexander R. 2014. "The Reticular Fallacy." 26 October 2014. Accessed 24 January 2015. http://cultureandcommunication.org/galloway/the-reticular-fallacy.

Ganesh, Shiv, and Cynthia Stohl. 2010. "Qualifying Engagement: A Study of Information and Communication Technology and the Global Social Justice Movement in Aotearoa New Zealand." *Communication Monographs* 77 (1): 51–74. Accessed 12 December 2014. doi:10.1080/03637750903514284.

Gómez García, Rodrigo, and Emiliano Treré. 2014. "The #YoSoy132 Movement and the Struggle for Media Democratization in Mexico." *Convergence: The International Journal of*

Research into New Media Technologies 20 (4): 496–510. Accessed 12 December 2014. doi: 10.1177/1354856514541744.

Hands, Joss. 2011. *@ Is for Activism: Dissent, Resistance and Rebellion in a Digital Culture.* London: Pluto Press.

Huerta-Wong, Juan Enrique, and Rodrigo Gómez García. 2013. "Concentración y diversidad de los medios de comunicación y las telecomunicaciones en México." *Comunicación y Sociedad* 19:113–52. Accessed 12 December 2014.

Huesca, Robert. 2001. "Conceptual Contributions of New Social Movements to Development Communication Research." *Communication Theory* 11:415–33. Accessed 12 December 2014. doi: 10.1111/j.1468-2885.2001.tb00251.x.

Juris, Jeffrey S. 2008. *Networking Futures: The Movements against Corporate Globalization.* Durham, NC and London: Duke University Press.

Islas, Octavio, and Amaia Arribas. 2012. "Enseñanza y ejemplo de la primavera mexicana." *Razón y Palabra* 17(80). Accessed 12 December 2014.

Kellner, Douglas. 1989. *Critical Theory, Marxism and Modernity.* Cambridge: Polity Press.

Lasén, Amparo, and Iñaki Martínez de Albeniz. 2011. "'An Original Protest, at Least.' Mediality and Participation." In *Cultures of Participation: Media Practices, Cultures and Literacy,* edited by Hajo Greif, Larissa Hjorth, Amparo Lasén and Claire Lobet-Maris, 141–58. Berlin: Peter Lang.

Latour, Bruno. 2002. "Morality and Technology: The End of the Means." *Theory, Culture & Society* 19 (5/6): 247–60. Accessed 12 December 2014. doi: 10.1177/026327602761899246.

Mattoni, Alice. 2013. "Repertoires of Communication in Social Movement Processes." In *Mediation and Protest Movements,* edited by Bart Cammaerts, Alice Mattoni and Patrick McCurdy, 39–56. Bristol: Intellect.

Morozov, Evgeny. 2011. *The Net Delusion: The Dark Side of Internet Freedom.* New York: Public Affairs.

Nardi, Bonnie A., and Vicki L. O'Day. 1999. *Information Ecologies: Using Technology with Heart.* Boston: MIT Press.

Ratkiewicz, Jacob, Michael Conover, Mark Meiss, Bruno Gonçalves, Alessandro Flammini and Filippo Menczer. 2011. "Detecting and Tracking Political Abuse in Social Media." In *ICWSM: 5th International AAAI Conference on Weblogs and Social Media,* 297–304.

Red, Magdelana. 2013. "Rocking the Vote in Mexico's 2012 Presidential Election: Mexico's Popular Music Scene's Use of Social Media in a Post–Arab Spring Context." *International Journal of Communication* 7. Retrieved from http://ijoc.org/index.php/ijoc/article/view/1874.

Reguillo, Rossana. 2012. "Reflexiones iniciales en torno a #YoSoy132". *Magis,* 28 May.

Ricaurte Quijano, Paola. 2011. "Acarreados digitales", *El Universal,* 23 June. Accessed 28 January 2015. http://bit.ly/ii9VmP.

Ricaurte Quijano, Paola. 2013. "Tan cerca de Twitter y tan lejos de los votantes: las estrategias de los candidatos presidenciales mexicanos durante la campaña electoral de 2012." *Versión* 31:118-132. Accessed 12 December 2014.

Ricaurte Quijano, Paola, Jacobo Nájera Valdez and Jesús Robles Maloof. 2014. "Sociedades de control: tecnovigilancia de Estado y resistencia civil en México." *Teknokultura. Revista de Cultura Digital y Movimientos Sociales* 11 (2): 259–82.

Rovira Sancho, Guiomar. 2012. "México, #YoSoy132: ¡No había nadie haciendo el movimiento más que nosotros!" In *Anuari del conflicte social 2012.* Observatori del conflicte social, 423–48. Barcelona: Universitat de Barcelona.

Sosa Plata, Gabriel. 2012. "#YoSoy132: jóvenes frente a las redes sociales y la democratización de los medios de comunicación." In *Esfera pública y tecnologías de la información y la comunicación.* México, DF: Instituto Electoral del Distrito Federal.

Stalder, Felix. 2006. *Manuel Castells and the Theory of Network Society.* Cambridge: Polity Press.

Trejo Delarbre, Raul. 2004. *Poderes salvajes. Mediocracia sin contrapesos.* México, DF: Cal y Arena.

Treré, Emiliano, and Alejandro Barranquero Carretero. 2013. "De mitos y sublimes digitales: movimientos sociales y tecnologías de la comunicación desde una perspectiva histórica". *Redes.com* 8:27–47. Accessed 12 December 2014.

Tuckman, Jo. 2012. "Mexican Media Scandal: Secretive Televisa Unit Promoted PRI Candidate." *Guardian*, 26 June.

Uzelman, Scott. 2011. "Dangerous Practices: 'Determinism of Technique' in Alternative Media and Their Literature." *International Journal of Media and Cultural Politics* 7 (1): 21–35. Accessed 12 December 2014. doi: 10.1386/mcp.7.1.21_1.

Villamil, Jenaro. 2010. *El sexenio de Televisa: Conjuras del poder mediático*. México, DF: Grijalbo.

———. 2012. *Peña Nieto: el gran montaje*. México, DF: Grijalbo.

Chapter Ten

Social Media and the 2013 Protests in Brazil

The Contradictory Nature of Political Mobilization in the Digital Era

Mauro P. Porto and João Brant

In June 2013, a wave of massive street demonstrations took place in Brazil, establishing the country's largest protest movement in more than two decades. The first demonstrations emerged in opposition to a 20-cents (about 9 cents of the US dollar) rise in public transportation fares. There was also widespread discontent with the economic and social costs of Brazil's decision to host the 2014 FIFA World Cup. These first protests faced violent police repression and negative media coverage. Despite this, the movement grew very quickly. At the peak of the protests, on 20 June 2013, more than 1.4 million people in at least 140 cities went to the streets bearing a profusion of agendas. By then, the initial focus on public transportation fares and on the impact of mega sport events had been replaced by a much more diversified and complex agenda and set of demands.

The rise of this mass movement was a remarkable and quite unexpected development in Brazil's recent history. Among its many features, the intense use of digital platforms—including Facebook, Twitter and YouTube—figured prominently. The goal of this chapter is to advance a critical analysis of the role of social media in the emergence and development of the 2013 protests in Brazil. While evidence suggests that online platforms played significant roles in calling and facilitating street mobilizations in Brazil and elsewhere, the contradictory nature of internet-based political activism has received less attention. We are still a long way from more consistent theorizations about the relationship between online forms of political contestation and the broader political context. We also need analytical frameworks that consider how strategies of self-presentation deployed by social media users affect the development of political subjectivities and agendas within protest movements.

This chapter examines key features of the political context that are essential to understand the scope and significance of the demonstrations, including Brazil's recent political history and the role of political actors, civil society organizations and the mainstream media. The chapter also highlights the contradictory effects of political contestation by 'individualized publics' (Bennett and Segerberg 2013) in the digital era, arguing that the fragmentation of the movement's agenda was related to the structure of communication processes held within social networks and to online strategies adopted by some key players. These and other factors help explain why initial progressive and critical actors and demands that were central in the first demonstrations became less influential as the movement grew in scope and strength.

SOCIAL MEDIA AND PROTEST: A CONTEXTUALIST APPROACH

The role of social media in shaping collective action and political protest has been the object of intensive scholarly debate. Much of the early literature on the relationship between internet and political mobilization was characterized by a dichotomy between 'cyber-enthusiasts' and 'cyber-skeptics' (see Joseph 2012; Wolfsfeld, Segev and Sheafer 2013). Enthusiasts often express optimism about the ability of new media to empower individuals and political organizations. In one of the most sophisticated and insightful works in this line, Benkler (2006) emphasizes the internet's 'liberalizing effects' in providing anyone with an outlet to speak and in creating decentralized approaches to political debate and organization that establish a unique 'networked public sphere'. Sceptics, on the other hand, tend to downplay the significance of the impact of new technologies. Gladwell (2010), for example, argues that social media connections promote weak ties and low-risk activism, creating loose and leaderless networks that lack political efficacy.

More recently, several scholars have insisted on the need for more nuanced perspectives that can move beyond this basic dichotomy (Bennett and Segerberg 2013; Juris 2012; Wolfsfeld, Segev and Sheafer 2013). The dramatic events of the so-called 'Arab Spring' offer a good illustration of major controversies about the political role of social media. For some, new digital technologies played a major role in the wave of protests that spread over the Middle East, offering activists coordination tools that were already embedded in networks of family and friends (e.g., Howard and Hussain, 2011). Other scholars question the view that the massive wave of protests of the Arab Spring can be interpreted in terms of social media impact. Wolfsfeld, Segev and Sheafer (2013) argue that it is a mistake to attempt to understand the role of any media in any political process without consideration of the surrounding political environment. The authors note, however, that both 'cyber-enthusiasts' and 'cyber-skeptics' generally fail to integrate political variables into the analysis of the role of social media in political mobilization and protest. To overcome this lacuna in the literature, Wolfsfeld, Segev and Sheafer propose a third approach that they label 'contextualism'. According to this perspective, it is essential to emphasize the impact of political, social and economic variables when examining the role of social media in collective action (Wolfsfeld, Segev and Sheafer 2013). Similarly, James Curran (2012) insists on the importance of the external context in enabling or disabling the realization of the technological potential of the internet.

This chapter seeks to advance this line of inquiry by contextualizing the 2013 protests in Brazil in relation to broader political, social and economic environments. More specifically, we identify seven variables of the political context that are essential to understanding the recent wave of street demonstrations and the role social media played in them. We argue that such a 'contextualist' approach is essential to avoid overestimating or misunderstanding the role of digital platforms in processes of political mobilization.

CONTRADICTIONS IN ONLINE MOBILIZATIONS OF INDIVIDUALIZED PUBLICS

Besides emphasizing the importance of contextualizing social media in relation to the broader political environment, recent scholarship also offers valuable tools to examine the different logics of distinct forms of online political mobilization. In his ethnographic analysis of the dynamics of the #occupy movement in Boston, Juris (2012) stresses that different networking tools produce varying effects given their distinct sociotechnical affordances. For example, social media platforms like Facebook and Twitter allow individuals to quickly, cheaply and effectively disseminate vast amounts of information and coordinate protests in person-to-person networks, producing a sense of connectedness and copresence that has the potential of strengthening political mobilization. However, social media are far less effective than other online tools, such as listservs, for facilitating complex, interactive discussions regarding politics, identity, strategy and tactics. Thus, while Facebook and Twitter facilitate mass aggregation of individuals within concrete locations through viral communication flows, they are less suitable to generate stable organizational networks. As a result, rather than establishing a 'logic of networks', the use of Facebook and Twitter within social movements is characterized by a 'logic of aggregation' that tends to generate 'crowds of individuals' (Juris 2012, 267).

In their insightful analysis of economic justice and climate change movements in the postindustrial world, Bennett and Segerberg (2013) develop a similar approach.[1] The authors argue that the new forms of contentious action that have emerged since the late 1990s are associated with the rise of more highly 'individualized publics'. According to them, such publics are made up of large numbers of concerned citizens who are not inclined or able to join formal political organizations and whose political engagement is characterized instead by simple, everyday discourses anchored in lifestyles and shared with social networks. Bennett and Segerberg (2013) identify two main types of connective action. In 'organizationally enabled' connective action, loosely tied networks of organizations sponsor multiple actions and causes around a general set of issues in which followers are invited to personalize their engagement on their own terms. In 'crowd-enabled' connective action, dense networks of individuals deploy digital platforms to establish dynamic organizations in which crowds allocate resources and respond to external events (Bennett and Segerberg 2013). While nongovernmental organizations (NGOs) and social movements play a more significant leadership role in the first type of connective action, there is a high level of personalization and decentralization in the second.

Bennett and Segerberg praise organizations forming loose networks for allowing citizens to personalize their involvement with issues in creative and interactive ways. According to them, this type of personalized connective action has several advantages when compared to more conventional protest movements, including their ability to: scale up quickly; produce large and sometimes record-breaking mobilizations; display unusual flexibility in tracking targets and bridging different issues; build up adaptive protest repertoires; share open-source software development and embrace an ethos of inclusiveness (Bennett and Segerberg 2013, 25).

Questions remain, however, about the nature and political consequences of connective action, especially in its more individualized, crowd-enabled form. Bennett and Segerberg (2013, 191–92) recognize that organizationally enabled networks seem to have a better performance in sustaining focused messages and efforts in the long term, while crowd-enabled networks show a stronger adaptive capacity, enabled by technologies, to aggregate and filter huge volumes of individual inputs. However, the authors do not fully theorize the contradictory aspects of highly individualized forms of online mobilization that compromise the networks' ability to keep agenda consistency and ensure sustainability.

Several authors identify problematic political outcomes that are associated to personalized forms of online mobilization that rely heavily on social media. Juris (2012) argues that the individualized nature of participation in movements such as #occupy presents a particular challenge in terms of developing common proposals. Such forms of collective action often mobilize actors with little previous experience or with diverse ideological orientations, making it more difficult to establish a uniform set of demands (Juris 2012, 272–73). When examining academic discourses about the Arab Spring, Markham (2014) notes a tendency to value individual creativity and expression, while ignoring the fact that individualized engagements with social media can undermine a movement's sense of collective identity. For example, social media can lead movements to lose their ability to constrain and direct members' attention, communication and interaction (see also Fenton and Barassi 2011). Thus, creative acts of individuation do not always deliver substantive political change, since copresence in digital rituals and communication does not necessarily mean that participants are working together to build a common political subjectivity.

These and other critics highlight the contradictory nature of online political mobilizations, especially those that rely more heavily on social media platforms. We argue that the 2013 protests in Brazil illustrate these contradictions. As discussed in more detail below, platforms like Facebook and Twitter were instrumental in producing large record-breaking mobilizations in a short period of time and in creating and disseminating alternative political discourses and information. However, such platforms also played a significant role in fragmenting the agenda of the protests, diluting the political and ideological identity of participants, and in marginalizing the organizations that had played a leading role in the initial demonstrations. But before developing a more detailed analysis of the 2013 protests in Brazil, it is worth presenting a brief overview of the main events.

THE POLITICAL CONTEXT OF THE PROTESTS

One of the central arguments of this chapter is that the role of social media in political protest cannot be understood without careful and systematic consideration of the broader political, economic and social context. While not pretending to exhaust all the relevant variables that played a central role in the 2013 political mobilizations, we present seven factors that should be taken into account when explaining the dramatic events of June 2013. But before presenting the contextual factors, we introduce a basic timeline of the main events.

The demonstrations had specificities in each city and developed in direct connection with local contexts. Moreover, although the chronology presented below emphasizes protests that took place in June, especially in São Paulo, it is important to stress that the Free Fare Movement (MPL by its Portuguese acronym) had organized previous mobilizations in several other cities. Considering these caveats, we highlight the following events:

- The MPL organized the first major demonstration against the rise of bus fares in São Paulo on 6 June. Demonstrations were then held successively, with a few days' interval between them.
- From 6 June to 11 June, demonstrations gathered relatively small crowds, from two to five thousand participants each.
- On 13 June, a demonstration in São Paulo faced severe police repression, with several cases of aggression against protestors and journalists.
- On 15 June, the Confederations Cup started with the soccer match between Brazil and Japan, in Brasília, Brazil's capital. The match takes place under strong protests.
- On 17 June, large demonstrations took place in several cities, including São Paulo, Rio de Janeiro, Brasília, Belo Horizonte and Belém. On this day, the broadening of the scope of protests becomes clear. Bus fares and the World Cup now share posters and slogans with many other themes, such as the fight against corruption and the demand for improvements in healthcare and education systems.
- On 13 June, the mayor of Goiânia is the first one to revoke the fare increase. On 18 June, authorities in Cuiabá, Porto Alegre, Recife and João Pessoa did the same. In the following day, officials in São Paulo and Rio de Janeiro, Brazil's largest metropolitan areas, also announced the return to the previous bus fare value.
- On 20 June, the protests reached their peak, even though mayors had already revoked the bus fare increases. According to conservative estimates, over 1.4 million people protested in more than 140 cities, with about two hundred thousand taking the streets in São Paulo and three hundred thousand in Rio de Janeiro, Brazil's largest metropolitan areas (Roman 2013, 9).
- On 21 June, President Dilma Rousseff used a prime-time televised address to discuss the movement publicly for the first time.
- From 22 June onwards, attendance to protests starts to decline, although the scenario of public agitation remains.

Taking into consideration this dramatic chain of events, we identify seven factors of the political context within which the 2013 protests took place. We begin highlighting *timing as political opportunity*. In Brazil, public transportation fares are the responsibility of state and municipal governments[2] and increases usually take place in January. In 2013, however, President Dilma Rousseff requested other public officials to postpone the increase in order to contain the threat of rising inflation. As a result, several municipal and state administrations planned the rise of fares for May. Unlike the month of January, when students and a significant part of the workforce are on vacation, the country was in full speed by May. The postponement of bus fare increases for the months of May and June offered these groups an unusual opportunity for political mobilization.

The period of the protests also coincided with the beginning of the Confederations Cup. The tournament was organized by the International Federation of Association Football (FIFA) and was held in six Brazilian cities between 14 and 30 June. FIFA organized the event in preparation for the World Cup, which Brazil was scheduled to host the following year. The tournament became the stage for protests organized by the World Cup Popular Committees, which emerged in opposition to forced evictions of mostly low-income communities, as well as to the misuse of public funds in construction works of stadiums and urban infrastructure related to the 2014 FIFA World Cup.

The second contextual factor was *discontent with traditional mechanisms of political representation.* The political scenario in Brazil at the time of the outbreak of the demonstrations did not suggest that a mass protest movement could emerge. Unlike other countries that witnessed similar protests, Brazil was not experiencing significant economic problems or facing political tensions (Conde and Jazeel 2013; Fonsêca 2013; Roman 2013). However, trends in the country's recent political history contributed to set the stage for the mobilizations. It is impossible to explain the events of June without considering the growing discontent with traditional mechanisms of political representation. Indeed, a survey with protestors from eight capital cities on 20 June revealed that 89 percent of them did not feel represented by politicians and 83 percent did not feel represented by political parties.[3] Some episodes in 2013 point to an intensification of clientelistic practices in the political system, which contributed to further disseminate dissatisfaction among key publics. On 1 February, the Federal Senate elected Renan Calheiros as its new president. Senator Calheiros had been involved in several political scandals and was seen by many as an unethical politician. His appointment was opposed by a mass mobilization demanding his impeachment, which included an online petition that by 11 February, had more than 1.3 million signatures, or 1 percent of the electorate.[4] In March, the Committee on Human and Minority Rights of the Chamber of Deputies elected conservative Congressman Marco Feliciano as its new Chairman. Congressman Feliciano is an evangelical pastor who has expressed intolerant views against gays and other stigmatized groups. In both cases, civil society groups and concerned citizens mobilized to oppose clientelistic and authoritarian tendencies in representative institutions.

The influence of global protest networks is another relevant contextual factor. International protest movements affected the development of the June 2013 events in Brazil in at least two important ways. First, the creation of the Free Fare Movement–MPL, the organization that called and led the initial demonstrations against the bus fare increase, was heavily influenced by the antiglobalization movement of the late 1990s and early 2000s. The MPL emerged in 2005 when activists from all over the country gathered in the city of Porto Alegre for the World Social Forum. Second, the global wave of mass demonstrations that swept several regions of the world since 2010 offered local activists new models of political protest. The events of the so-called 'Arab spring' in the Middle East and different types of political and social protest in other regions of the world became important 'repertoires of political action' that inspired local groups.

We emphasize the *recent history of mobilizations about public transportation* as a fourth contextual factor. Since the first half of the twentieth century, public transport fare increases have sparked significant processes of popular mobilization. In the last fifteen years, however, protests around this issue have increased in scope and strength (see Fonsêca 2013). In 2003, students from the Northeastern capital city of Salvador revolted against the bus fare increase and paralysed the city for three weeks. They failed to force authorities to cancel the rise, but the movement demonstrated the ability of the cause to mobilize concerned citizens, especially young people. In 2004 and 2005, similar demonstrations took place in the Southern city of Florianópolis. This time, protestors succeeded in cancelling the increase. In January 2011, the Free Fare Movement–MPL led street mobilizations against the rise in public transportation fares in São Paulo. There were at least seven major rallies in that period, which gathered between three thousand and five thousand demonstrators each. São Paulo's City Hall did not give in and the movement eventually lost steam. It is therefore important to recognize that the 2013 protests did not emerge in a vacuum. There was already a significant history of political mobilization around public transportation in some key urban areas.

Public discontent with the World Cup is another significant variable. The decision of Brazilian authorities to host the 2014 World Cup and other mega sports events, such as the 2016 summer Olympics, created popular discontent and stimulated protests. Significant sectors of the population became outraged with the excessive costs and mismanagement of public funds related to construction projects for the World Cup. There was also significant indignation about the eviction of entire neighbourhoods (mostly low-income) to open way for these projects and about stringent rules and obligations imposed by FIFA. As a part of the resistance to these mega events, 'World Cup Popular Committees' were organized in twelve cities that hosted games for the World Cup. Taking the opportunity of the Confederations Cup, activists in six of these cities organized protests that gained visibility and gave momentum to the street protests.

Another decisive factor that helps explain the growth of the 2013 protest movement was *police violence against protestors and journalists*. This was particularly relevant in the city of São Paulo, location of the first demonstrations. During the 13 June demonstration, police violence increased, with unrestricted use of rubber bullets, tear gas and 'moral effect grenades' that disperse gas and release splinters. On that day, police officers purposely struck journalists covering the events, including reporter Giuliana Vallone from the newspaper *Folha de S. Paulo*. The images of the black-eyed reporter published the next day caused public outcry and contributed to increase public opinion support for the demonstrations.[5] It also forced the news media to review its stand propolice violence and the governor of the state to review orders given to the police force.[6] Similarly to developments in the #occupy movement in Boston (Juris 2012, 259), videos of aggressive police response which circulated widely on social and mainstream media generated widespread sympathy for the movement.

Finally, we emphasize the role played by *shifts in the attitude of the mainstream media*. From 6 June to 13 June, most newspapers and television networks covered the movement in a restricted and biased way, focusing on vandalism and on the difficulties that demonstrations caused to city traffic. However, police violence against protestors and journalists on 13 June and the realization that the population was becoming more aware and supportive of the movement and its demands led to a significant change in media coverage. After 13 June, the news media started to downplay vandalism, offering widespread support for the protests and their demands. The change in coverage was an adaptation of the media to the political context, especially in relation to an increase of public opinion support for the protests.[7] Moreover, there was also a dialectic element in the process, in which changes in media coverage contributed to reinforce positive public perceptions about the movement and to increase participation in the protests. Finally, positive media coverage after 13 June also reinforced the broadening of the movement's agenda, especially through a stronger emphasis on political corruption. For example, there was significant media sympathy for the movement against proposed Constitutional Amendment 37, which intended to remove the investigative powers of the Public Prosecutor's Office–MP.

SOCIAL MEDIA, POLITICAL MOBILIZATION AND ALTERNATIVE COMMUNICATION

In the remaining sections of this chapter, we examine the role of social media in the 2013 protests, with a focus on Twitter and Facebook. Prior to the rise of the 2013 protest movement, there was a significant growth in the user base and in use frequency of both platforms. In 2012, Twitter grew 23 percent in Brazil, achieving more than 41 million users.[8] Facebook penetration also increased dramatically. In 2013, there were 76 million registered users in

Brazil, with 47 million people reporting that they used the platform every day.[9]

The June protests demonstrated the mobilization capacity of social media. Platforms like Facebook and Twitter facilitated the mass aggregation of individuals within concrete locations through viral communication, creating a 'swarming effect'. A public opinion survey conducted in eight capital cities with 2,002 individuals that participated in the demonstrations showed that 62 percent of them found out about the demonstrations via Facebook and 75 percent used Facebook to invite friends to participate in the protests.[10]

The internet also became a relevant alternative source of political discourse and information. Widespread availability of mobile phones with cameras and internet access allowed a significant number of protestors to disseminate videos and messages in extended networks. Though initially dialoguing only with immediate networks, materials posted by some individuals gained high levels of visibility in online flows of communication. For example, when a military police officer was caught breaking the glass of his own car during a demonstration in São Paulo on 13 June, allegedly to blame it on protestors, a video of the scene posted by an ordinary citizen reached hundreds of thousands of views in a matter of hours.

During the protests, the online channel *Ninja Media* became a significant form of alternative media. The channel was established by the collective *Fora do Eixo* and became known for its 'straight from the frontline' coverage, with live and permanent broadcasts of the rallies and interviews with protestors, police officers and government officials. The rapid and significant impact of *Ninja Media* was facilitated by *Fora do Eixo*'s own network of activists and by wide dissemination in social media platforms. These networks allowed *Ninja Media* to compete with traditional media for the status of 'relevant source of information', an unusual feat for an alternative media outlet. Moreover, the mainstream media often used *Ninja Media*'s videos and photographs in their own coverage of the protests.

SOCIAL MEDIA, INDIVIDUALIZED PUBLICS AND AGENDA FRAGMENTATION

Social media were instrumental in the mobilization that led to the 2013 street protests and in establishing alternative sources of political discourse and information. However, they played a more ambiguous and contradictory role in terms of sustaining a coherent political platform. To examine this issue, we look at the evolution of the agenda of social media discussions related to the protests. We use data from the online platform *Causa Brasil*, which monitors discussions related to the protests in Facebook, Twitter, Instagram, YouTube and Google. The platform identifies 'mentions' to the protests in social media based on a list of hashtags and more than one hundred keywords directly related to the protests.

One of the limitations of the platform is that its data collection starts only on 16 June, ten days after the first demonstration in São Paulo against the increase of transportation fares. Despite the fact that the platform does not include the initial phase of the movement, it reveals important trends in social media discussions about the protests.

Figure 10.1 below presents the results of the classification of mentions to the protests in social media for three points in time: 16–17 June, 18–19 June and 20–21 June.[11] Since the number and size of street demonstrations decreased significantly after 22 June, the period between 16 June and 21 June includes the largest and most intense demonstrations. A first noteworthy aspect about the data is the difference in the volume of social media discussions identified by the platform: 2,879 mentions in 16–17 June; 54,401 mentions in 18–19 June; and 228,434 mentions in 20–21 June. The huge difference in the number of social media mentions to the protests in the three periods suggests that we should be careful when comparing them, since there is significant variation in sample size.

Figure 10.1 also shows important shifts in the agenda of social media discussions across time. The subject heading 'Transportation Quality and Cost' faced a 50 percent decline in the period, from 36.1 percent of all mentions in 16–17 June to 18.1 percent in 20–21 June. Although not facing the same dramatic decrease, the subject heading 'Public spending and World Cup cost' also declines over time, from 8.7 percent of mentions to 6.0 percent. Thus, the more the movement grew in scope and strength, the more marginal its original agenda became. At the same time, discussions about public services (Health and Education) and about corruption (Corruption and Constitutional Amendment 37) gradually started to dominate social media discussions.

These significant shifts in the movement's agenda can be interpreted as a natural outcome of the political process. By 19 June, on the eve of the largest demonstrations and right before the last data period of Figure 10.1, government officials in all significant metropolitan areas had already cancelled public transportation fare increases. One of the protestors' central goals had been achieved and it seemed only natural that the movement would move on to incorporate other causes.

Mauro P. Porto and João Brant

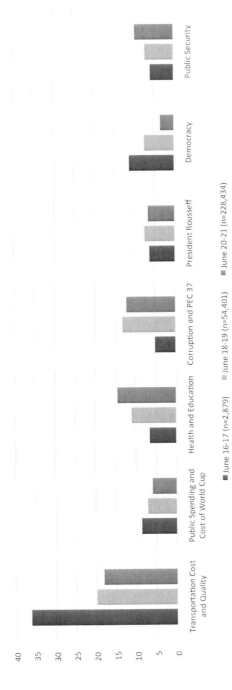

Figure 10.1.   See note 11 for details.

We argue, however, that social media played a major role in causing the shift in the movement's agenda. We highlight two mechanisms by which platforms like Facebook and Twitter affected the 2013 protests: the dissemination of individualized forms of self-expression by middle-class publics and the online strategies of key political actors.

Social Media and Individualized Self-Expression

Both in the streets and in social media platforms, individualized forms of expression predominated and they gradually replaced collective forms of discourse and political organization. Individual posters, more than large and collective banners, marked the environment of the rallies. One of the main target audiences of these individual posters were not other participants in the demonstration or bystanders, but rather the social media networks of family and friends that would see photographs and often validate the individual's creativity.

To understand the forms of individualized self-expression that came to dominate the movement, it is important to consider the specific demographics that took to the streets. Public opinion surveys show that protestors were much younger, considerably richer and better educated than the average citizen (Roman 2013, 11). This profile suggests that most individuals who joined the movement, especially after it grew in scope, had never occupied the streets before. Protestors also did not share a common ideological orientation. A survey with 551 protestors in the city of São Paulo on 20 June, day of the largest demonstrations, shows that 36.1 percent of them identified their political orientation as 'Left', 30.7 percent as 'Centre', 20.7 percent as 'Right', while 12.5 percent did not know. As Conde and Jazeel (2013, 443) note, protestors were not united by a common ideology or political belief. The same survey also showed a significant hostility to organized social movements and to political parties: only 34.3 percent considered trade unions important to defend workers' rights and only 24.6 percent identified with one of the political parties.[12]

The 2013 protests were therefore characterized by a strong participation of young and more affluent people with diverse ideological orientations, little previous political experience and a hostile attitude toward political parties and traditional social movements. One of the most common slogans in the streets, 'The giant has awakened', illustrates this common character of protestors. The overconfident expression suggests that society was dormant before the protests, endorsing a frame that effectively erases the history of intense political mobilization by civil society groups and social movements.

The hostility of the movement toward political parties became particularly controversial. During the largest demonstrations on 20 June, protestors attacked participants holding banners and flags of leftist political parties and trade unions, arguing that they were trying to hijack the movement and proclaiming slogans like 'My party is my country' (Conde and Jazeel 2013, 443). In response, the Free Pass Movement–MPL, the organization that had called and organized the first demonstrations, announced that they would stop participating in the protests.

Thus, the larger masses of protestors that joined the movement had little in common with the leftist vanguard organizations that led the first rallies and which had succeeded in putting the cost and quality of public transportation, as well as human rights violations related to the World Cup, at the centre of the national agenda. These new participants emphasized instead general, unspecific and less controversial demands for better education and health systems, while endorsing populist calls for the end of corruption.

These general demands for better social services were not simply the result of protestors' personal experiences with Brazil's problematic education and health systems. They are a reflection instead of the movement's middle- and upper-class perspective. Take, for example, public perceptions about Brazil's public health system, known as Unified Health System or SUS. The problems and deficiencies of the system are well documented, but a national survey that took place in September 2011 reveals interesting patterns in public opinion. According to this survey, 61 percent of the population evaluate public health as 'terrible' or 'bad'. However, the higher the income and educational level of the respondent, the more negative is the evaluation. In other words, people who can afford and use private health systems tend to evaluate the public system more negatively. Moreover, it is very revealing that respondents who use the public system evaluate it much more positively than those who do not. When those who had used SUS in the last twelve months were asked about its quality, 48 percent evaluated it as 'excellent' or 'good', in contrast to only 10 percent of the general population (CNI 2012).

Paradoxes in public perceptions about the public health system suggest that the movement's growing emphasis on general and noncontroversial issues like health and education is related to a middle- and upper-class sensibility, rather than to personal experiences with these systems. We argue that social media platforms like Facebook were instrumental in offering these publics a forum where this perspective could thrive and spread to the streets.

The protestors that gathered in the climax of the movement were predominantly young (43 percent were fourteen to twenty-four years old), highly educated (43 percent had a college degree) and more affluent (the family income of 49 percent of them corresponded to five or more minimum wages).[13] Sherry Turkle's (2011) research about social media use by similar publics in the United States shows that young people's subjectivity is often characterized by a 'collaborative self', in which feelings and thoughts are discovered and explored by sharing them in digital platforms like Facebook.

According to Turkle, such technologies encourage a sensibility in which validation of a feeling (and we would add, of a political opinion) becomes part of establishing it.

A 2013 national survey conducted in the United States by the Pew Research Center about the Snowden-NSA revelations provides further evidence of the contradictory nature of political discussions mediated by social media (Hampton et al. 2014). The study found that the only settings where most people were not willing to discuss their opinion on the issue were on Facebook and Twitter. The study therefore suggests that, compared to offline settings, social media are less welcoming to debate when the topic of discussion is controversial. The survey also suggests that Facebook users are more likely to share their views if they think their network of family and friends agrees with them. Moreover, people who used Facebook's 'like' button more frequently were more likely to think that friends and family members agreed with them. As the report about the survey states, '[r]eading content contributed by other users, actively clicking the like button, as well as receiving feedback in response to status updates, provides for enhanced observation of others and confirmatory feedback from friends and family' (Hampton et al. 2014, 23).

Although no similar data exists about the 2013 protests in Brazil, we argue that related dynamics can be identified. When developing strategies of self-presentation in platforms like Facebook and Twitter, young people often feel the pressure to post content that conforms to the logic of that particular platform and to perceived dominant values and opinions in online networks of friends. For example, users will often post messages, videos and photographs with the goal of attracting the largest possible amount of 'likes', comments, shares and retweets. This permanent search for validation tends to reinforce commonsensical political opinions among users. In a context where younger and more affluent individuals dominated online interactions, social media platforms were less welcoming to discussions about more 'controversial' and 'distant' topics, such as the quality and cost of public transportation or the human rights violations related to the World Cup. With the exception of the more restricted networks of activists linked to social movements and political parties, these topics were not likely to attract significant confirmatory feedback. Conversely, strategies of self-presentation that relied on the expression of opinions about nonspecific demands (such as 'better' and 'more' public education and health or less corruption), which in turn expressed the sensibilities of affluent groups, tended to be favoured in social media interactions. By posting pictures of creative posters with these banners, users were often able to receive broad endorsement from their middle- and upper-class peers, reinforcing the changes in the agenda of street demonstrations.

Online Strategies of Key Political Actors

The online strategies of key actors is another significant factor that helps explain the shifts in the agenda of social media discussions about the protests. One first aspect is the absence of a coordinated and sophisticated strategy of online mobilization by the social movements that organized the first demonstrations, particularly the Free Fare Movement–MPL. To organize the first demonstrations in early June, MPL launched Facebook pages with invitations that were able to attract significant levels of presence confirmation, including 20,500 confirmations for the 6 June rally, 6,200 confirmations for the 7 June rally, thirteen thousand confirmations for the 11 June rally and twenty-eight thousand confirmations for the 13 June rally (Pimentel and Amadeu, 2013). However, the Movement did not go much beyond that, failing to develop a strategy in the use of hashtags and other tools that would allow it to shape online discussions in a more systematic way. As a result, the MPL gradually lost ground as an 'authority' in social media discussions, since the percentage of people sharing its postings declined over time (Pimentel and Amadeu 2013).

While the MPL lost ground in social media debates, other actors became influential authorities by having a higher number of people share their postings in online networks. Some of these actors were created in the momentum of the protests, such as ChangeBrazil, which appeared on 15 June, combining criticism to politics and politicians. Others existed before, such as the Movement Against Corruption and AnonymousBrasil, but had a significant increase in their numbers of followers at this point. AnonymousBrasil was one of the profiles with greater ability to impact social media discussions and the agenda of the protests, especially after 18 June, when they disseminated a video entitled 'The five causes'. The video quickly reached over 1 million views and emphasized the following five demands: rejection of the Proposal of Constitutional Amendment–PEC 37, which intended to remove the investigative powers of the Public Prosecutor's Office–MP; the immediate removal of Renan Calheiros as President of the National Congress; immediate investigation and punishment of irregularities found in construction works for the World Cup; approval of a new law to classify corruption as a heinous crime. Through viral messages and videos like this, the Anonymous profile was able to remain as one of the top authorities in social media discussions through the most intense period of the demonstrations (Pimentel and Amadeu, 2013). The actors with a more sophisticated and systematic online strategy were able to generate a virtuous circle, incorporating ideas that emerged in the streets and in the mainstream media, while reinforcing their presence in the agenda of the demonstrations.

CONCLUSION

This chapter offers two main contributions to debates about the relationship between social media and political protest. First, its results corroborate research that identifies the strong mobilization potential of digital platforms. As in other recent processes of mass protest around the world (Juris 2012; Bennett and Segerberg 2013), platforms like Facebook and Twitter allowed Brazilian organizations and individuals to quickly, cheaply and effectively disseminate vast amounts of alternative information and to produce large, record-breaking mobilizations. However, we also suggest that the impact of social media should not be overestimated. The study highlights the importance of seven elements of the political context that help interpret the strength and scope of the 2013 protests in Brazil. Moreover, the intensification of social media use tended to follow, rather than precede, increases in protest participation. social media use alone cannot therefore explain the causes and consequences of the 2013 wave of political mobilization.

A second main contribution of this chapter is to highlight the contradictory nature of political contestation in the digital era. The mobilization of 'crowds of individuals' (Juris 2012) in 'crowd-enabled networks' (Bennett and Segerberg 2013) can result in the rise of massive street demonstrations. However, this type of contentious politics can also result in the mobilization of actors with little previous political experience and with diverse political orientations. In the 2013 protests in Brazil, this type of political mobilization fragmented the agenda of the protests, diluted the political and ideological identity of participants and marginalized organizations, such as the MPL, that had played a leading role in the initial demonstrations.

The creative acts of individuation that dominated social networks and the streets turned the movement more attractive to young and affluent individuals, but it also contributed to provoke substantial changes in its agenda. The larger crowds of protestors that joined the movement had little in common with the leftist vanguard organizations that led the first rallies. These organizations had previously succeeded in putting the cost and quality of public transportation, as well as human rights violations related to the World Cup, at the centre of the national agenda. However, the new publics that joined the movement tended to emphasize instead general, unspecific and less-controversial demands for better education and health systems, while endorsing populist calls for the end of corruption. Social media platforms allowed these 'crowds' to validate their strategies of self-presentation in online networks of family and friends, which in turn reinforced the shift in the movement's agenda. The absence of a coordinated and sophisticated strategy of online mobilization by the social movements that organized the first demonstrations, particularly the Free Fare Movement–MPL, also contributed to the fragmentation of the protests' agenda. This facilitated the growing influence of more internet-savvy groups in social media debates about the protests. In these and other ways, the 2013 protests in Brazil illustrate the contradictory nature of political mobilization in the digital era.

NOTES

1. As Bennett and Segerberg (2013, 205) themselves recognize, their concepts of 'organizationally enabled' and 'crowd-enabled' connective action is similar to Juris's concepts of 'logic of networks' and 'logic of aggregation'.

2. Buses are a responsibility of the municipalities, but in the case of metropolitan transportation systems, the responsibility rests with state governments. In São Paulo, for example, the subway is a state responsibility, while buses are a municipal one.

3. http://www.ibope.com.br/pt-br/conhecimento/Infograficos/Paginas/Levante-Popular. aspx

4. 'Brazil's zombie politicians: Unstoppable?' *The Economist*, 16 February 2003.

5. http://datafolha.folha.uol.com.br/opiniaopublica/2013/06/1295431-paulistanos-aprovam-protestos-mas-rejeitam-vandalismo-e-tarifa-zero.shtml

6. It is important to remember that repression and law enforcement in Brazil are exercised by the Military Police, a corporation that is controlled by state governors, not by the Federal Executive Branch.

7. http://datafolha.folha.uol.com.br/opiniaopublica/2013/06/1295431-paulistanos-aprovam-protestos-mas-rejeitam-vandalismo-e-tarifa-zero.shtml

8. http://pt.kioskea.net/faq/12500-twitter-atinge-o-meio-milhao-de-usuarios-o-brasil-chega-na-segunda-posicao

9. http://g1.globo.com/tecnologia/noticia/2013/09/brasil-e-o-2-pais-com-mais-usuarios-que-entram-diariamente-no-facebook.html

10. http://www.ibope.com.br/pt-br/conhecimento/Infograficos/Paginas/Levante-Popular. aspx

11. The platform Causa Brasil (http://www.causabrasil.com.br) was established by three companies that specialize in advertising and social media monitoring: W3haus, Seekr and HUIA. The platform presents the results of a classification of the topics of all 'mentions' related to the protests in Facebook, Twitter, Instagram, YouTube and Google. The system identifies these mentions based on a list of hashtags related to the protests, as well as on more than one hundred keywords related to the protests. Figure 10.1 presents the results of three periods: 16–17 June, 18–19 June and 20–21 June. It is important to stress that in each period the platform presents the results in more than one point of time. Figure 10.1 includes data time points with the highest number of mentions for the respective period: 3:00 p.m. for 16–17 June, which includes 2,879 mentions; 8:00 p.m. for 18–19 June, which includes 54,401 mentions; and 8:00 a.m. for 20–21 June, which includes 228,434 mentions. The following subject headings are the same used in the platform: 'President Rousseff' (Governo Dilma Rousseff); 'Democracy' (Democracia) and 'Public Security' (Segurança). The subject heading 'Transportation Quality and Cost' adds up the mentions to two topics: 'Transportation Fares' (Preço das Passagens) and 'Quality of Public Transportation' (Qualidade do Transporte Público). The subject heading 'Public Spending and World Cup Cost' adds up the mentions to two topics: 'Expenses of World Cup Construction Projects' (Gastos das Obras da Copa) and 'Public Spending' (Gastos Públicos). The category 'Health and Education' adds up the mentions to two topics: 'Health' (Saúde) and 'Education' (Educação). The subject heading 'Corruption and PEC 37' adds up the mentions for two topics: 'Fight against Corruption' (Combate à Corrupção) and 'PEC 37'. Although the selected subject headings of Figure 10.1 do not exhaust all the topics of online discussions, they account for the great majority of them: 79.8 percent of all mentions in 16–17 June; 73.4 percent of all mentions in 18–19 June and 70.5 percent of all mentions in 20–21 June.

12. Encarte Tendências (2013). *Opinião Pública 19*(2) novembro, 475–85.

13. http://www.ibope.com.br/pt-br/conhecimento/Infograficos/Paginas/Levante-Popular. aspx

REFERENCES

Benkler, Y. (2006). *The wealth of networks*. New Haven, CT: Yale University Press.

Bennett, L., and Segerberg, A. (2013). *The logic of connective action: Digital media and the personalization of contentious politics*. New York: Cambridge University Press.

CNI. (2012). *Pesquisa CNI-IBOPE: Retratos da sociedade brasileira: Saúde pública*. Brasilia: CNI.

Conde, M., and Jazeel, T. (2013). Kicking off in Brazil: Manifesting democracy. *Journal of Latin American Cultural Studies 22*(4), 437–50.

Curran, James (2012). Reinterpreting the Internet. In J. Curran, N. Fenton and D. Freedman (Eds.), *Misunderstanding the Internet* (pp. 3–33). New York: Routledge.

Fenton, N., and Barassi, V. (2011). Alternative media and social networking sites: The politics of individuation and political participation. *The Communication Review 14*(3), 179–96.

Fonsêca, D. (2013). *You cannot not see: The media in the June 2013 demonstrations*. São Paulo: Friedrich Ebert Stiftung.

Gladwell, M. (2010). Small change. *New Yorker*, 4 October, 42–49.

Hampton, K. N., Rainie, L., Lu, W., Dwyer, M., Shin, I. and Purcell, K. (2014). *Social media and the 'spiral of silence'*. Washington, DC: Pew Research Center. Available at http://www.pewinternet.org/2014/08/26/social media-and-the-spiral-of-silence/.

Howard, P., and Hussain, M. (2011). The upheavals in Egypt and Tunisia: The role of digital media. *Journal of Democracy 22*(3), 35–48.

Joseph, S. (2012). Social media, political change, and human rights. *Boston College International and Comparative Law Review 35*(1), 145–88.

Juris, J. (2012). Reflections on #Occupy Everywhere: Social media, public space, and emerging logics of aggregation. *American Ethnologist 39*(2), 259–79.

Markham, T. (2014). Social media, protest cultures and political subjectivities of the Arab spring. *Media, Culture and Society 36*(1), 89–104.

Pimentel, T., and Amadeu, S. (2013). Cartografia de espaços híbridos: As manifestações de junho de 2013. Available at http://interagentes.net/?p=62.

Roman, A. (2013). *The class cleavage, minority influence, and Brazil's 2013 protests*. Paper presented at the ECPR General Conference, Bordeaux.

Turkle, S. (2011). *Alone together*. New York: Basic Books.

Wolfsfeld, G., Segev, E. and Sheafer, T. (2013). Social media and the Arab Spring: Politics comes first. *The International Journal of Press/Politics 18*(2), 115–37.

V

Myths and Organizational Trajectories

Chapter Eleven

Social Media and the 'New Authenticity' of Protest

Lina Dencik

Debates around social media and protest movements have grown significantly in recent years with waves of uprisings across the world leading to renewed understandings of the relationship between media technologies and social change. In particular, we have seen an attempt to understand recent events as representing 'new' types of movements, distinct in their emergence and nature from traditional forms of political activism. Central to this, it is claimed, is a prominent role of social media that has allowed for new possibilities and opportunities to mobilize and organize protest in easier ways at lower cost. The power of social media is said to lie in the spontaneous and unpredictable ways in which networks of protest and solidarity can emerge. These technologies allow for a new type of political activism to come to the fore, one that is said to be more participatory, horizontal and autonomous in nature (cf. Castells 2012). What is more, these platforms tap into a much broader base of support, moving activist communication and practices out of the radical 'ghettos' and into the mainstream, allowing for protest to be sustained by popular and majoritarian claims on social justice (Gerbaudo 2014).

   Drawing on research carried out on the recent and ongoing fast food workers protests in the United States, commonly known as Fast Food Forward, this chapter explores these debates on social media protest and makes the argument that there has emerged a particular discourse of 'authenticity' regarding the use of social media by protest movements. Looking to current debates on social media in journalism studies and in corporate branding that have highlighted the use of social media as a strategic tool to create a *perception* of authenticity, I make the case that some of these discussions need to form part of our understanding of social media protest. This becomes particularly evident in the case of more traditional forms of political organization, such as trade unions, that engage with this so-called 'new' protest environment at a significant point of transformation and crisis. In such a context, the emphasis on social media forms part of a broader communication strategy to legitimize and authenticate campaigns by abstracting protests from institutional 'baggage' and organizational interests and agendas. Although such a strategy is a way to engage sympathetic mainstream media coverage of dissent that otherwise struggles to enter public debate, the branding of authenticity that social media affords also serves to obscure important underlying aspects and dynamics of how protest movements emerge and are organized that need to be properly understood.

SOCIAL MEDIA AND PROTEST

The question of the relationship between protest movements and social media has exploded as a field of research in the last couple of years with uprisings like the Arab Spring, the Indignados, Occupy, Gezi Park in Turkey, the Free Fare Movement in Brazil and more recently, the Umbrella movement in Hong Kong (see Haunss in this volume). There has been much discussion around the ways in which social media provides new opportunities for political activism, for people to organize and mobilize in new and easier ways with fewer necessary resources. Castells (2009; 2012) has been at the forefront of this view, advancing an ongoing argument about the shifting nature of power in a 'network society' that sees communication tools as being central: 'power relies on the control of communication, as counterpower depends on breaking through such control' (Castells 2009). The rise of new media technologies and social media, or the rise of 'networks of mass self-communication' as he describes them, offers new opportunities for autonomous communication between individuals and groups that can facilitate precisely such counterpower. The movements of recent years, he claims, can be explained by the material support of social networking sites and the internet more broadly that support a new type of political participation, a participation that is based on horizontal networks, leaderless organization, political autonomy and borderless solidarity (Castells 2012). Bennett and Segerberg (2012) have presented a more complex picture of this interaction by focusing on how these digitally enabled political protest movements engage in a form of 'connective action' that stands in juxtaposition to the 'collective action' of traditional forms of political organizations such as political parties or trade unions. Such 'connective action' is marked by personalized, individualized and technologically organized processes that come to replace the requirement of collective identity framing or formal organizational structures that usually require a lot of resources for membership. Drawing on Diani, Bennett and Segerberg note that networks are not just precursors or building blocks of collective action: they are in themselves organizational structures that can transcend the elemental units of organizations and individuals. These organizational structures made up of digital communication, in turn, are much better suited to contemporary forms of political engagement (Bennett and Segerberg 2012). Indeed, the opportunities that these technologies have facilitated for political activism to flourish have been explored across a range of both scholarly and media discourse (cf. Shirky 2008; Mason 2012; Ghonim 2012), sometimes even heralding platforms of social media as the defining feature of uprisings as in the BBC documentary series on the Arab Spring called *How Facebook Changed the World* (BBC 2011).

Inevitably, more critical accounts have accompanied and followed such discourse, foregrounding not only broader historical and social developments in any explanation of protests (Curran et al. 2012), the significance of face-to-face interaction in mobilization (Juris 2012), and shared physical space (Gerbaudo 2012), but also the problems with assumptions around autonomy, horizontalism and connectivity that surrounds the narrative of social media protests (Gerbaudo 2012; Barassi and Fenton 2011; Cammaerts et al. 2012; Fuchs 2012). Rather, these technologies are affecting political imagination and practices in quite contradictory ways (Barassi and Treré 2012) that speaks to a very complex and convoluted emerging protest environment. As Fuchs (2012) has argued, the media—social media, the internet and all other media—are contradictory because we live in a contradictory society. As a consequence, their effects are actually contradictory, they can dampen/forestall or amplify/advance protest or have not much effect at all. And the media, in turn, stand in contradictory relation and power struggle with not only each other, but also with politics and culture and ideology that also influence the conditions of protest.

This point of the contingent nature of protest movements, as has always been the case, is important because the emphasis on a 'new' protest environment with the emergence of social media has allowed for a particular discourse to emerge that seeks to provide a coherent and continuous narrative of recent uprisings that has become especially prominent in news reporting. That journalists will seek to simplify and find continuity in diverse, complex and relatively simultaneous events is part of standard analyses of news values and journalistic practices that help us understand how events are organized into news (Galtung and Ruge 1965). Journalists will often seek to select events to report on based on an understanding of how these fit within a broader narrative and will seek to limit ambiguity by highlighting particular aspects of an issue or event. However, by making social media the point of simplification and continuity in our understanding of recent protests, certain qualities are attributed to these technologies in and of themselves that become the entry-point into which we are to evaluate the nature of emerging movements. The argument made here is that this has become particularly prominent in how we view the legitimacy of protesters' claims and the authenticity of any given movement.

SOCIAL MEDIA AND AUTHENTICITY

Although relatively neglected in debates on social movements and protest, the topic of how social media relates to understandings of authenticity is something that is gaining increasing interest in parallel fields, particularly in journalism studies and in studies on corporate branding and consumer culture. In fact, as Banet-Weiser points out in her book *Authentic™* (2012), the question of authenticity is becoming evermore important in an age that hungers for anything that *feels* authentic, just as we lament more and more that it is a world of inauthenticity. Faced with a crisis of trust in central institutions of contemporary democracy, social and political actors are struggling to manifest societal positions on legitimate grounds. The relationship between social media and journalism has become an interesting example of this struggle. At the same time as much debate, certainly at the beginning of the dawn of social media, has been concerned with the ways in which these technologies have come to undermine the practice of professional journalism, a more recent debate has emerged about the ways in which social media has rather become incorporated into professional news practices in strategic ways. This has especially been prominent in 'crisis reporting' where journalists have relied on elements of 'citizen witnessing' (Allan 2013) in news reporting, often drawing on social media content. This type of content increasingly forms part of how we come to learn about different kinds of crises, be they disasters or acts of extreme violence such as terror attacks (Pantti et al. 2012). Studies have shown that audiences respond well to the inclusion of social media content as they perceive these platforms very differently from that of traditional news outlets with content produced by journalists. Williams et al. (2011) found in their focus group research with audiences of BBC user-generated content that the high audience approval for the inclusion of amateur content is linked to a perception of it being authentic, more 'real' and less 'packaged' than news produced solely by journalists. This perception of increased realism is closely linked to the idea that such news is considered more immediate and that it adds drama and human emotion to a cultural form, which is often understood to be dry and distanced from 'ordinary people'. Indeed, Chouliaraki and Blaagaard (2013) have argued that social media technologies have afforded a 'new authenticity' of new media journalism towards its public that can potentially allow for the construct of new solidarities and cosmopolitanist identities. That is, these technologies play a part in our ability to empathize and engage with others who are reported to be suffering around us. Interestingly, however, Williams et al. (2011) found in their further interviews with reporters that this 'perceived authenticity' of user-generated content is highly valued by journalists and, in the case of reporting news, it is strategically used by journalists to enliven conventional news reports and construct the *impression* of authenticity.

This trend towards creating impressions of authenticity has become a central part of contemporary culture and social and political processes are embedded in this quest. Naomi Klein famously argued back in 2000 with her book *No Logo* that we are increasingly engaging simultaneously in the production of culture through the very processes of consumption, as products have attained meaning in the form of brands as experience, as lifestyle. In advertising and corporate branding, social media have become crucial technologies for developing these brands. In particular, the shift has focused entirely from the product or service itself towards the relationship between the producer and consumer that engulf the product or service (Terranova 2000). For some, this is celebrated as a new dawn of consumer empowerment as in this age of the 'social brand', communicative relationships are prioritized and corporate activities are under unprecedented scrutiny with the ability for consumers to voice concern and demands, forcing businesses to uphold ethical and socially responsible standards (cf. Jones 2012). However, as Banet-Weiser (2012) points out, what really comes to matter in the age of the social brand is that these communicative relationships come to *feel* authentic, regardless of actual corporate activities and consumer voice. Importantly, she argues that this manufacturing of authenticity has become central not only to corporate brands, but is increasingly also the model for politics and movements of social change. The previous binary link between the commercial and inauthentic and the noncommercial and authentic is therefore too simple for contemporary society. Rather, authenticity is itself now a brand and 'authentic' spaces have become branded (Banet-Weiser 2012, 11). This also includes spaces of politics and political activism, evidenced particularly for Banet-Weiser in the growth of ethical consumption and new media technologies that allow for consumers to reimagine and further—and therefore validate—the brand (Banet-Weiser 2012, 152).

AUTHENTICITY OF PROTEST

Although the question of authenticity is becoming ever more pressing in our understanding of different aspects of social life, it has yet to form a substantial part of our analysis of contemporary forms of protest. This is despite political protests arguably becoming 'mainstream', expanding the parameters of the 'political' in contemporary civil society (Cottle 2008). However, as

Birks (2014) has illustrated in her study of the coverage of recent protests in British news media, our understanding and analysis of protest movements are continuously being negotiated around different claims to legitimacy presented in news coverage of protesters, including the authenticity of their argumentation. Drawing on Habermas's notion of legitimacy in the public sphere, Birks looks at the ways in which judgments of protests are made in news media based on legal, political, social and personal claims to legitimacy, often in very complex and contradictory ways. The role of the media audience, she argues, is to distinguish between established organizations that appear 'before the public' (representing sectional interests and identities) and less formally organized actors who 'emerge from' the public and are more 'authentic' because they are less distorted by vested interests (Birks 2014, 47). Here, she particularly looks at questions of violence, organizational structures, public opinion and the ability for protesters to present themselves as victims with emotional responses when determining the legitimation and delegitimation (and authenticity and inauthenticity) of protests in news coverage.

The point I want to make here is that the discourse surrounding social media, and the affordances of social media technologies, particularly with regard to protest, has also come to play an important part in the legitimation and perceived authenticity of protesters and social movements. This goes beyond the types of legitimacy claims as outlined by Birks, and borrows, instead, from some of the debates we have seen in journalism studies and corporate branding with regard to the authenticity granted social media platforms as communicative networks. Partly, perhaps, due to journalists' own interest in it, a discourse around social media and protests has emerged that suggests not only that social media is integral to the organizing and mobilizing of people, but also that movements that are closely associated with social media activity are somehow more horizontal, more inclusive and participatory, broadly free from top-down institutional agendas and interests, and as such ultimately more 'authentic'. To borrow from Habermas's distinction between actors appearing 'before the public' and actors 'emerging from the public' in our judgement of their interests and, related to that, their authenticity, the discourse of social media activities has predominantly emphasized their roots in the less formal actors 'emerging from the public'. As Couldry (2013) has argued, social media companies and commentators have jointly advanced a 'myth of us'—the generating of the idea that platforms like Facebook underpin a kind of natural collectivity. In this myth, media (and other) institutions seem to drop out altogether from the picture and the story is focused on what 'we' do naturally. In this way, the institutional frameworks that surround social media platforms are removed from the equation. Of course, one problematic consequence of this is that the political economy of social media platforms, and their *institutional* architectures, that come to shape, censor and put political activity under continuous surveillance (Hintz 2013; Dencik 2014; see also Hintz, Leistert and Redden in this volume) are entirely obscured under this myth. However, the point that is important to emphasize in this context is that this 'myth of us' also obscures the *movement* architectures and organizational structures that often underpin protest and political activism. Instead, social media-driven protest becomes abstracted from institutional interests and is granted a 'new authenticity' towards the public. It therefore becomes part of a branding exercise rather than offering an actual analysis of the nature and structures behind contemporary uprisings and campaigns for social justice and interweaves with more familiar forms of protest legitimation around protesters as subjects as discussed above.

FAST FOOD FORWARD

An interesting example to illustrate this dynamic between social media and the 'new authenticity' of protest is to look at how traditional forms of political organization have engaged with what is being considered a changing protest environment in order to participate and be heard in public debate. Here, I want to draw particularly on research into labour movements and trade unions that are currently going through significant transformations and reassessments about their role and practices in the contemporary global political economy (Dencik and Wilkin 2015). A pertinent case study in this regard is the case of the fast food workers protests in the United States that were first staged in November 2012. The analysis presented here is predominantly based on reports, media coverage and social media content, as well as seven semistructured interviews conducted during fieldwork carried out in New York in December 2013 (one of the interviews was carried out via Skype in January 2014) with a range of actors including campaign organizers (anonymized with fake names in this chapter), public relations officers, journalists and labour activists. Analysis is also based on participant observation during the Fast Food Forward strike and rally on 5 December 2013, in New York City, which was part of a national one-day strike with fast food workers taking place in one hundred US cities simultaneously. During this, field notes were taken from participating in the strike protests and rally, observing activities throughout the day and speaking with attending fast food workers and organizers.

   In forty years, the fast food industry has grown from a $6 billion industry to more than $170 billion in annual revenues in the United States alone (Bernstein 2011). There are about 3.5 million fast food workers in the United States—55,000 fast food workers are based in New York City. Importantly, almost half of those jobs were created in the past decade. In fact, the US economy has been rebuilding itself as a low-wage economy, particularly since the financial crisis in 2008, alongside a minority of very high-wage jobs, creating a stark 'job polarisation' in the US labour market (Boehm 2014). A big class of low-wage workers now work in very uncertain working conditions with few entitlements and rights—and are largely nonunionized. This growth in the industry has also seen a significant change in the demographic of the fast food workforce. Traditionally, fast food work was carried out by high-school students or graduates, looking for part-time and temporary work to supplement other primary incomes in the household. That has changed. Today, workers in fast food restaurants are usually over the age of twenty, often bringing up a child and in as many as 68 percent of cases they are the main wage-earner in the family (Allegretto et al. 2013). At the same time, wages for the bottom 70 percent of the wage ladder have either stagnated or declined in the past decade (Mishel and Shierholz 2013). As of 2012, when the protests started, the federal minimum wage was $7.25 an hour, which comes to an annual income of about $15,000 for full-time work. The median pay for core frontline fast food jobs is $8.69, with many jobs paying at or near the minimum wage. Benefits are also scarce for these workers; an estimated 87 percent of front-line fast food workers do not receive health benefits through their employer (Allegretto et al. 2013). This context is important for understanding the background and timeliness of the fast food worker protests within the United States.

The campaign for higher wages for fast food workers started in early 2012 with the Service Employees International Union (SEIU) setting out a strategy to mobilize fast food workers through community organizing. SEIU is one of the biggest unions in the United States with around 2 million members, focusing mainly on workers in the health sector, public services and property services (including janitors and food service workers). Due to the precarious nature of the work, fast food workers have historically been close to impossible to organize and have largely been placed outside the union framework. However, with the changing demographic and growth of the sector, along with rising inequality, conditions for mobilizing this workforce have been gradually emerging. SEIU has been the primary funder of the campaign, and spent in excess of $10 million on the initiative in its first year alone (Gupta 2013). The organizing drive came via a number of community groups that SEIU funded to mobilize workers in the community around wage issues. The main player in this was New York Communities for Change (NYCC), which approached people using petitions on issues relating to affordable housing and 'stop and frisk' (a practice in which police officers stop, question and search paedestrians without warrant), which are both key issues in several lower-income communities in New York. An organizer from NYCC explained how the data collected on people from petitions was then used for phone-calling, asking further 'no-brainer' questions around issues of cost of living. The aim was that these types of questions would lead to calls for higher wages ('John', former NYCC organizer). This would then be followed up with meetings with fast food workers in and around their workplaces. In doing this, the mobilization of workers came to be seen as part of a community drive rather than as a union drive. As the organizer pointed out, 'the word "union" was sort of a last resort, we weren't really allowed to mention the word "union" at the very beginning. It wasn't until sometime late Spring that we started talking about unionization' ('John', former NYCC organizer). This speaks to a recurring theme in the campaign, one in which unions are seen to carry too much 'baggage' to be able to organize and mobilize workers and are therefore kept in the background (Gupta 2013).

Alongside other community and social groups such as MaketheRoad and United NY, faith leaders and local politicians, NYCC funded and guided by SEIU created the New York chapter of the campaign under the name Fast Food Forward. The demands of the campaign have been clear and concise: fast food workers should get paid $15 an hour and have the right to organize without retaliation. The first action of the campaign took place in November 2012 in New York with a one-day strike action with around two hundred nonunionized fast food workers. This was then followed by further similar actions in other major cities such as Chicago, Washington and Los Angeles in Spring and Summer of 2013 where other chapters of the campaign were established under the broad banner 'Fight for 15'. A large coordinated one-day strike action across sixty cities took place on 29 August 2013 to coincide with the anniversary of the civil rights march in Washington in 1963. This was then followed by an even bigger action on 5 December 2013 with a coordinated one-day strike taking place across one hundred cities, the largest strike action in the history of the fast food industry in the United States at the time. Further big actions have since followed, with recent efforts to globalize the campaign.

What is significant about these events is that they have been described as 'socially organised' and not union-led (Helmore 2013). Rather, they are considered to have emerged out of a coalition of unions, community groups, faith leaders and local politicians collectively supporting these nonunionized workers engaging in direct action (McVeigh 2013). What is more, the protests have received a significant amount of media coverage—and sympathetic media coverage—marking them out from how labour movements have historically been reported in corporate media (Birks 2014; Dencik and Wilkin 2015). Several editorials in the *New York Times* and the *Washington Post* were dedicated to the movement. For example, a *New York Times* piece stated: 'victory for the lowest-wage workers will have a positive impact on wages for everyone . . . well-intentioned people often ask me what they can do to help improve our food system. Here's an easy one: When you see that picket line next week, don't cross it. In fact, join it' (Bittman 2013). Similarly, an article in the *Washington Post* argued: 'The protests have the benefit of putting low-wage workers in the media spotlight, a place they're almost never found in a world more interested in the antics of Miley Cyrus and Donald Trump' (Dionne Jr. 2013). What is more, these events are considered to have had real impact. The minimum wage was raised in several cities following the protests; in SeaTac, near Seattle, they even went for the $15 wage-floor, which some attribute to the fast food campaign (cf. Dean 2014). In President Obama's State of the Union address in January 2014, he announced he was going to raise the minimum wage of federal workers to $10.10 an hour, encouraging corporations to follow suit and singling out particularly the plight of fast food workers (O'Connor 2014).

MEDIA PRACTICES AND BRANDING AUTHENTICITY

The impact of the fast food workers protests is of course a result of a complex multitude of factors where many different elements have played a part. Here I want to focus on some of the media practices of the movement that highlight how the discourse surrounding social media protest has become a 'brand' of authenticity that can be strategically used to advance protest campaigns. The fast food workers protests in some ways mark a significant moment in the labour movement, particularly within the United States, but also in other advanced capitalist societies such as Britain, partly because of its emphasis on strategies to garner media attention. Not only did SEIU 'contract' community groups for mobilizing and organizing fast food workers (leading labour activist/historian Immanuel Ness to describe this in an interview as a kind of 'sub-contracting unionism' in which organizing is outsourced to nonunion organizations that are considered more capable), but it also decided to invest significant amounts of resources in professionalizing communications for the campaign. Several public relations companies were hired to market Fast Food Forward, most prominently the PR agency *Berlin Rosen*, famous for running the successful campaign for New York mayor Bill de Blasio, amongst others. Another interesting communications company hired for the campaign was the venture *Purpose*, a PR agency that describes itself as a technology and social movements specialist. This heavy media focus has led to some organizers describing the campaign as a 'march on the media'—in contrast to a 'march on the boss' as is familiar in more traditional union practices (Gupta 2013).

A key aspect of the communication strategies of Fast Food Forward as a protest movement has been about the use of social media in different ways. First of all, designated social media coordinators were hired for the campaign to increase the visibility of the protests and surrounding activities by engaging in 'Twitter rallies', Facebook memes and various forms of 'streaming' strikes and rallies through micro-blogging. This is a function of social media we have become familiar with in our understanding of contemporary protest in which social media platforms come to be seen as amplifying movements and campaigns (Tufekci and Wilson 2012). However, in the case of Fast Food Forward, social media practices took on further significance in advancing the movement in public debate. Amplifying the visibility of the protests became important not just because of how protesters are historically marginalized in mainstream corporate media without the creation of spectacle and noise, but also because the actual number of fast food workers involved in the strikes has been relatively small. In interviews, the organizers pointed out that fast food workers themselves have made up a minority in the protests, which have been dominated by paid organizers and union officials. Crucially, also, the turnover of fast food workers from one action to the next has been incredibly high. As one organizer said: 'Say there were a hundred workers last year who went on strike, I would be shocked to find that there are thirty of them who are still involved.' Partly this is due to the intensive fear-mongering and union-busting techniques that corporations like fast food companies have engaged in for years, making workers very scared and fearful of taking action and losing their jobs, but it also speaks to the lack of actual workplace organizing within the campaign. Indeed, behind closed doors, SEIU officials themselves have outlined that the power of the campaign lies in public image, not in industrial power ('Nick', SEIU official, private communication).

Social media has in this context served to make the movement seem bigger than it actually is in order to grant Fast Food Forward greater legitimacy. What is more, this legitimacy is also enforced through social media by the content produced on these platforms purporting to be the voice of fast food workers. By using predominantly social media platforms to spread messages from the protests through a combination of a few fast food workers and community-group-affiliated social media coordinators, the institutional 'baggage' of historically top-down and hierarchical trade unions has been removed from the identity of the campaign. The protests therefore come to signify something that is not controlled by strategic interests and agendas, but rather something that can be considered 'raw' and 'more real' (to echo the BBC audience focus groups mentioned above). One organizer epitomized this notion with the statement: 'We basically used Twitter to make the scripted things that workers said seem spontaneous' ('Judy', social media coordinator for #Fightfor15). This allowed for the very micro-managed protests (noted also during participant observation) to be mediated as autonomous and worker-led actions, free from any particular organizational structure, in order to grant the campaign a sense of authenticity. This was also the sentiment expressed by organizer and social media coordinator 'Judy' in her interview: 'I think [SEIU] wanted to give the image that this is a worker-driven campaign and that they are not actually pulling the strings but that it's the workers who have taken the lead and taken the initiative to start the campaign and then continue to take the lead and I think the SEIU is just essentially using that as a way to give the campaign an air of credibility'.

Importantly, therefore, social media has also been presented as being the key instigator in the organization and mobilization of fast food workers rather than this mobilization being part of longer-term SEIU strategy. Despite organizers pointing out in interviews that social media activities were incorporated at a later stage in the campaign and that notes during participant observation outline that social media did not seem to have played a role in mobilizing the fast food workers present at the 5 December protests (rather, they had been approached by organizers at or around the workplace), the notion that social media has been instrumental in both the organization and mobilization of the movement has become a central part of the Fast Food Forward narrative. It has been a narrative jointly advanced by journalists and communications officers involved in the campaign. One of the key people at *Berlin Rosen* responsible for the campaign said in a phone conversation when asked about the role of social media in the movement that 'this is the way most workers have come to us' (Daniel Massey, public relations officer at *Berlin Rosen*). From a news perspective, subscribing to this notion of the protests being 'socially organized' and driven by social media technologies allows for the coverage of Fast Food Forward to be situated within a longer continuous narrative of 'new' protest movements and emerging social uprisings. Moreover, these protest movements have been granted legitimacy in large parts due to the broader discourse that surrounds social media protest. In particular, in the context of the United States, this has manifested itself with frequent references to the Occupy movement in the media reporting of the fast food workers protests, also strongly encouraged by campaign organizers who have deliberately sought to incorporate protest tactics and discourse that imitate that of Occupy Wall Street. For example, uses of 'human microphones' in which a person's speech will be echoed by the surrounding crowd, references to the 99 percent as well as slogans highlighting income inequality and the bailing out of banks all have a close association with Occupy and have been widely incorporated into the mediation of the fast food workers protests. By adopting the tactics of such 'new' protest movements, continuing their narrative and emphasizing particularly the role of social media in the mobilization and organization of the protests, fast food workers have in this way become the most recent symbols of economic inequality and the new (authentic) voices of social injustice permeating American society. And they have done so in a way that some consider a 'stunning success for organized labour' (Weissman 2014).

CONCLUSION

The relationship between social media and protest is a rich and growing field of research and debate. However, it is also one that suffers a great deal from misconceptions and blinkered views that have come to have significant social and political consequences. A particular discourse has come to accompany our understanding of 'new' protest movements that centres on a very specific, and very problematic, account of social media technologies. In our quest to find continuity—and perhaps thereby make sense of—complex disparate moments of social and political change, social media has come to provide a possible focus for creating a connected and coherent narrative for contemporary social uprisings. However, in so doing, this narrative comes to attribute particular affordances to social media that lead to the abstraction of these technologies—and the protest movements that incorporate them into their repertoires of action—from important structural and institutional dynamics that are associated with particular interests and agendas. As a consequence, social media has come to occupy a position of 'authenticity' in our evaluation and understanding of 'new' protest movements.

This quality of 'authenticity' attributed to social media platforms has received increasing attention in the fields of journalism studies and corporate branding that have illustrated the strategic ways in which authenticity can therefore be constructed through the use of social media. These discussions need to be incorporated into debates on social media and protest as well, in order to advance our understanding of the ways in which movements are mediated and perceived in public debate. This suggests a need to explore different ways of looking at the construction of legitimacy claims amongst protesters that is less about the content of campaign messages or the nature of activist personalities, and rather foregrounds the *technological means* of movement communication as grounds upon which protests are perceived as authentic or inauthentic. What we have seen in the case of the fast food workers protests in the United States is that such attribution of authenticity allows for social media technologies to be incorporated into broader public relations strategies as modes of communication that represent certain (legitimating) qualities in and of themselves. In particular, they suggest a sense of movement spontaneity, grassroots-driven and horizontal in nature that all contribute to a protest 'authenticity'.

Fast Food Forward illustrates how the use of social media as a type of protest authenticity has been very fruitful for organized labour at a time of significant transformation and crisis by successfully entering and becoming incorporated into the discourse surrounding 'new' protest movements. This is despite the protests actually being instigated and managed by SEIU, which, as a large mainstream trade union, is a traditional form of political organization frequently dismissed as irrelevant in such discourse (cf. Bennett and Segerberg 2012). Although the strategic use of social media authenticity in these circumstances could therefore be considered an opportunity for otherwise marginalized protest movements to make claims to legitimacy, it is important to highlight that this authenticity has been manufactured on the basis of a 'myth of us', an alienating aspect of social media protest that fundamentally obscures significant social, political and economic processes that must form part of our analysis for the relationship between social media and protest. By ignoring these, we not only run the risk of turning a blind eye to the very problematic conditions under which social media *institutions* operate, but we also come to foreground communicative technologies as a way of understanding movement infrastructures, essentially turning social media protest into a PR exercise which, as seen with the case of Fast Food Forward, can only ever provide a very limited analysis.

REFERENCES

Allan, S. (2013). *Citizen Witnessing: Revisioning Journalism in Times of Crisis*. Cambridge: Polity.
Allegretto, S. et al. (2013). Fast Food, Poverty Wages: The Public Cost of Low-Wage Jobs in the fast food Industry. Report by UC Berkeley Labor Center and University of Illinois at Urbana-Champaign.
Banet-Weiser, S. (2012). *Authentic™*. New York and London: New York University Press.
Barassi, V., and Fenton, N. (2011). Alternative Media and Social Networking Sites: The Politics of Individuation and Political Participation. *The Communication Review* 14(3): 179–96.
Barassi, V., and Treré, E. (2012). Does Web 3.0 follow Web 2.0? Deconstructing Theoretical Assumptions through Practice. *New Media and Society* 14(8): 1269–85.
BBC (2011). *How Facebook Changed the World*. Series on BBC 2. September.
Bennett, L., and Segerberg, A. (2012). The Logic of Connective Action: Digital Media and the Personalization of Contentious Politics. *Information, Communication & Society*, 15(5): 739–68.
Bernstein, S. (2011). fast food Industry Is Quietly Defeating Happy Meal Bans. *Los Angeles Times*, 18 May.
Birks, J. (2014). *News and Civil Society*. Farnham and Burlington, VT: Ashgate.
Bittman, M. (2013). Fast Food, Low Pay. *New York Times*, 25 July.
Boehm, M. (2014). Job Polarization and Middle-Class Workers' Wages. *VoxEU*. Available at: http://www.voxeu.org/article/job-polarisation-and-decline-middle-class-workers-wages (accessed 24 March 2014).
Cammaerts, B. et al. (eds.) (2012). *Mediation and Protest Movements*. Chicago: Intellect Books.
Castells, M. (2009). *Communication Power*. New York: Oxford University Press.
———. (2012). *Networks of Outrage and Hope: Social Movements in the Internet Age*. Polity.
Chouliaraki, L., and Blaagaard, B. (2013). Cosmopolitanism and the New News Media. *Journalism Studies* 14(2): 150–55.
Cottle, S. (2008). Reporting Demonstrations: The Changing Media Politics of Dissent. *Media, Culture & Society* 30(6): 853–72.
Couldry, N. (2013). A Necessary Disenchantment: Myth, Agency and Injustice in a Digital World. *Inaugural Lecture*, London School of Economics and Political Science. Available at: http://www.lse.ac.uk/media@lse/documents/MPP/Nick-Couldrys-LSE-INAUGURAL-SCRIPT.pdf (accessed 24 March 2014).
Curran, J. et al. (2012). *Misunderstanding the Internet*. London and New York: Routledge.

Dean, A. B. (2014). 'People Make Up Our City': Why Seattle's $15 Minimum Wage Is a Sign of Things to Come. *Truthout*, 28 June. Available at: http://www.truth-out.org/news/item/24608-people-make-up-our-city-why-seattles-$15-minimum-wage-is-a-sign-of-things-to-come (accessed 18 July 2014).

Dencik, L. (2014). Why Facebook Censorship Matters. *JOMEC@Cardiff University*. Available at: http://www.jomec.co.uk/blog/why-facebook-censorship-matters/ (accessed 24 March 2014).

Dencik, L., and Wilkin, P. (2015). *Worker Resistance and Media: Challenging Global Corporate Power in the 21st Century*. New York: Peter Lang.

Dionne Jr., E. J. (2013). New Life for Labor. *Washington Post*, 1 September.

Fuchs, C. (2012). Some Reflections on Manuel Castells' Book Networks of Outrage and Hope: Social Movements in the Internet Age. *Communication, Capitalism and Critique* 10(2).

Galtung, J., and Ruge, M. (1965). The Structure of Foreign News. *Journal of Peace Research* 2(1): 64–90.

Gerbaudo, P. (2012). *Tweets and the Streets: Social Media and Contemporary Activism*. London: Pluto Press.

———. (2014). Occupying the Digital Mainstream. *The Occupied Times*, 27 March. Available at: http://theoccupiedtimes.org/?p=12853 (accessed 9 November 2014).

Ghonim, W. (2012). *Revolution 2.0: The Power of the People Is Greater than the People in Power*. New York: Houghton Mifflin Harcourt.

Gupta, A. (2013). Fight for 15 Confidential. *In These Times*. Available at: http://inthesetimes.com/article/15826/fight_for_15_confidential (accessed 24 March 2014).

Helmore, E. (2013). US fast food Workers in Vanguard of Growing Protests at 'Starvation' Wages. *Observer*, 10 August.

Hintz, A. (2013). Dimensions of Modern Freedom of Expression: WikiLeaks, Policyhacking, and Digital Freedoms. In Brevini, B. et al., (eds.), *Beyond WikiLeaks: Implications for the Future of Communications, Journalism and Society*, 146–65. Basingstoke: Palgrave Macmillan.

Jones, D. (2012). *Who Cares Wins: Why Good Business Is Better Business*. London: Pearson.

Juris, J. (2012). Reflections on #Occupy Everywhere: Social Media, Public Space, and Emerging Logics of Aggregation. *American Ethnologist* 39(2): 259–79.

Klein, N. (2000). *No Logo*. London: Fourth Estate.

Mason, P. (2012). *Why It's Kicking Off Everywhere: The New Global Revolutions*. London and New York: Verso.

McVeigh, K. (2013). Fast Food Workers Continue Fight against Low Wages: 'This Is Our Right'. *Guardian*, 29 August. Available at: http://www.theguardian.com/world/2013/aug/29/fast-food-workers-low-pay-nationwide-walkout (accessed 9 November 2014).

Mishel, L., and Shierholz, H. (2013). A Decade of Flat Wages: The Key Barrier to Shared Prosperity and a Rising Middle Class. Briefing Paper #365. *Economic Policy Institute*, 21 August. Available at: http://s1.epi.org/files/2013/BP365.pdf (accessed 21 August 2015).

O'Connor, C. (2014). With Minimum Wage on State of the Union Agenda, Fast Food Workers Are Guests of Honor. *Forbes*, 28 January. Available at: http://www.forbes.com/sites/clareoconnor/2014/01/28/with-minimum-wage-on-state-of-the-union-agenda-fast food-workers-are-guests-of-honor/ (accessed 18 July 2014).

Pantti, M. et al. (2012). *Disasters and the Media*. New York: Peter Lang.

Shirky, C. (2008). *Here Comes Everybody: The Power of Organising without Organisations*. London: Allen Lane.

Terranova, T. (2000). Free Labor: Producing Culture for the Digital Economy. *Social Text*, 18(2): 33–58.

Tufekci, Z., and Wilson, C. (2012). Social Media and the Decision to Participate in Political Protest: Observations From Tahrir Square. *Journal of Communication* 62(2): 363–79.

Weissman, J. (2014). The fast food Strikes Have Been a Stunning Success for Organized Labor. *Slate*, 7 September. Available at: http://www.slate.com/blogs/moneybox/2014/09/07/the_fast_food_strikes_a_stunning_success_for_organized_labor.html (accessed 9 November 2014).

Williams, A. et al. (2011). 'More Real and Less Packaged': Audience Discourse on Amateur News Content and Its Effects on Journalism Practice. In Anden-Papadopoulous, K. and Pantti, M. (eds.), *Amateur Images and Global News*, 193–210. Bristol: Intellect.

Chapter Twelve

Network Cultures and the Architecture of Decision

Geert Lovink and Ned Rossiter

Far more dreadful are social milieus, with their supple texture, their gossip, and their informal hierarchies.

—The Invisible Committee, *The Coming Insurrection*, 2009

Please do not share this announcement with any journalists. I have selected your profile as a trusted node of connection in the cultural professional networks and would hereby like to invite you to access a platform of pirated daily financial news.

—Confidential announcement, 2014

The diversity of the movement, the informality and speed of the network, the rituals of the assembly and the formal power of the party: each political form has its distinct features and dynamics. Medium theory always taught us that expression is shaped by the contours and material properties of communication technologies. The same can be said for these organizational political forms. They hold a capacity to mediate and conform to an extent dictated by their typology, enabling certain processes while frustrating others. No matter their internal variation—there are many different kinds of networks, just as there are assemblies and so forth—there is something distinct about their organizational forms.

Lately, there is growing discontent over event-centred movements. The question of how to reach a critical mass that goes beyond the celebration of temporary euphoria is essential here. How can we get over the obvious statements about the weather and other meta fluctuations (from Zeitgeist to astrology)? Instead of contrasting the Leninist party model with the anarcho-horizontalist celebration of the general assembly, we propose to integrate the general network intellect into the organization debate. We've moved on a good 150 years since the Marx–Bakunin debates.

We should start sabotaging the pressure to update and grow our networks. Strategies, if not devices, are required that shortcut the implicit competition that so often compels us to act. The proposal here is to intensify what's already there and collaborate—instead of merely communicate—in ways that ensure existence is a political force to be reckoned with. Call it a lingering passion to invent. Organized networks, also called 'orgnets', are first and foremost unidentified theoretical objects. Read it as a proposal to undermine the fear of missing out.

Amalgamating the words 'organization' and 'network', the concept of 'orgnets' is something we developed in 2005 as a response to the rise of the 'social networking' paradigm and orthodox ideas in management circles about the 'networked organization' (Lovink and Rossiter 2005; Lovink 2007; Rossiter 2006). The term can be read as a variation and upgrade of the popularity and mystique that surrounds 'organized crime', while intersecting with the more imaginative but slightly conceptual term 'organized inno-cence' (as described by pseudonymous collective Adilkno in their book *Media Archive* from 1998). Needless to say, orgnets are both virtual and real. They are as much living data, crunching away on hard disks, as they are hardcore urban tribes and nonidentities, invisible for nonmembers.

Orgnets have grown in response to European offline romanticism and assembly strategies from Occupy activists. Meeting in-real-life is cute but expensive and often impossible to arrange on the hop. Most collaborations these days, if serious, are not touristic in nature anyway. Leave those junkets for the coterie clinging to the vestige of power bestowed upon boardrooms. There is a tragic, harsh element in the fact that more often than not we don't coincide in the same room, building, city or continent. This is the rotten reality of our global existence. Organized networks are out there. They exist. But they should still be read as a proposal. This is why we emphasize the design element. Please come on board to collectively define what orgnets could be all about. The concept is an open invitation to rethink how we structure our social lives.

Whereas it is possible to interpret the rich history of humankind as org-nets, from clans and villages to secret societies, collectives and smart mobs, we prefer to emphasize the twenty-first-century blend of technology and the social. Orgnets have appeared on the scene in a time of high uncertainty. Not only do we have the catastrophe of planetary life driving fear into the soul of the future, but we also have what seems a broader social incapacity to act. And this is partly a result of the problem of traditional institutional forms grappling with the challenge—still—of a world that is deeply networked by digital media. Witness, for example, the crisis of conventional organizations such as the trade union, the political party, the church and the social movement. Losing credibility by the day, increasingly decoupled from their constituencies and no longer able to galvanize collective passion to mobilize action, the primary pillars of social organization that defined the nineteenth and twentieth centuries have struggled to reinvent themselves to address the complexities that define our times. This is where orgnets step in.

How to comprehend the emergence of large global protests and the rise of networked movements? The concept of organized networks can neither explain such phenomena, nor is it a response to them. First and foremost, organized networks arise from the growing discontent with social media and their presumed role as the motor behind the current popularity of protest. But perhaps more importantly, organized networks ('orgnets') are a response to the problem of organization and institutional form, and have to be understood as a response to the current contradictions. The abstraction of democracy is not so often a motivating force that brings bodies and brains to the street. The 2014 Hong Kong uprising is a clear case in point, where the experience of economic misery projected into the future was a powerful enough catalyst for political action and the production of subjectivity.

Four primary features define the current situation of communication systems for orgnets. First, short-term communication that evaporates after resolving task-based organization. Second, mobilization that is focused on connecting core organizers with politicized masses. Third, the facilitation of deliberation, discussion and debate. And fourth, processes of decision making that demonstrate populist governance at work (e.g., assemblies). The concept and practice of organized networks is only one of a whole range of possibilities circulating in the field of political design.[1] Our thesis is that the current wave of protests is key to the production of new forms of organization beyond traditional forms such as trade unions, tribes and even social movements.

THE NETWORK DECISION

The question of decision is one we see as central to the organizational form of networks. For Jodi Dean, this is the function of the party. 'The primary organizational question, then, is what might a party look like for us? What features might install in it the necessary discipline, flexibility, and consistency necessary for building communist power?' (Dean 2014, 834). The assembly attempts to do what Dean desires for the party, namely the instantiation of the moment of decision making through consensus building. As a form of direct democracy, people try to go beyond the particular—single issues, the core topic, the fragmentation of desire, will, cause and so forth. The assembly form tries to sideline mediation. There is an implicit critique of social media here, and a desire for the corporeal as the pure scene of social relations.

For Dean and the Communist Co. (Žižek, Badiou and their droves of disciples), democracy is a messianic moment, driven by a passionate urgency, undiluted and unadulterated by the technical, which is about exclusive knowledge (engineers) and political economy (the dirty corporation driven by commercial interest). This sentiment is shared by the 'assembly' advocates, even though the political form of the assembly is considerably more experimental. It operates according to the logic and immediacy of the event, while the party is the established organizational structure that has proven its form as a device for deliberation and organized power throughout modern history.

This is no less the case today, as the political form of the party adapts its operations, techniques of reproduction and processes of decision making to the 'metric-driven' experimentation of data analytics, enabling a real-time modulation of the relation between parties and populations (Tufekci 2014). As noted by Zeynep Tufekci, technical infrastructures consisting of 'blogs, micro-blogs and online social media and social networking platforms' foreground a new system of algorithmic governance overseen by a 'small cadre of technical professionals'. The technical expertise and algorithmic operations special to such modes of governance results in a party-form whose machinations are even more obscure, abstract and removed from processes of accountability and any public comprehension of how policy making, for example, is developed out of a relation with the supposed empirical qualities of lived experience. Metrics, and what architectural theorist Reinhold Martin terms a 'numerical imaginary', function as the new mediators of our machinic relation to material phenomena and the modulation of desire (Martin 2014, 1).

The act of decision is determined by the politics of parameters, whose expression as architecture in the form of algorithmic operations establishes a correlation between the party as an organizational entity and other systems dependent on complex computational procedures, such as high-frequency trading. A paradox emerges in which data analytics makes possible the reinvention of the party form within a paradigm of social network media, while also serving to effectively deontologize twentieth-century organizational forms such as the political party and the trade union in such a way that makes its decision-making processes indistinct from any number of other social, economic or political system driven by algorithmic operations. The sovereignty of the algorithm, in other words, renders the borders and functional capacity of organizational forms in ways that are indifferent to an ontology of the visible. This is why a correlation can be made between what otherwise seem entirely different, even incompatible, organizations (as operational systems). Organizational forms whose acts of decision have not yet been captured by the power of the algorithm and data analytics remain a social-political force to be reckoned with. An ontology prevails, one that is defined by the unruly and conflictual relation between the social and the technical.

For venture capitalist Peter Thiel, the PayPal founder who is on the board of directors of Facebook, the social is a conspiracy of invisible bonds, of old boys networks (Thiel 2014). It is not sufficient for an organization to have good people, the best in their field and so on. The assumption that tribal bonds of efficiency result in strength and organizational power cannot be guaranteed by assembling the leading experts in one room. This lesson was made clear in the recent film adaptation of Michael Lewis's *Moneyball* (2011) with Brad Pitt and Philip Seymour Hoffman. In that story, the best possible baseball team was assembled not through the acquisition of star players, but rather through the algorithmic selection of a team whose aggregate performance complemented and transcended what were otherwise assumed to be individual weaknesses. The lesson here for organized networks is to build on that totality of strong ties that advance a particular cause or movement and not succumb to the allure of diversification and the dilution of talents that all too often defines the democratic gesture. When manifest in the party, such modes of organization stagnate with a cohort of brilliance whose individualized desolation is unable to commit to the collective decision of the project or movement.

In this age of social network media, it really isn't conceivable any longer for the party to emerge from within itself. In other words, the plebiscitary of the networked conversations is the dominant social-technical form, which means the party can only emerge from within the culture of networks. As Rodrigo Nunes writes: '*Even if* a return to the party-form were found to be the solution, the party would no doubt have to emerge from existing networks' (Nunes 2014, 11). A populist party such as Podemos, for example, will always carry the trace of the network in its myth of origin: the movement of the squares (M15) serves as a core component of its organizational ontology, despite its image of an electoral war machine under the leadership of Pablo Iglesias. The network logic has redefined the delicate balance of unity and diversity. That's the lesson learned: irrespective of where you want to end up as far as your preferred organizational form goes, in order to know your object you will necessarily start to diagnose your network. There are two dimensions to this: technical and social. All too often the technical remains insufficiently addressed and too easily dismissed. The social, on the other hand, is privileged as the primary logic of networks—at least within social media where the precept of interface design is to accumulate more friends whose data entrails feed an economy of extraction and recombination.

In the case of networks there are, broadly speaking, social media platforms that are closed proprietary worlds at the technical level. The attempts to generate alternatives have to date been limited. Diaspora* was a case of an open source network that entered campaign mode dependent on crowd-sourced funding, short mobilizations and global protests to garner mass attention with the hope of signing up enough users to make an operational claim as a viable alternative to commercial providers (https://joindiaspora.com). The difficulty for Diaspora* has been that it could not scale up and become adopted by a movement galvanized by the event. It also wasn't sufficient at a design and technical level to copy or mimic the juggernaut of Facebook.[2]

The scalar strategy has to be questioned because such old broadcasting tactics all too often lead to weak ties with little impact. We know how to scale and the world of PR and advertising does it all the time. So do orgnets (as concept/practice) become a form of retreat or an elite avant-garde strategy to prepare and anticipate change and future implementation? Do they offer new forms of social interaction? Is it ridiculous to think of a Bauhaus of net-culture that provides the blueprint for future mass production and distribution? The network protocols have a similar and bigger impact—more general than IKEA. They are not a lifestyle. There is currently no choice in the adoption of media architectures.

Post-Snowden and the PRISM revelations, social media software is tasked with the additional demand to ensure encryption. The March 2014 hype around the ad-free social network Ello (https://ello.co/beta-public-profiles) showed there was a great need for an alternative to the Facebook and Twitter monopoly. The problem here was that, as often is the case, the platform launched too early and became overhyped through the traditional media. Because of the premature release the developers hadn't built a solid foundation of early users and adopters. The larger issue here for developers of network software is the pressure from users for a post-PRISM alternative, resulting in insufficient time for developers to fine-tune the software. The demand for instantaneous solutions has resulted in half-baked, bug-ridden products being unleashed with a near certainty to fail, crippling many efforts to build new networks.

We also need to address developments coming out of the right-wing, techno-libertarian start-up movements. Many of these proponents hold ideas and proposals not so different from those of the open source movement, academic left and even the art world. The call, for example, by the conservative tech revolutionary Peter Thiel to dismantle formal university training and college education is one that chimes frequently within groups gathering around free and public universities. Thiel prefers the commitment-to-cause inside cults to the nihilism and nonengagement of the consultancy class. He proposes to 'take cultures of extreme dedication seriously. Is a lukewarm attitude to one's work a sign of mental health? Is a merely professional attitude the only sane approach?' (Thiel 2014, 124).

While the sentiment may share a similar distaste for state power and the society of crippling debt—manifest also in the 'sharing' economy such as Airbnb and Uber,[3] which strive to promote services unshackled from the regulatory control of the state—the political agenda of the start-up world is often obscure, presenting itself as a space of neutral-free tools. But this is far from the case, and all too often radical left-wing movements sign up unwittingly to a techno-political ideology of libertarianism that is, if nothing else, massively contradicting the political sentiments of movements. This is because the movements are largely disconnected from development and consider technology simply as a functionary tool when in fact it profoundly shapes the production of subjectivity and instils practices with political values that are far from neutral. This only becomes really visible on the surface in a city such as San Francisco where these political tendencies collide, with activists attacking the Google bus which transports tech-designers in the secure world of a charter bus.

THE INVISIBLE ORGANIZATION

The invisible is not the virtual. Thanks to the Snowden revelations, we continue to live through the trauma of materiality accompanying the seemingly invisible realm of what was fondly referred to in the 1990s as 'cyberspace'. The utopian spark of the Hong Kong protests and occupation brought off-the-grid organization to widespread attention. While this practice ensured a mode of connection not dependent on commercial infrastructures, it was not without implications for the sustainability of orgnets. Blue-tooth communications using applications such as FireChat are inherently insecure and indeed invite the enemy to infiltrate what might otherwise have been secret planning sessions (see, for example, Cohen 2014; Bland 2014).

The other aspect of off-the-grid computing concerns the relation between memory, archives and the sustainability of movements. Without a common repository, off-the-grid computing lends itself to the task of organization but not the storage of collective history. One exception can be found in the collective archives of political dissent such as MayDay Rooms (http://maydayrooms.org/), which exemplify the work of collaborative constitution and the mediation of memory for social-political movements. Moreover, projects such as these acknowledge the socio-technical logics of retrieval: the power not of the net and its infrastructures but of the network-form itself.

Short encryption services that operate like a secure free local SMS used by thousands on a particular location accommodate the rumour-like forwarding of event announcements and actions. But is this sufficient to the task of organization? This indeed was one limit-horizon experienced by core organizers in recent uprisings the world over. Again, we refer to the political demonstrations in Hong Kong in 2014, which were mobilized through off-the-grid computing and the use of the Bluetooth app FireChat. Here, the use of an open access system meant authorities were just as informed as movements. And without the technical capacity of archiving communication, the Hong Kong movements leave open the question of how to galvanize future movements and constitute subjectivities without reference to an archive of dissent.

Does the invisible organization have an invisible committee? Occupy circles do not like to talk about the informal groups behind their spectacle-type assembly meetings. And it's not hip to discuss who's in charge of the agenda-setting of their consensus theatre productions. Orgnets? In the case of classic guerrilla organization as depicted in Gillo Pontecorvo's film *The Battle of Algiers* (1966), anticolonial insurgents are organized across a network of cells whose relations to each other are structured according to a triangular logic, thus protecting but also obscuring the central management. This social form of invisible organization is not readily duplicated within the logic of networks whose technical parameters may section off core organizers and administrators from members and participants, but does not guarantee the sort of structure of security and invisibility afforded by predigital techniques of social-political organization. Outside of encryption, the digital at the level of everyday popular use is a technology of transparency. Yet at the level of infrastructure, the digital is more often enclosed within the black box of proprietary regimes and heavily securitized data centres.

This prompts the question of alternative (tech) infrastructures and the need to share expertise about what works and what doesn't (how to deal with trolls and spies, domain name disputes, email overload, at what point switch to crypto, etc.). The future of organization in a post-Snowden landscape requires the generation of new protocols and perhaps off-the-grid computing made secure. To create new protocols within the sort of techno-political environment just described, however, is another task altogether. Part of this work requires attention to devising strategies and tactics that facilitate and sustain political intervention over time. But crucially, such work must also address the question of organization coupled with technical and infrastructural issues related to social media use, something we see missing from the sort of campaign handbooks written by LSE civil liberties activist Simon Davies (2014). His campaign ideas fail to register the political stakes of organization among noncitizens who may reside in the territorial borders of the nation-state, but hold none of the privileges accorded to the citizen-subject. Moreover, his toolkit of strategies and tactics for campaigning is wedded to a media logic of representation. He has nothing to say about how media forms and organizational networks play a core role in the sort of campaigning he advocates. It's almost like we never left the broadcast age and its conspiratorial moves behind the scenes, aimed to 'manufacture public opinion'. These days 'ideas for change' should explicitly deal with the distributed nature of both organizations and mass communication. The internet is not a black box anymore.

German media archaeologist Siegfried Zielinski does not believe in the 'protocol' approach that locates the centre of power in code, while turning this insight into a political strategy. This is the core of the nerdist philosophy: it is neither content nor interface that determine our situation. Zielinski: '. . . I acknowledge my powerlessness. The position from which I believe it is still or is again possible to formulate criticism is located on the periphery, not in the centre' (Zielinski 2013, 21). We do not believe that either the nerd or the artist will enlighten us with the Truth. Key for us is not the perpetuation of tinkering on the margins of obscurity but in fact focusing very clearly on the network architectures at the centre of power. For Zielinski, there is a political periphery of informality dedicated to art initiatives, counterdesigns, alternative interfaces and so on. However, we take our cue from the various companies such as Red Hat, Canonical and SUSE involved in the Linux enterprise who, among others, located their businesses in the centre of technological development in Silicon Valley despite the general Linux radical agenda of a free, open and distributed communication architecture.

The design of alternative protocols must first reckon with the architecture of communication and control. This political economic geography of centres, not margins, extends to the infrastructure of storage, transmission and processing: namely the highly securitized, hidden territory of data centres (also known as server farms or colocation centres). Until we know more about the technical operations, communication protocols, legal regimes, design principles and social-economic impact of such infrastructure, the capacity of movements to make informed decisions about how to organize in ways that both support and secure their interests and agendas will remain severely circumscribed. Orgnets may have an important role to play here in terms of coordinating collective endeavours of critical research into such infrastructures of power.

INTRODUCING THE POSTDIGITAL ORGANIZATION

Organized networks always take place in informational settings and this is why the postdigital becomes a relevant topic and condition to address. The questions of organization and 'political design' these days cannot be separated anymore from the IT realm. The concerns of the informational carry over. This is not good news for the development of organized networks, where so many of the alternatives in the making are abandoned as the supremacy of templates takes command. Postdigital organization in such a context is also then about knowledge organization. The university has been an institution whose autonomy is undermined, in question and so forth and this is only made clearer in a post-Snowden context.

According to Rotterdam media theorist Florian Cramer, '"Post-digital" first of all describes any media aesthetics leaving behind those clean high tech and high fidelity connotations' (Cramer 2014). It is no longer the remit of engineers. Postdigital = Postdigitization. The phase of digitization is complete as a process of implementation and integration. We are no longer speculating about the arrival of the new. The systems are in place. Our task is now to map its impact, in real-time: instant theory. When the scanning is done and records logged, meta-tagged and uploaded in the database, the bureaucratic end of digitization takes command. The transition is over and the story can begin in which the hidden dream of a postdigital renaissance where the old values of humanistic inquiry would resurface and once again supply society with the moral compass and grand stories through which to conduct life.

The postdigital is not about less digital, it's about the digital pushed to the background (Cramer) in part because it is made invisible and integrated into everyday life, but also because we've mastered it (or should have). The digital was never about the digital precisely because no one ever knew what was in the background. It just worked as general infrastructure in much the same way that electricity does—the magical cyberspace that was connected. The postdigital therefore needs to be understood as a process of demystification—part of the *Entzauberung der Welt* (Schiller). Disenchantment does not capture the mythical element. There is a lyrical element that is erased in the process of normalization and the rise of technocratic culture and the administrative world (*die verwaltete Welt*).[4] And here, we can say that the postdigital is coincident with the logistical worlds of global supply chains because they too are very much about calculating activity and the repetition of movement within enterprise architectures with the aim of extracting value from the accumulation, analysis and commercial sale of data.

We can note the place of digital humanities in this phase of digitization where much of the debate has now moved on to data analytics, visualization and the development of dynamic research methods. Amidst issues around data securitization are a concern for institutions, including those engaged in higher education, hosting these projects not only for reasons of sound ethical practice with regard to data management. Of perhaps greater concern is the potential market value and consequent proprietarization of data generated within quasipublic institutions where the logic of data is increasingly understood in economistic terms. The lesson of social media in other words has migrated over to the disciplines and the production of knowledge. We can only sense what 'platform capitalism' will have to offer us in the near future in terms of brutal yet invisible destruction of the social.

For Cramer, the new normality of the postdigital corresponds with ordinary, everyday use of template software. The postdigital sits comfortably with off-the-shelf aesthetics and preformatted cultural expression. Such a condition frequently carries over to the organization of networks, where social-technical nondynamics are the default mode of coordination and communication. Template culture for political movements results in a certain indistinction across what are otherwise enormously varied social collectives and movements who are responding quite often to very particular social and political issues. The template mode of organization shifts authority in some respects from the engineering class to the networked multitudes who need to self-administrate their dreams in Excel sheets.

The roaring 90s were bedazzled by the allure of shiny interfaces of multimedia projects, even if their execution was frequently short of the mark and poor at the level of content. Within the postdigital scene, aesthetics is drifting off to the 'maker' culture, which is notable for two key developments. First, is a media aesthetics of nostalgia for a 1980s DIY digital culture. And this taps into the second prevailing feature of the postdigital, namely an experimental interface aesthetics that bridges the material with the digital and creates new one-off hybrids ('new aesthetics') (see Berry and Dieter 2015).

The postdigital is beyond the dialectics of old and new media, since with digitization all communication forms are computational in nature (appearances might be different). We can definitely say the digital has been enormously powerful at the level of the imaginary. The postdigital therefore implies a time and space within which new imaginaries can emerge that are not beholden to the mysteries of engineers or the obscurity of internet governance circles and geek enclaves such as GitHub. So a politics of the postdigital would be one that confronts and makes visible the submersion of communication into the vaults of secret data centres scattered about the globe. Rational technocratic organizational culture can only be more horrendous when it disappears as an object of fear and force of control. This is not to get conspiratorial and whatnot, but rather to know how communication, culture and economy are operative in a digital world. Otherwise it's the story of a great somatic slumber.

We have often asked how something comes into being as a singular event. The question should now focus on the materiality of the continuum. Media and cultural studies can only study an object or phenomenon once it's there. But today that's not enough if you are always running behind the facts. This is the weak point. The alternative is not predictive analytics of big data. Pattern recognition supposes equivalence between data, its algorithmic organization and external referents within the world. And even though there's increasingly an integration of data, technology and life (Internet of Things), it is at least for now not totalizing. Life still escapes. So while we can say media are constitutive of the experience of communication and even produce unforeseen effects, there is an outside to media. And a postdigital theory of media therefore has to know not just what it incorporates (as in the measuring of systems) but it also needs to know that which is external to it since these will be the new spaces of capture in the design of media architectures that drive capitalism.

The postdigital is a form of submission. The ubiquity of the digital, its thorough integration into the routines of daily life, signals acquiescence to the hegemony of standards and protocols. In its generalization, the postdigital withdraws into the background. We are no longer conscious, or even less conscious than say we were during the 1990s, of the architectures which support communication and practice. Often the presence of technology would be sufficient to prompt an address. But with the slide into the background of sensation, we have no clue what constitutes the media as an object of communication, which operates on a spectrum outside human cognition and perception. The rise of big data registers the limits of human cognisance when set against computational power.

Can we say there is equivalence between the postdigital and the posthuman? For Nicholas Carr, human agency prevails as the invisible remainder following the automation of economy and society (Carr 2014). The human is the last resort and upholder of an ethical existence and the necessary component for the system to survive. Since Taylorism and Fordism, the human was consigned to a future of redundancy and eventual obliteration. This scenario has played out within a networked, informational paradigm through the figure of 'free labour', where value is extracted from social relations made possible by digital media of connection. Once this horizon is eclipsed, which we start to see with the rise of the quantified self movement, there is no resource left for capital accumulation, since time also has been effectively eradicated with the nano-speed of high frequency trading, which generates something in the vicinity of 80 percent of global financial transactions. At the end of the day, the inert body of the human persists and retains a capacity for thought and action, which include importantly for techno-capitalism the power to decide, which is power to distinguish. Paradoxically, the loss of agency through automation conditions the vitality of what remains of the human.

New schools of literacy for the invisible will emerge to address the power of automation and the postdigital. The Snowden effect is just one index of a nascent awareness of technologies of capture supported by the selective openness of enormous datasets collected on behalf of the dominant IT companies for the techno-surveillance complex. To shift your operations to less noticeable IT providers is of course a false security, since they are harnessed to the infrastructure of power such as data centres.

To summarize, we propose to shift attention away from mobilization and event making to collaboration in order to provide rapidly emerging social movements and 'global uprisings' with more sustainable organizational tools. This includes producing concepts that correspond with the social-technical dynamics of practice, and which operate as an architecture through which things get done. The social ties within protests are tightened through the work of organizing networks. Focusing on the consensus spectacle of the assembly or the nostalgic return to the form of the political party is fine if you are seeking distraction *because movements are temporary and cannot make decisions.*

NOTES

1. Possible solutions would require a mix between offline practices such as the assembly (as discussed by David Graeber in *The Democracy Project: A History, a Crisis, a Movement* (2013) and Marina Sitrin and Dario Azzellini in their book *They Can't Represent Us! Reinventing Democracy from Greece to Occupy* (2014) and technical online experiments such as the LiquidFeedback decision-making software (see http://liquidfeedback.org/ and the work of Anja Adler from the NRW School of Governance in Duisburg, Germany), or the Loomio decision-making software which assists groups in collaborative decision-making processes in an attempt to overcome the short lifespan of social phenomena such as swarms and smart mobs.

2. Since 2011, the Unlike Us network has been collecting and discussing experiences with alternative social media platforms. Besides three conferences and a reader, this has mainly been done on the Unlike Us email list: http://networkcultures.org/unlikeus/.

3. See the extraordinary ongoing reporting by Paul Carr for PandoDaily (http://pando.com/) on Uber and the more general analysis of Sebastian Olma (2014) and Trebor Scholz (2014).

4. See https://de.wikipedia.org/wiki/Verwaltete_Welt.

REFERENCES

Adilkno. 1998. "Contemporary Nihilism: On Innocence Organized." *Media Archive: The World Edition*, 165–69. New York: Autonomedia.

Berry, David M., and Michael Dieter (eds). 2015. *Postdigital Aesthetics: Art, Computation and Design.* London: Palgrave Macmillan.

Bland, Archie. 2014. "FireChat: The Messaging App that's Powering the Hong Kong Protests." *Guardian.* 29 September. http://www.theguardian.com/world/2014/sep/29/firechat-messaging-app-powering-hong-kong-protests.

Carr, Nicholas. 2014. *The Glass Cage: Automation and Us.* New York: Norton.

Cohen, Noam. 2014. "Hong Kong Protests Propel FireChat Phone-to-Phone App." *New York Times.* 5 October. http://www.nytimes.com/2014/10/06/technology/hong-kong-protests-propel-a-phone-to-phone-app-.html.

Cramer, Florian. 2014. "What Is Post-Digital?" *APRJA: A Peer Reviewed Journal About // Post-Digital Research* 3 (1). http://www.aprja.net/?p=1318 .

Davies, Simon. 2014. *Ideas for Change: Campaign Principles that Shift the World.* December. http://www.privacysurgeon.org/resources/ideas-for-change/.

Dean, Jodi. 2014. "The Question of Organization." *South Atlantic Quarterly* 113 (4).

Graeber, David. 2013. *The Democracy Project: A History, a Crisis, a Movement.* London: Allen Lane.

Lovink, Geert. 2007. "Introducing Organized Networks: The Quest for Sustainable Concepts." In *Zero Comments: Blogging and Critical Internet Culture*, 239–55. New York: Routledge.

Lovink, Geert, and Ned Rossiter. 2005. "Dawn of the Organised Networks." *Fibreculture Journal* 5. http://journal.fibreculture.org/issue5/lovink_rossiter.html.

Martin, Reinhold. 2014. *Mediators: Aesthetics, Politics and the City*. Minneapolis: University of Minnesota Press.

Nunes, Rodrigo. 2014. *Organisation of the Organisationless: Collective Action after Networks*. Lüneburg: Leuphana, Mute and Post-Media Lab.

Olma, Sebastian. 2014. "Never Mind the Sharing Economy, Here's Platform Capitalism." 16 October. http://networkcultures.org/mycreativity/2014/10/16/never-mind-the-sharing-economy-heres-platform-capitalism/.

Rossiter, Ned. 2006. *Organized Networks: Media Theory, Creative Labour, New Institutions*. Rotterdam: NAi.

Scholz, Trebor. 2014. "The Politics of the Sharing Economy." 19 May. http://collectivate.net/journalisms/2014/5/19/the-politics-of-the-sharing-economy.html.

Sitrin, Marina, and Dario Azzellini. 2014. *They Can't Represent Us! Reinventing Democracy from Greece to Occupy*. London and New York: Verso.

Thiel, Peter, with Blake Masters. 2014. *Zero to One: Notes on Startups, or, How to Build the Future*. London: Penguin Random House.

Tufekci, Zeynep. 2014. "Engineering the Public: Big Data, Surveillance and Computational Politics." *First Monday* 19 (7). http://firstmonday.org/ojs/index.php/fm/article/view/4901/4097.

Zielinksi, Siegfried. 2013. *[. . . After the Media]*. Trans. Gloria Custance. Minneapolis: University of Minneapolis Press.

Index